W9-BLN-481

The German Lied
and Its Poetry

The German Lied
and Its Poetry

ELAINE BRODY AND ROBERT A. FOWKES

NEW YORK, *New York University Press*, 1971

Preface

In the following pages we have discussed poetry and music of various nineteenth-century lieder, many of which have achieved today the status of representative works in the genre. A listener hears each song as a self-contained single work of art. He is unaware of the consummate difficulties involved in mating two distinctly different art forms. The musician approaches song with a need to analyze the diversified elements—melody, harmony, rhythm, sound, and texture—which are common to all musical compositions. For him the text is but one additional feature that he will consider when treating melodic style, range, text underlay, and text reflection. The philologist will read the lines, observe the meter and rhyme scheme, explain the original meaning of words or phrases which today may be obsolete or restricted in their usage, and interpret the imagery or symbolism inherent in the poetry.

A few years ago, we joined forces to offer a course on *The German Lied and Its Poetry*. Our investigations into the overlapping areas of our two disciplines resulted in our collaboration on this book. Understanding the synthesis of music and poetry demands the efforts of two specialists. For this reason, we decided that each of us would deal with the subject primarily in his own area of expertise, venturing into the other's territory only when specific circumstances warranted it. Each of us treated the lied from his own vantage point, after which we collated our findings.

Most lieder composers chose their texts with great care, selecting only the better poems of the most significant poets. They sought to endow these texts with music that would heighten the expression of the words and thus make the poem even more meaningful. Among the great poems that have been enhanced through their union with music, we might cite *Erlkönig*, *Gretchen am Spinnrade*, *Der Doppelgänger*, and Mignon's songs from

Wilhelm Meister. These songs reflect the success of their creators in raising them beyond the mere sonority of words.

Occasionally we come across a beautiful lied that was based on a second-rate poem, but this situation does not obtain too often. It is true that Goethe believed only inferior poems would benefit from being set to music, and he therefore resented Schubert's settings of his poetry. He claimed that the accompaniments distracted the listener and added unnecessary embellishment to an already finished work. The poet preferred instead the settings of Zelter and Reichardt, lesser-known contemporaries of Schubert, none of whose innocuous music could possibly add to or detract from the original poetry.

We have been able to discuss only a few examples from among hundreds of fine lieder. This kind of explication, however, could be applied to any song. We ask, for example, what was the poet's intention? What do the words mean? Do they themselves have a melody? A rhythm? Has the composer captured or destroyed the original meaning? Or has he perhaps intensified the statement? How has he accomplished this feat? Which are the musical elements that he stresses to underline a point? Finding the answers to these questions helps to increase our enjoyment of the work.

The space allotted a particular lied is not a reflection of its aesthetic value. Sometimes a superb song needed relatively little explanation beyond calling the listener's attention to techniques he may have overlooked. Then too, because art is indefinable, we might cite several effective techniques but be unable to say why this particular concinnity of disparate elements produced a masterpiece. At times a lied that is not among the finest of our examples presented us with the opportunity to show different processes at work. This song therefore received increased attention. Always we have tried to indicate how the best of the lieder represent a synthesis of words and music in a way that each without the other is incomplete.

E. B. and R. A. F.

New York City   August 27, 1970

We are very much indebted to Mrs. Barbara A. Petersen, who not only prepared the final copy but also typed the entire manuscript.

The Authors

Contents

I. MUSICAL AND LITERARY FORERUNNERS
Music and Poetry of the Minnesingers and the Master-singers. *Bar* form. The Chorale and the Polyphonic Lied. The Continuo Lied. The *volkstümliches* Lied. The Romantic Lied 3

II. THE EARLY ROMANTIC LIED
Form and Style in the Nineteenth-century Lied. Goethe. Beethoven 10

III. THE HIGH ROMANTIC LIED
Schubert. Schubert's Goethe Lieder. Songs to poems by other poets. Wilhelm Müller and Schubert's cycles. Heine. Schubert's Heine songs 20

IV. THE NEW STYLE OF PIANO ACCOMPANIMENT
Schumann. Schumann's *Dichterliebe.* Chamisso. Schumann's *Frauenliebe und -leben.* Eichendorff. Schumann's *Liederkreis.* Songs to poems by other poets. Mendelssohn. Goethe and Heine songs 99

V. THE ROMANTIC BALLAD AND RHAPSODY
The Ballad. Loewe. Herder's *Stimmen der Völker.* Loewe's Goethe Ballads. The Supernatural. Liszt. Gypsy elements. Heine, Schiller, and other poets 182

VI. MINOR POEMS AND MAJOR LIEDER
     Brahms. The Introspective Lieder. Hölty. Storm. Daumer.
     Groth. Wenzig. Heine. The lighter songs. Kugler. Uhland.
     Wiegenlied. Vergebliches Ständchen 225

VII. FOLK INFLUENCE
      Mahler. Arnim and Brentano, *Des Knaben Wunderhorn.*
      Leander 251

VIII. POEMS FOR VOICE AND PIANO
       Wolf. Mörike. Wolf's Mörike Lieder. Eichendorff Lieder.
       Goethe Lieder. Italian and Spanish Songbooks. Summary . . 259

BIBLIOGRAPHY 300

INDEX 303

SONG INDEX 311

The German Lied
and Its Poetry

I

Musical and Literary Forerunners

Previous to the eleventh century written German literature was almost entirely in the hands of the Church. Worldly themes, when employed, were made to serve a didactic purpose and point a moral. It was as a result of conversion to Christianity that the Germanic peoples acquired the art of writing, and that art was long associated with the clergy as a sort of ecclesiastical monopoly.

Yet there existed simultaneously a large body of unwritten poetry, pagan in origin and orally transmitted. Only a microscopic part of that poetry was committed to writing; still less has been preserved until the present day. It may never have occurred to the poets or reciters that such literature was a suitable subject for written form. In fact, many cultures have produced tremendous literatures that never saw writing or print (until, in some cases, meddling scholars collected and transcribed them).

In the period called Middle High German (roughly from 1050 to 1350), although the power of the Church can hardly be said to have diminished, its influence on German literature waned, and worldly themes came to be favored. The authors themselves were no longer predominantly Churchmen. In the thirteenth century there was a flowering of German poetry, both epic and lyrical, that has, in the opinion of many enthusiasts, not been surpassed in subsequent ages. The lengthy epics, some of them Arthurian romances, others of native Germanic origin, do not concern us here, for, excellent as many were (e.g., *Parzival, Tristan und Isolde, Das Nibelungenlied*), they are not directly involved in the development of the German lied.

The kind of poetry called "minnesong," however, is of prime importance to us. (*Minne* is the medieval German word for "love.") It owes its origin to many sources. In part, it goes back to the native Germanic love poetry of oral tradition; an art form emerged after a long development of the earlier folk poem. To some degree, its growth is due to the influence of French poets, especially the Provençal trouvères-troubadours whom the German minnesingers met on the Crusades and elsewhere. The rich mine of lyrical expression in Provence, the South of France, liberally plundered by poets from many other parts of Europe, was itself clearly related to, if not precipitated by, Arabic lyrical poetry. Church songs, particularly hymns to the Virgin Mary, lent additional elements to the verse of the minnesingers, and the blending of all of these ingredients, plus the particular genius of each individual poet, resulted in the characteristic phenomenon of minnesong. The poets were also composers; they created words, melody, and accompaniment. They also sang the songs, usually to fiddle accompaniment, because they were often instrumentalists, too.

The power of the influence exerted by the various elements entering into minnesong varied according to geographic area: the troubadour influence is most perceptible in the West (the Rhineland, for example), that of folk poetry in the East (Austria and Bavaria).

In its most rigid form minnesong was utilized in the service of a stiff social code, a conventional game. The poet (a knight) is in an unnatural relation to an exalted lady, usually the wife of another and therefore unattainable; sometimes she is the wife of the liege lord of the poet himself. Her name must never be mentioned in verse. The poet complains of her cruelty, and protests his own loyalty and merit. False friends, intrigues, spies, and traitors are themes of much of minnesong, but all belong to the game. Despite the contrived nature of the poems, some authors obviously endow their verse with the genuine poetry of experience. And a poet like Walther von der Vogelweide (1165-1230) shows a spontaneity of expression and a genuine depth of emotion that is far removed from the artificial sentiments of the "hothouse poetry" of some of his predecessors. He also does not confine himself to the theme of unrequited or unattainable love. Later minnesingers—e.g., Neidhart von Reuenthal (Nîthart von Riuwental in the medieval spelling), c.1180-c.1240—often gave up entirely the whole pretense of "courtly love" and bragged about conquests, real or fancied, of village beauties, conquests sometimes involving fisticuffs with rustic yokels who disputed the right to such trophies. Neidhart's poetry has been designated *höfische Dorfpoesie* ("courtly village poetry"), which would have been a contradiction in terms during the period of strictest minnesong.

Yet the words are apropos for him, for he goes among the peasants and joins in their festivities *unter dem Lindenbaum,* while his style ranks him among the minnesingers. He also excels in nature poetry and is said to have left his mark on German song for several centuries. A Bavarian nobleman, he often reveals his own dialect in his poems, mainly in the consonantism (e.g., *p t k* for *b d g*), less in the vocabulary.

Neidhart von Reuenthal's minnesong *Willekommen mayenschein* is a typical example of the genre. It features the musical format most often used by the minnesingers: the *Bar* form, which comprises two *Stollen* (stanzas) and one *Abgesang* (refrain). (See Ex. 1.) The composition offers unity and variety: two stanzas use the same music, and the refrain relates to these stanzas by concluding with the same final pitches.

Ex. 1

NEIDHART VON REUENTHAL: *Willekommen Mayenschein*

The text here concerns nature, not love, and welcomes the month of May (cf. Schumann's *Dichterliebe,* No. 1). The composer uses a conjunct, stepwise melody, a syllabic text setting (i.e., one syllable to one note), a limited range, no text repetition, and a regularly repeated rhythmic figure, seemingly in duple meter. Centuries later, many of these characteristics appear in eighteenth-century lieder, particularly those inserted in the *Singspiel* (German comic opera). More significant, however, the *Bar* form (schematically represented as *a a b*) remained a favorite of German composers from J. S. Bach (1685-1750), whose chorale cantatas and chorale preludes are shaped in this mold, to Richard Wagner (1813-1883).

THE MASTERSINGERS

When chivalry died, minnesong died with it. The new age, with the rise of the towns and the ascendancy of prosperous burghers, saw a different kind of poetic activity, the product of the mastersingers, even though they regarded themselves as the successors to the minnesingers. These mastersingers were not exclusively poets; they were also artisans. And they attempted to turn the art of poetry into a learnable trade. It became an artificial thing, based upon the mastery of rules and the imitation of models. A boy who was apprenticed to a shoemaker or carpenter would simultaneously be sent to the local *Singschule* for instruction in singing and versifying. The lessons would be imparted by a master, usually unpaid, who had been through the same course of training himself. Just as the craftsman went through the successive stages of apprentice, journeyman, master, etc., the mastersinger was first a *Schüler*, then a *Schulfreund*, a *Singer*, a *Dichter*, and, finally, a *Meister*. (The specific titles and number of ranks varied somewhat from place to place.)

A *Schulfreund* had to memorize the complicated set of rules; a *Singer* had to be able to sing a certain number of prescribed "tones" or tunes; a *Dichter* had to compose a new text for one of the traditional tunes; and the title of *Meister* was bestowed on one who had himself composed a new tune. Little esteem was accorded originality or genius in words or music; conformity was the treasured aim.

Poets competed, sometimes after issuing challenges to each other (there had been a precedent for this in the battles of the bards in medieval times). The competition was judged by a *Merker*, who concentrated on detecting trivial violations of the code (cf. Richard Wagner's Beckmesser).

If blind obedience was the stern demand of mastersong on its devotees, it is little wonder that genuine poetical creation was extremely rare. Yet Hans Sachs (1494-1576) was a poet in spite of the system. Not that all of his works bear the stamp of genius; they could not be expected to, for his productiveness was virtually unstoppable. In 1567 he took inventory of what he had written until then. He counted 4,275 mastersongs, 18 volumes of other poetry, 200 plays, and still had nine years to live!

Hans Sachs was, in the opinion of many, far better as the author of *Fastnachtsspiele* (Shrovetide or Mardi Gras plays) than as a poet; these comedies are often hilariously good. Goethe revived Hans Sachs's prestige by calling him a kindred spirit and fellow poet.

It is easy to belittle such movements as mastersong, and sufficient scorn has been heaped upon the German poets of that period by some literary historians. But others have realized the salubrious effect of a movement which produced a vital involvement in literary activity on the part of people who, in other ages, would never have had such interest. The literary guilds which arose in the fifteenth and sixteenth centuries gave the impetus to favorable development in many genres of German literature.

Finally, during the periods of minnesong and mastersong, as well as throughout other vogues and fads, the *Volkslied* continued to enjoy its own independent existence, sometimes flourishing when all other forms of literature presented a dreary picture.

Martin Luther's hymns spring from the vast tradition of German *Volkslieder* and their unaffected sincerity and simplicity of utterance are their outstanding qualities. Both folk songs and hymns were generally written to be sung *a cappella*. Occasionally, as indicated in the discussion about minnesingers, accompaniments were performed ad libitum. These instrumental figurations were probably improvised on the spot and not written down. The vast majority of both sacred and secular vocal music right through the Middle Ages lacks any instrumental accompaniment and consists simply of one line of music, called "monophonic" music. We use this term regardless of how many persons sing the melody, provided that all sing the same notes in the same rhythm at the same time.

Although we can continue to find numerous examples of secular monophonic music, particularly folk songs, in the Renaissance, the predominant musical texture of this period was polyphonic. In polyphony, independent voice parts present important melodies simultaneously, thus providing a richly varied musical palette of far greater density than had appeared in the vocal compositions of earlier times. The monophonic songs of the mastersingers are, therefore, exceptional because they represent a continuation of the same techniques of the minnesingers of the thirteenth century.

A monophonic example from the vast repertory of Hans Sachs is his *Gesangsweise*. (See Carl Parrish, editor, *A Treasury of Early Music*, No. 22.) Sachs uses the *Bar* form, a limited range, and syllabic text setting, varied by occasional melodic flourishes, or *Blumen,* at cadences and also at the beginning of a song in order to embellish the text. Despite the development of precise rhythmic notation by this time, the correct rhythm of the piece eludes us. The repeated rhythmic patterns and duple meter have been determined from the text. The words, like those of many other mastersongs, come from the Bible (here the Psalms), but the piece is still nonliturgical.

The polyphonic textures of the Renaissance had created the need for keyboard instruments at which one performer could simultaneously play several independent melodies. As a result, this epoch saw the invention of many different instruments, among them the virginal, clavichord, and harpsichord, all forerunners of the piano. Composers began to develop idiomatic figurations suitable to the sound of these keyboard instruments. Later, in the baroque era, some musicians sought to combine vocal and instrumental style within the same composition. Musical history moves in cycles. By the seventeenth century, opera, a new genre, was gaining importance. With the development of opera came the demand for clear and expressive declamation of the text. This emphasis on the words resulted in the eventual polarization of the many strands of musical texture into two basic lines: a primary melody for the singer, and a bass line that incorporated all the other (now subordinate) melodies. Thus in the German solo song, or continuo lied, of the baroque period, the musical material was reduced to two basic parts: the singer's melody and the accompaniment. The accompaniment, or continuo, as it was often called, was performed by two players: a harpsichordist and a cellist, or bassoonist, who doubled the harpsichordist's bass (lowest) part. The sonority of the harpsichord as well as the aesthetic taste of the period limited the kind and style of the accompanimental figures. The use of figured bass, or shorthand notation, for the accompaniments of this period, while tending toward more harmonic richness and ultimate definition of tonalities, restricted the more imaginative figurations for the accompaniment.

By the eighteenth century, the *volkstümliches Lied,* the immediate precursor of the significant romantic lied, began to appear in the *Singspiel.* Here, in addition to the overture, entr'acte music, and dances, these self-contained songs, occasionally to preexistent melodies, offered relief from the continuous dialogue. These songs were usually very tuneful, with melodies whose pitches could be anticipated and easily remembered. Phrasing and meter were regular, and harmonization was routine. The songs were written for the most part on two staves, a treble and a bass. The treble offered the single line of the vocal melody; the bass contained the full chords or arpeggios of the supporting harmony. When accompanying a singer, the pianist used his left hand to supply the harmony, while his right hand merely doubled the singer's melody. Interest was thus focused on the melodic line, and after one or two renditions of the song, most members of the audience could sing the tune themselves.

Independent collections of songs began to appear before the middle of the eighteenth century. Often the melodies were well known, and the editor merely included several stanzas of a poem that could be sung to the printed music. The text was not set in position under the music. The editor assumed that those people who used the book would be sufficiently familiar with the texts to sing the proper words to the suitable pitches.

The romantic lied, a very specialized musical form, is first encountered in the late eighteenth century in a few works of the Viennese classical masters. The art of lieder composition, however, reached its zenith during the nineteenth century, principally in the vocal compositions of Schubert, Schumann, Brahms, and Hugo Wolf. It is their lieder, as well as those by some other German composers, which will be the focal point of our study.

II

The Early Romantic Lied

As we shall define it for use in this book, the lied is the German art song of the nineteenth century. It is usually a short composition for solo voice with piano accompaniment, based on a poetic text and composed in a fairly simple style designed to enhance the significance of the text. The lied—differing from the folk song, which is usually unaccompanied, anonymously composed, and transmitted by oral tradition—is the personal creation of an individual composer aiming at artistic perfection. In its deceptive simplicity, the lied conceals the artfulness with which its creator has fused the three elements of text, melody, and accompaniment into a unified whole.

Several different musical forms have been used in the composition of these songs. The basic types are these:

1 *Strophic:* The same music is repeated for each stanza of the text (*a a a a*).

2 *Strophic variation:* The melody is virtually the same for each stanza, but the accompaniment undergoes slight changes (*a a¹ a² a³*).

3 *Modified strophic:* Essentially the same structure and much the same music are used for each stanza, but the voice as well as the accompaniment has changes (also *a a¹ a² a³*).

4 *Ternary:* This form is made up of three sections, with the middle one contrasting in elements such as key, meter, style, mood, etc. The third section need not be an exact repetition of the first, but it uses basically the same material (*a b a* or *a b a¹*).

5 *Through-composed* or *durchkomponiert:* The melody and accom-

paniment follow the meaning and mood of the text, changing with each such change in the poetry. There may be some repetitions of sections or phrases in this form, but it is generally in several contrasting sections (*a b c d*).

Of course, the number of stanzas in each instance is variable.

Each form poses different problems. In strophic form the limitations imposed by the use of the same music for several different stanzas of a poem, while apparently simple, often create an insuperable challenge. Here, as the same pitches are required to underline different words, the entire meaning (as reflected in the music) may be distorted. The composer favoring the strophic form must somehow capture the basic mood of the poem within the framework of one melody, repeated perhaps four or five times, and yet avoid monotony. The strophic-variation and modified strophic forms allow the composer some freedom in setting individual words, but the restrictive scheme still involves much repetition. Ternary form allows a greater contrast, but requires that the text of the first and third sections be set to the same, or nearly the same, music. Understandably, the through-composed form allows the composer greater freedom in his accompaniments and in expression of the text. A combination of the above forms is sometimes the best solution. A good example of this can be heard in Schubert's *Die Forelle,* where, when the trout is finally caught, the strophic patterns change to fit the text.

The responsibility for setting the mood of the poem, commenting on the action, elaborating the vocalist's line through the anticipation or echo of a phrase, providing an interlude between stanzas, or concluding the song with an instrumental postlude rests with the accompaniment. Through the years, the significance of the piano accompaniment presented a problem to composers and critics concerned with the relative importance of words and music in the lied. Earlier writers indicated the interpretation of the text as the duty of the singer. By the late eighteenth century, however, the piano accompaniments began to share in the support of the vocal melody, sometimes through increased harmonic activities, other times through enrichment of the texture or embellishment of the melodic line. Mozart, in the example of his single Goethe lied, highlights the changing lines of the text through changes in the piano figurations. Schubert entrusts to the piano all manner of effects, increasing thereby not only the importance of the accompaniment but also the vitality of the song and its potential expressiveness. Schumann goes even further. He lifts the accompaniment to the level of the vocal melody and occasionally beyond it. Technological advances in the new piano enabled the composers to use it to mirror the changing moods of a poem.

To summarize, several factors contributed to the flourishing of the lied at the end of the eighteenth century. First, the new profusion of lyrical poetry, the best of which appeared in the works of Goethe; second, the significant technological advances in the new keyboard instrument, the piano; third, the existence of a group of composers, beginning with Beethoven, whose subjective approach to music required greater freedom of expression and a need to reflect their intimate sentiments in compositions that blended words and music. Finally, still another sociological change hastened the trend toward lieder composition: the growth of a middle class in which the women, instead of working, spent their time in pursuit of cultural activities—i.e., learning to play the piano (now found increasingly in private residences), singing, and buying the increased quantities of music distributed by the new commercial entrepreneurs, the music publishers.

In succeeding pages, beginning with Mozart's setting of Goethe's *Das Veilchen,* we shall discuss the meaning of the poem, examine specific details of the text, and comment on the success or failure of a composer's synthesis of words and music in his composition of the lied. Occasionally the words are stressed, at other times the music. We have not aimed at consistency. Rather, we have sought to emphasize the multiple facets of the text and music which together have made the piece an important example of the lied.

We shall feature the lieder of approximately ten composers, who have set to music poems written by about forty poets. Biographical material on most of the composers is readily accessible to readers; information on many of the poets is more difficult to acquire. For this reason we have included significant biographical data on the writers of the poems. Because Goethe is the poet whose works have been set by the largest number of composers, we shall first review his contribution.

JOHANN WOLFGANG VON GOETHE (1749-1832)

When historians look for what they call the last "universal man"— the last person who was a master of all known fields in his age—Goethe is always high on the list of candidates. Evincing all the versatility of his own character Faust, without the criminal Mephistophelian connections, he was, in addition to being the outstanding German literary figure of his day—and one of worldwide stature—a botanist, zoologist, geologist, physicist, painter, actor, statesman, supervisor of mines of the duchy of Weimar, attorney; and that does not exhaust the catalogue of his activities. Surely no major or minor poet since Goethe can present a comparable curriculum vitae. He wrote some two hundred books: plays, novels, novelettes, poetry, science, travel. His lyrical poems have attracted the best composers; there are about three thousand musical settings of Goethe's poems by Beethoven, Brahms, Mendelssohn, Schubert, Schumann, Wolf, and scores of others. Ironically enough, his understanding of music seems to have been less than profound.

Goethe's view of the literary process was an extremely personal one. On one occasion he stated that all his works were fragments of a great confession. He saw the beginning and end of literary activity as the reproduction of the world that surrounds the poet by means of a world that is *in* him, all things being perceived, related, re-created, molded, and reconstructed in a highly personal form and an original manner. This must cause some annoyance in those quarters where it is considered unforgivable to read into an author's works anything of his life. If it is true that literary works must stand on their own merits, it is equally true that the poetry of a very personal, subjective writer, such as Goethe indubitably was, cannot be fully grasped without some knowledge of the experience behind it and in it.

Despite the worship of the Goethe cult, which still thrives, his works cannot all be branded unadulterated masterpieces. How could they be, in view of their very profusion? Yet many of them are most rewarding to the person who brings something to their reading. He is no author for rapid readers. Often a line will have four or more levels of significance; one cannot coast along and at the same time really read Goethe. This may be what antagonizes those who have called him pretentious and stuffy. At times he is. But much of his literary creation wears extremely well and can occupy serious readers for many years, for Goethe was more than one literary figure; he was an age, or several ages, too varied and too profound to be pigeonholed in any movement or period. Yet every movement claimed him: rococo, *Sturm und Drang* (Storm and Stress), classicism, romanticism; he belonged to all but was monopolized by none. He led all and outgrew all. His best-known work is certainly the unclassifiable *Faust* (called by him a tragedy, though hardly fitting that label); most readers seem to know only Part I of *Faust,* whereas the great drama hardly begins until the mighty second part. Among his plays of the *Sturm und Drang* period one can mention *Götz von Berlichingen* and *Clavigo.* The novelette which took the world by storm, but no longer can, is *Die Leiden des jungen Werthers* (often incorrectly translated "The Sorrows of Young Werther," although *Leiden* means "sufferings"). His classical play par excellence is perhaps *Iphigenie.* A historical drama based on a critical period in the history of the Netherlands is *Egmont.* An idyllic poem in hexameters, with the fate of the refugees at the time of the French Revolution as its theme, is *Hermann und Dorothea.* His lengthy novel is *Wilhelm Meister,* his most renowned book of travel, *Italienische Reise.* Hardly one of the above works has been without its significance for music. And his lyrical poems have been a gold mine for the German lied, for it is scarcely an exaggeration to say that the German lyric achieved in Goethe's hands a higher perfection than ever before. His most spontaneous writing, the lyrical poem, usually seems to require no planning or cogitation. Even the choice of a specific meter or rhyme scheme seems to occur without forethought. It was not only the most natural thing for Goethe to express his own emotional experiences in poetry; it was almost an irresistible necessity. He "wrote himself out of" painful events in his life and transformed every significant experience into a poem which conveyed to the reader or hearer much of the essence of that experience. Speaking not specifically of himself but of the theoretical "genius" (a classification to which the none too modest Goethe would regard himself as belonging), he maintained that "everything that a genius creates, as a genius, is done unconsciously." There may be considerable debate whether this can apply to all his works. *Faust,* for example, took the greater part of a long lifetime to write, and there were many changes and reworkings of that masterpiece, but the statement may well hold true for most of his lyrical poems. Some of the best of these seemed to come to him in a flash of inspiration, while on a solitary walk, but equally as often in crowded company. Sometimes he arose from a fitful sleep and was able to regain repose only after committing to writing an insistent poem that virtually demanded to be born. The amazing diversity of his poetry also strikes us. His lyrical works cannot be contained in one or two categories; he essayed almost every conceivable type of poetry, often with consummate success.

Das Veilchen

Ein Veilchen auf der Wiese stand,
Gebückt in sich und unbekannt;
Es war ein herzigs Veilchen.
Da kam eine junge Schäferin,
Mit leichtem Schritt und munterm Sinn,
Daher, daher,
Die Wiese her, und sang.

Ach! denkt das Veilchen, wär' ich nur
Die schönste Blume der Natur,
Ach, nur ein kleines Weilchen,
Bis mich das Liebchen abgepflückt
Und an dem Busen mattgedrückt!
Ach nur, ach nur
Ein Viertelstündchen lang!

Ach! aber ach! das Mädchen kam
Und nicht in acht das Veilchen nahm,
Ertrat das arme Veilchen.
Es sank und starb und freut' sich noch:
Und sterb' ich denn, so sterb' ich doch
Durch sie, durch sie,
Zu ihren Füssen doch.

The poem is from a *Singspiel, Erwin und Elmire* (1775). The poem itself was written in 1773. Goethe revised it a few times, contrary to his customary procedure; in the original version it is sung by Elmire, the reluctant heroine. She believes it to have been written by Erwin, the hapless hero whom she has treated coldly. As she sings, she perceives the obvious symbolism. The song has the effect of melting her heart and ultimately inducing her to show poor Erwin a modicum of pity. This is obviously not the most spontaneous of Goethe's poems.

There is a cross-cultural difficulty in accepting the violet as representative of a man. In English this is impossible. In Italian it would be just as difficult, for *violetta* is feminine and is also the name of a girl. German *Veilchen*, however, being neuter (because a diminutive), may represent either sex. Here it is made the symbol of an ill-treated male.

The violet is solitary; it is a modest, unassuming flower (*gebückt in sich und unbekannt*), yet it arouses affection, and perhaps pity (*es war ein herzigs Veilchen*). Then a young shepherdess comes by, and as soon as we see *Schäferin* in a poem we expect the artificiality of pastoral verse. This pastoral lass is both carefree and careless. The poor violet wishes that he were, for a moment, the loveliest flower in creation, so that she might pick him and press him to her bosom. But, alas (and there are more than enough *ach*'s), the maiden pays no attention to him as she comes by and unthinkingly tramples him. As he dies, the violet expresses gratification that he dies because of her, at her feet. In the *Singspiel* the man does not die but wins the girl. Since practically everything Goethe wrote was autobiographical, he had in mind, perhaps, a real girl and a real incident.

Notes on the text:

1   *Veilchen:* note that the initial sound is "f."
3   *herzigs (herziges):* "lovely, sweet, appealing to the heart," not "hearty."
6   *Daher, daher:* belongs with *kam; kam daher* "came along."
7   *Die Wiese her:* "along the meadow, across the meadow."
10   *Weilchen:* a rhyme that is almost too close for comfort; it rhymes with *Veilchen* (lines 3 and 17) in an irregular interstrophic scheme.
14   *Viertelstündchen:* the peculiarly mathematical "only a quarter of an hour" is somewhat jarring, being rescued from being completely prosaic, perhaps, by the diminutive ending.
17   *ertrat:* for the more usual *zertrat* "trampled."

The last two lines of Mozart's setting are not the ending of Goethe's poem.

Mozart was not by nature a composer of lieder. Instead he wrote operas, most of which show his complete assimilation of the Italian vocal style. His self-contained songs are relatively few, and they tend to sound more like operatic scenas or arias. *Das Veilchen*, an exception, has become one of the prototypes of the nineteenth-century lied. For his German opera, *Die Zauberflöte*, however, Mozart wrote two *Volkslieder, Ein Vogelfänger bin ich ja* and *Ein Mädchen oder Weibchen*, both sung by Papageno. These are models of the strophic song, with predictable rhythms and phrasing, easily remembered tunes, and within the grasp of any amateur singer.

Mozart's Goethe lied includes many characteristics of the contemporary aria of his day. For example, the piano prelude presents the entire first portion of the vocal melody before the singer begins, thus giving him the proper pitch and also setting the mood of the poem. When the voice enters, the piano repeats its opening phrase, at the same time doubling the voice (Ex. 2-a). The composer highlights the text as the shepherdess trips gaily along (Ex. 2-b). After a new figuration in the piano interlude, he emphasizes the violet's apprehension with a modulation to the minor mode (Ex. 2-c). This completely new texture in the accompaniment now changes the mood of the song.

Notice the descending chromatic scale at *sank und starb* and the quasi-recitative vocal style in the concluding measures. The text is set syllabically, one note to each syllable, and only a few words are repeated. *Das Veilchen* is *durchkomponiert,* the music changing with the text, much in the manner of an aria.

Ex. 2

MOZART: *Das Veilchen*

Ein Veil - chen auf der Wie - se stand ge - bückt in sich und un - be - kannt:

a.

leich - tem Schritt und mun - term Sinn da -

b.

"Ach!" denkt das Veil - chen, _____

C.

Wonne der Wehmut

Trocknet nicht, trocknet nicht,
Tränen der ewigen Liebe!
Ach, nur dem halbgetrockneten Auge
Wie öde, wie tot die Welt ihm erscheint!
Trocknet nicht, trocknet nicht,
Tränen unglücklicher Liebe!

Like Mozart, Beethoven was not primarily a lieder composer. On the other hand, he did make a significant formal contribution to the literature in his song cycle *An die ferne Geliebte,* a setting of six unrelated poems by A. Jeitteles, a Viennese Jewish medical student. In these songs, the piano joins the individual poems by continuing uninterruptedly throughout the cycle. In other words, when the singer has concluded a song, the pianist plays a postlude that holds the listener's attention and carries him into the next number. This kind of continuity, however, was not employed by any of the major lieder composers. But another feature, Beethoven's repetition of the melody of the first song in the last stanza of the final song, anticipates Schumann's technique in the last lied of his *Frauenliebe und -leben.* Unfortunately, the quality of the poetry of *An die ferne Geliebte* does not match that of the music. Beethoven also set a few of Goethe's poems, which provide a welcome contrast to the poetry of Jeitteles. One of the best of these Goethe lieder is *Wonne der Wehmut.*

In mood and attitude the poem *Wonne der Wehmut* belongs to the sentimental phase of *Sturm und Drang,* rather than to the aspect of that movement that insisted on action and rebellion. It is reminiscent of the weepy passages of *Werther,* although its lachrymose excesses are less extreme. The sense is that life is much harder to bear if tears are suppressed, or even half checked. It is only when they are allowed to flow unimpeded that the sufferer will experience the emotional release that makes the desolate world endurable. The poet pretends that the love which is the source of these tears is eternal (line 2); at the end he calls it unhappy; hence we are asked to believe that this is a case of lasting, unrequited love. Will the tears, then, never cease? But the title implies that the very melancholy from which release is sought is itself a pleasure.

The unrhymed verses seem to point to an earlier period of Goethe's *Sturm und Drang* than does the record of its date of writing (middle of the 1780's). The irregular meter is essentially dactylic, with the number of feet per line varying between two and four.

Beethoven has here extended the length of the original poem by means of text repetition. Notice the flowing tears reflected by the running notes in the accompaniment (Ex. 3). The sobs and sighs increase in intensity until the final measure, where the descending scale figure is the longest of the entire lied. The highest pitch of the melody is at the G natural on *Tränen* (bar 17). The singer then can settle down into the final notes. Beethoven uses a syllabic text setting, often doubling the vocal line in the accompaniment. Observe the appoggiaturas (dissonant notes on accented beats) that underline the cries of the unhappy lover in bars 1, 2, and 6.

Ex. 3

BEETHOVEN: *Wonne der Wehmut*

III

The High Romantic Lied

SCHUBERT (1797-1828)

By the sheer weight of their numbers (over 600), Schubert's lieder occupy a disproportionately large position in the repertory. And by virtue of their quality, many outshine those of his foremost successors and all of his predecessors. To the songs of his two cycles, both to poems by Wilhelm Müller, we cannot give unstinting praise. Some settings are delightful, others poignant; but still others do not rank with the best that their composer has left us. *Die Winterreise,* written in 1827, when Schubert was at the height of his powers, surpasses the earlier *Die schöne Müllerin* (1823). In both cycles, the songs are interrelated principally by extramusical means: in the 1823 cycle, the adventures of the young miller who, inspired by the motion of the millstream, decides to see more of the world; in the later cycle, the young man's sad journey as he leaves his native village, rejected by his sweetheart. In each, the interest is cumulative; the songs should not be sung out of context. Coursing through both collections is the nature music we have come to associate with Schubert, particularly his water figures. At no time does Schubert use recurrent musical motives. Yet each cycle presents a tightly knit, cohesive musical unit. The composer omitted the prologue and epilogue of *Die schöne Müllerin,* as well as three of Müller's poems, setting twenty of the total twenty-five in a rearranged sequence. He set all twenty-four poems of *Die Winterreise.*

Limitations of space prevent a discussion of the two Müller cycles. (See p. 83 for comments on one song, *Das Wandern,* the opening of *Die schöne Müllerin.*) Within each, however, we can find a wide variety of piano figurations, many never before used by the composer. Schubert created fresh material for his lieder accompaniments. Unlike Schumann, he did not write his large-scale piano works and then begin to tackle the lied. Lieder and piano pieces appeared within the same few years. Only in the last two years of his life (1826-28)—the period that saw the completion of the two Piano Trios, the C Major Symphony, and the C Major String Quintet—did his work undergo a distinct change of style. This change is most noticeable in his lieder and chamber works.

The Heine songs of *Schwanengesang* (composed in 1828), the cycle put together by the publisher Haslinger after Schubert's death, rate with the finest of all his lieder. We do not believe that these were meant to be part of a cycle; they are often sung separately.

Schubert's treatment of the accompaniment was unique for his time. Conceivably he was influenced in his choice of figurations by the new style of piano writing that he heard in Beethoven's sonatas. Schubert extends the function of the piano accompaniment beyond that of any earlier song composer. The piano sets the scene, comments on the actions, anticipates or echoes the vocal phrase, and sometimes provides a prelude, postlude, or interlude between stanzas. Most important, it supplies the ingredient that unifies the several stanzas of a poem.

Despite its newfound importance, however, the accompaniment is never meant to overwhelm the singer. The piano in Schubert's lieder is subordinate to the voice; it offers support to the singer. The melodic line is usually complete in the vocal part. Only rarely does the pianist conclude a phrase that originated with the voice; nor is the melody fragmented between voice and piano, as we so often find it in Schumann's lieder.

Schubert's imitations of nature, his water figures, storm scenes, whistling wind, and rustling leaves and flowers represent fine examples of *Tonmalerei*, tone painting. Although many of the accompaniments are fairly difficult for the average pianist to play, we must remember that Schubert was not a virtuoso and thus was not aiming at pyrotechnical feats. A keen sense of rhythm is a requisite for good performances, however, because often pianist and singer are active on different rhythmic levels.

In his 600-odd songs, Schubert set the poems of approximately ninety poets. We shall examine only a few of his lieder, but each will be shown to include several unusual aspects of lieder composition. Because the Goethe poems are among the earliest of his many remarkable settings, we shall discuss them first.

Gretchen am Spinnrade

Meine Ruh ist hin,
Mein Herz ist schwer,
Ich finde sie nimmer
Und nimmermehr.

Wo ich ihn nicht hab',
Ist mir das Grab,
Die ganze Welt
Ist mir vergällt.

Mein armer Kopf
Ist mir verrückt,
Mein armer Sinn
Ist mir zerstückt.

Meine Ruh ist hin,
Mein Herz ist schwer,
Ich finde sie nimmer
Und nimmermehr.

Nach ihm nur schau ich
Zum Fenster hinaus,
Nach ihm nur geh' ich
Aus dem Haus.

Sein hoher Gang,
Sein' edle Gestalt,
Seines Mundes Lächeln,
Seiner Augen Gewalt,

Und seiner Rede
Zauberfluss,
Sein Händedruck,
Und ach, sein Kuss!

Meine Ruh ist hin,
Mein Herz ist schwer,
Ich finde sie nimmer
Und nimmermehr.

Mein Busen drängt
Sich nach ihm hin.
Ach dürft'ich fassen
Und halten ihn,

Und küssen ihn,
So wie ich wollt',
An seinen Küssen
Vergehen sollt'!

Meine Ruh ist hin,
Mein Herz ist schwer,
Ich finde sie nimmer
Und nimmermehr.

Those who know *Faust* only through Gounod's opera, or even Marlowe's play, have very little notion of the nature of Goethe's drama, which took most of his life to write. Goethe knew the old traditions, also a *Faust* puppet play, a *Volksbuch* ("chapbook"), and conceivably Marlowe's version. But there is little resemblance in Goethe's *Faust* to the old story of the disillusioned, aging professor who sells his soul to the devil in return for pleasure and power, and who agrees to be dragged off to hell after a stipulated length of time—usually twenty-four years.

There were various forms and versions of Goethe's *Faust: Faust, ein Fragment,* the *Urfaust* (discovered after Goethe's death), etc. In its final form, *Faust* is introduced by three successive prologues:

(1) *Zueignung* ("Dedication"). Recollection of the voices and figures of the past, friends now gone who were still alive when Goethe began work on the drama.

(2) *Vorspiel auf dem Theater* (suggested by the Sanskrit drama *Šakuntala* by the Indian author Kalidasa). Three figures concerned in the theatrical venture get together and discuss plans: the manager, the poet, the clown. The manager wants effects that will bring in money; the clown is anxious to make people laugh; the poet has a far different plan in mind. This *Vorspiel* provides a link between the drama and the stage, the boards.

(3) *Prolog im Himmel.* The idea comes from the Book of Job. Mephistopheles appears in heaven and manages to exact from the Lord the permission to tempt Faust, being sure that he, like any other man, will prove to be a puny wretch with his face in the mud, unworthy of God's trust. Mephisto is no longer a traditional devil. "I am the spirit that always negates, a part of that force which always wants evil yet always creates good." He is sardonic and blasphemous, like the traditional devil, granted. He says, "I like to see the Old Man [God] now and then, and I am careful to keep relations between us civil. It's actually very decent of

a mighty lord to be so 'human' in talking to the devil."

The first scene in Faust's study reveals a high-vaulted, narrow Gothic chamber full of manuscripts, books, paraphernalia. Faust is still a relatively young man; as he says, he has been teaching "going on ten years." Fed up with book knowledge and with all of his subjects, which give him no satisfactory answers to his questions, he has resorted to magic. He opens a magic tome and looks at the sign of the macrocosm, but the experience is too overpowering and he cannot bear even the sight of that symbol. He then succeeds in summoning the Earth Spirit. But he is unable to endure the sight of this spirit either, and he is told to associate with his own kind or with a spirit that he can comprehend. His mood hits the depths of despair, and he is aroused from it only by the knocking of his famulus, or assistant—Wagner—who begs to be permitted to enter and to listen to Faust. Wagner thinks Faust is declaiming a Greek drama, and he would like to profit from observing this, for "such things make a great impression nowadays." He reveals himself to be the very antithesis of Faust: smug, satisfied with the "great progress" that man has made, delighted in his musty manuscripts and tomes. After he has left, Faust looks toward a vial with a brown potion and contemplates ending his life. But at that moment the Easter chimes and the Easter chorus prevent him from taking that decisive step. Not that he "gets religion." Rather, he is recalled to a happier time of childhood, when doubts did not assail him, when there was real joy in life, and he is, for the time being, won back: *Die Erde hat mich wieder* ("Earth has me once again").

In the next scene *Vor dem Tor* ("Outside the city gates"), Faust joins Wagner and most of the townspeople on a bright Easter Sunday. Able to enjoy at a distance some of the more obviously genuine pleasures of the people, Faust nevertheless becomes more and more estranged from the world, especially the scholarly world and the dry pedantry represented by Wagner. As the shadows lengthen, Faust notices a peculiar black poodle, which keeps running in circles around the two but coming ever closer. Wagner sees in the beast a common mutt, but Faust is strangely fascinated and surmises something unusual in the canine capers. He takes the dog home with him. The dog rests temporarily behind the stove while Faust returns to a long-abandoned task: the translation of the Bible. He wrestles with the first chapter of John and has trouble rendering the Greek *lógos,* which predecessors have translated "word" ("In the beginning was the Word"). He makes a few attempts at finding a good German equivalent, much to the annoyance of the poodle, it seems, who growls ferociously as Faust continues his scriptural activity. Then Faust hits upon the word

Tat ("the deed") as the most appropriate. The poodle then goes through a strange metamorphosis. He swells up, assumes various forms, becomes as huge as a hippopotamus—and looks like one—until he explodes, and a rather dudish scholar steps out. It is, of course, one manifestation of Mephistopheles. He brings the conversation around to his favorite theme. Foolishly, he offers to serve Faust in this life if Faust will return the favor in the beyond. Faust is not much concerned with the hereafter. Then Mephisto promises him more pleasure than any man has known before: fine living, money, women, honor, glory. Faust is bored at all this, although not entirely. He insists that he is not interested in these things alone; he wants rather to experience everything that mankind has experienced— pleasure *and* pain, ecstasy *and* suffering, fruition *and* frustration. And now he offers his own bargain. "You may provide me with all that you can. And if I ever lie on a bed of ease, if ever the pleasure you provide me is so great that I wish that moment to last forever, I've lost. I'm yours." Mephistopheles, somewhat perplexed, agrees. But he wants the pact to be signed in blood. Faust is amused at the legalistic pedantry of the devil. A gentlemen's agreement will not satisfy the diabolic chap. *Blut ist ein ganz besonderer Saft*—"Blood is a very special fluid"—says Mephisto.

Shortly thereafter Mephisto leads Faust into the student life of a tavern. ("The Song of the Flea" is Mephisto's contribution to the festivities, also some magic and hocus-pocus.) The two leave, airborne, on a barrel, Faust being profoundly bored.

A weird interlude is the *Hexenküche,* the Witches' Kitchen. Disgusting sights, fantastic allurements, revolting apes, a magic mirror in which Faust sees Margarete's face, and the potion which "makes him feel as if he has lost twenty years" are the principal features of this complicated scene.

Later he sees Margarete—Gretchen—as she returns home from church. He has never felt so attracted to a girl. She pretends to be offended at his attempt to pick her up, but she continues to think about him as she goes home. Then comes Faust's first request of Mephistopheles: "Get me that girl!" "That one? It's not in my power; she has just come from confession and is cleared of all sin. Her sins were hardly worth mentioning, anyway. I have no power over a girl like that." Faust replies, "We have a deal. Get me that girl!" "It takes time! I need two weeks to prepare the way." "What? I could do the job in a few hours." Mephisto does manage to smuggle Faust into Gretchen's room, where he remains for a few blissful moments. To his chagrin, the lecherous impulses that seemed to dominate him a few minutes ago vanish, and he feels almost as if he were in a church.

He leaves before she comes. But Mephisto has left there a marvelous chest of jewels, which the girl straightway takes to the priest.

This ecclesiastical destination of the jewelry almost drives Mephistopheles out of his mind. He tries to curse by all that is diabolical. He would fain give himself over to the devil, if he did not occupy that post himself. Faust calmly informs him that he must provide another chest of jewels at once. "Of course, Professor, everything is child's play to you!" Faust demands immediate action, or the entire deal is over.

We next see Gretchen at the house of her neighbor, Frau Marthe, a woman who would apparently stop at almost nothing to achieve her aims. She learns that Gretchen has found another chest of jewels, far more dazzling than the first. "Keep them" is her advice.

Later, Mephistopheles arrives and gives a report, real or false, of the demise of Frau Marthe's husband, of whom she has heard nothing for a long time. She wants a death certificate; like Mephisto, she is legalistic. Another witness is required. Mephisto has a friend, a fine gentleman; he'll witness the signature.

On the next visit, Faust and Gretchen meet and are obviously madly attracted to each other. And Marthe does her best to capture Mephisto. He finds it time to leave. There are subsequent meetings, and Gretchen is head over heels in love. Faust, too, has never felt this way.

Suddenly, for reasons not made clear, but surely as a result of the machinations of Mephistopheles, Faust feels he must leave town for a while and get close to nature. He becomes a kind of hermit in a cave in the forest. Here he reassesses his philosophical thinking. Gretchen is temporarily not on his mind. But he is on hers. Mephisto comes to Faust and maliciously tells him how wretched the poor girl is. "She thinks you have deserted her, and you have, in a way."

To Faust, love is a more complicated passion than the simple emotion felt by Gretchen. Yet, simple or not, her love is all-consuming. As she sings at the spinning wheel (the accompaniment of many a lovelorn maid in German song), she admits that without Faust's love—spiritual and physical—life is not worth living. This represents an overwhelming transformation in a pious girl, for she reveals that even her strong sense of traditional morality has been overcome by the magic of that love. And her repetition of the words *Meine Ruh ist hin, mein Herz ist schwer* indicates that she is completely occupied by this one emotion and lives only for her beloved's return.

Notes on the text:

> Title. Goethe does not give the song a name in *Faust;* there is merely a stage direction: *Gretchen am Spinnrade allein.*

> 1   *hin:* "gone."
> 3   *sie:* refers to *meine Ruh(e).*
> 3   *nimmer:* archaic for *nie* ("never")—from *nie mehr* ("nevermore") —which would render *nimmermehr* tautologous, were it not for the fact that the etymological identity of *nimmer* and *nie mehr* is not remembered.
> 5   *wo:* can be spatial "where" and temporal "when," and probably both senses are contained here.
> 10   *verrückt:* not specifically the adjective "crazy," although the latter is derived from this word, but rather the past participle *verrückt*— from *ver-* ("mis-") plus *rücken* ("move")—"displace, disarrange, derange, disturb, confuse."
> 25   *seiner Rede:* genitive, "of his speech."
> 40   *vergehen:* die. Gretchen's mental disturbance seems reflected in the confused syntax of the last two lines (for *Da sollt' ich . . .* or the like).

Young Schubert had been reading *Faust* for several weeks when, struck by the pathos of the young girl deserted by her lover, he wrote this song in a single day. With this one lied the seventeen-year-old boy created a landmark in the history of the art song. The constant accompanying figure, the sound of the spinning wheel (Ex. 4-a), remains basically the same throughout the piece, stopping only when Gretchen is overcome by the thought of her lover's kiss (Ex. 4-b). After she begins work once again, the accompaniment resumes, slowly gathering speed until it reaches Tempo primo.

The recurrent figuration in the piano part and the repeated *Meine Ruh ist hin, mein Herz ist schwer* in the vocal line produce the effect of a strophic setting. Musically the refrain comes at the beginning, twice more, and only partially at the end. The stanzas between refrains, however, are not treated strophically, but in through-composed fashion. In this way Schubert creates a combination of unity and variety. Throughout most of the song, the bass supports the running sixteenth notes in the treble in a

Ex. 4

SCHUBERT: *Gretchen am Spinnrade*

a.

b.

manner that suggests a feeling of uneasiness that would not be evoked by the same dominant-tonic alternation if sounded by full chords. Observe that the two hands are together only on the first and third of each group of three eighth notes.

Beginning at *Sein hoher Gang* (bar 51), Schubert changes the bass figure and increases the tension by raising the pitches in the melody until reaching a G at *Kuss*. Another rise is essayed at *Ach, dürft'* (bar 89), but

it is not sustained. The anguished climax of the text finds reflection in the
highest pitch of the entire vocal melody, A at *vergehen.* It occurs twice,
bars 107 and 111, before the conclusion. For musical reasons, Schubert
adds the refrain *Meine Ruh,* etc., at the close. Notice how this refrain
always begins on an upbeat (last beat of the bar) so that the significant
words *Ruh* and *Herz* fall on the accented beat (first note in each bar),
sometimes lengthened for emphasis.

Der König in Thule

Es war ein König in Thule,
Gar treu bis an das Grab,
Dem sterbend seine Buhle
Einen goldnen Becher gab.

Es ging ihm nichts darüber,
Er leert' ihn jeden Schmaus;
Die Augen gingen ihm über ,
So oft er trank daraus.

Und als er kam zu sterben,
Zählt' er seine Städt' im Reich,
Gönnt' alles seinen Erben,
Den Becher nicht zugleich.

Er sass beim Königsmahle,
Die Ritter um ihn her,
Auf hohem Vätersaale,
Dort auf dem Schloss am Meer.

Dort stand der alte Zecher,
Trank letzte Lebensglut,
Und warf den heil'gen Becher
Hinunter in die Flut.

Er sah ihn stürzen, trinken
Und sinken tief ins Meer.
Die Augen täten ihm sinken ;
Trank nie einen Tropfen mehr.

Probably written in 1773 or 1774, this poem was recited by Goethe to
friends in Cologne while on a trip through the Rhineland in 1774. It was
incorporated into the first draft of *Faust* (the *Urfaust*) and remains in the
final version.

Gretchen is addressed by a rather forward stranger (Faust) as she leaves church. She rebuffs him, as decent maidens are expected to do, and goes home. But she cannot forget him, and, while thinking about him at home, she sings this song. She is not to be regarded as aware of the profounder significance for her own life, for she is no prophetess, but she does reveal unwittingly something of the tragedy that is to come.

The golden cup symbolizes love that lasts beyond the grave. It, like the memory of his love, belongs to the King alone. He casts the cup into the sea so that no one else may gain possession of it. The gloomy, mysterious mood of the poem is reminiscent of many Scots ballads, of which Goethe was especially fond.

Notes on the text:

1   *Thule:* the Ultima Thule of the Romans was supposedly the most northerly isle beyond Britain, and there have been numerous claimants to the title. Some say it was Iceland; others, one of the Hebrides; still others identify it as Greenland. It was said by ancient geographers to be a six-day ocean journey beyond Britain.

5   *Es ging ihm nichts darüber:* "to him, nothing surpassed it, nothing was more precious to him."

6   *Schmaus:* "banquet, feast." Perhaps every meal in the palace was a *Schmaus.*

13-16   All the expressions employed in this strophe are traditional elements of one type of ballad—*beim Königsmahle, die Ritter um ihn her, Vätersaale* (the lofty ancestral hall)—the Castle by the Sea.

21-22   *stürzen, trinken, sinken:* first it plunges (*stürzen*), then it fills (*trinken*), then it sinks (*sinken*).

23   *Die Augen täten ihm sinken: täten* is not a subjunctive but an old form of the past indicative. As in English, the verb "do" used to be common as an auxiliary in colloquial German ("his eyes, they did drop").

Whereas *Gretchen am Spinnrade* clearly relates to the drama of *Faust, Der König in Thule* seems not to belong to the story at all. This ballad, however, caught the fancy of numerous musicians, among them Liszt and Berlioz, besides Schubert. In fact, Zelter (1758-1832), one of Schubert's foremost musical forebears, wrote a strophic version of the poem in 1812. Goethe himself declared the strophic form to be the best type of setting for a ballad of this sort, and most of the settings are strophic ones. Gounod, in the third act of his *Faust,* wrote the *Chanson du roi de Thulé* in an attempt to place a self-contained song in the continuous musical fabric of opera. He interrupted the stanzas with recitative, but the fundamental stanzaic outlines are clearly distinguishable.

Curiously, Schubert favors the older *Bar* form again, *a a b* for each verse. The folklike melody sounds somewhat like a dirge; the plodding bass octaves, one to each measure until the final bars of each phrase, emphasize the essentially melancholy mood. In this relatively thin-textured lied, Schubert shows good rhythmic balance: the bass moves in half notes, the treble in quarters, while the voice is the most varied of all.

Heidenröslein

Sah ein Knab' ein Röslein stehn
Röslein auf der Heiden,
War so jung und morgenschön,
Lief er schnell, es nah zu sehn,
Sah's mit vielen Freuden.
Röslein, Röslein, Röslein rot,
Röslein auf der Heiden.

Knabe sprach: Ich breche dich,
Röslein auf der Heiden!
Röslein sprach: Ich steche dich,
Dass du ewig denkst an mich,
Und ich will's nicht leiden·
Röslein, Röslein, Röslein rot,
Röslein auf der Heiden.

Und der wilde Knabe brach
's Röslein auf der Heiden;
Röslein wehrte sich und stach,
Half ihm doch kein Weh und Ach,
Musst'es eben leiden.
Röslein, Röslein, Röslein rot,
Röslein auf der Heiden.

People who expend time and ink on such matters have waged a battle concerning the origin of this poem, a battle which has never been entirely decided until this day. There seems to be no doubt that Goethe's poem is based on a folk song, one form of which is found in a collection by Paul van der Aelst (1602). Goethe apparently recited his version of the poem to Herder, who published it, from memory, in two different works, in neither case attributing it to an author. In one instance he designates it as being *aus der mündlichen Sage* (by oral transmission). When Goethe later included the poem in his own works, some authorities accused Herder of having suppressed the name of the author. Others may have suspected Goethe of plagiarism.

The whole matter is a tempest in a teapot. Goethe has reworked, stylistically and aesthetically, a poem of popular origin, imparting to it a new form and creating out of the earlier folk song what amounts to an art song. He also, as usual, applies it to his own experience, and it belongs to that group of poems owing their inspiration to his love for Friederike Brion, the pretty daughter of the pastor of Sesenheim, an Alsatian village near Strasbourg. This most idyllic affair of his student days began, if we are to believe his account, as love at first sight, but ended abruptly when Goethe contemplated with sudden terror the thought of marriage, which must have been in the girl's mind. Goethe showed many times later in life that he was able to love them and leave them. But there seems to have been long-lasting remorse over this ill treatment of a girl who deserved something much better. Goethe exploited this love affair in a number of poems which, while slight of substance, are something new in German lyrics. They evince a freshness and melodiousness, a freedom from pedantry of rules, but, nevertheless, an artistic finish such as had not been seen for centuries—some overexuberant critics of short memory say not since Walther von der Vogelweide.

Friederike is also, in part, the model for Gretchen in *Faust* and contributes to other characters in Goethe's plays. *Heidenröslein* is usually regarded as a companion piece to *Das Veilchen*. The wild rose (also a diminutive) here designates the girl. The affair is more painful, and there is more resistance. The *Veilchen* hoped that his beloved would pick him; the *Röslein* threatens, "I'll stick you so that you'll never forget me." The boy picks the wild rose, notwithstanding, and is badly pricked by her thorns. And Goethe suffered pangs of conscience for many years because of his calculated separation from Friederike Brion. *Heidenröslein,* although a reworked *Volkslied,* is a personal poem. Its counterpart, *Das Veilchen,* is less obviously so and is a trifle too sentimental.

Notes on the text:

Title. *Heide:* "heath"; *Röslein* (diminutive of *Rose*): "little heath rose," actually "wild rose."

1 *sah ein Knab':* here, as in 3, 4, and 5, the word order is that of the folk song (verb first). *Knabe* is now obsolete.
2 *Heiden:* an archaic dative singular (now *Heide*).
3 The absence of a subject is unusual.
    morgenschön: "morning-fair, lovely as morning," probably a compound of Goethe's own coinage. He contributed many such to the language.
6 *Röslein rot:* an ancient word order, with uninflected adjective following the noun.
8 *Knabe:* the lack of a definite article is unusual. It almost looks as if *Knabe* and *Röslein* were treated as dramatis personae in this miniature drama.
16 *'s: das.* Any temptation in the performance of this song to pause after *brach 's* will result in violence to the sense.
18 *ihm:* refers to the rose (*Röslein,* neuter) and not to the boy. This line has often been misunderstood by students of German.

Whether or not Goethe himself wrote this poem or based it on a folk song, Schubert's music does have the flavor of a folk tune. Although another setting, Heinrich Werner's song of 1827, has remained popular in Germany, it is through Schubert's composition that *Heidenröslein* is universally known. Characterized by clear-cut strophic form, syllabic text underlay, and a lightly tripping figure in the piano that serves to tie together the repeated stanzas, *Heidenröslein* is a foil for *Das Veilchen*. Whereas the violet is destroyed by the young shepherdess as she steps on it, in *Heidenröslein* the rose pricks the boy who picks it and makes him suffer for his actions. Schubert's preference for strophic form in *Heidenröslein* contrasts with Mozart's use of *durchkomponiert* technique in *Das Veilchen*.

Because of the limitations of a strophic setting, *Freuden* and *leiden* fall on the same notes (a tritone at bars 10 and 26). Are joy and sorrow closely associated? Schubert's irregular phrase groups also suggest the designs of folk song. For example, in the normal classical style the first four bars, or antecedent phrase, would be followed by a subsequent phrase, also of four bars. Schubert extends the phrase by two bars (Ex. 5-a), bring-ing the rhythmic activity to a climax here with the running sixteenth notes. Compare also bar 4 with bar 12, and notice how Schubert supports the repeated *Röslein* with smaller note values, filling in the gap in the interval between D and G. The phrase *Röslein auf der Heiden* features an accompanying figure (see * in Ex. 5-b) that Schubert often employs to reflect naïveté or simplicity. He concludes with a postlude that echoes the voice part and leads into the next stanza.

Ex. 5

a.

b.

Erlkönig

Wer reitet so spät durch Nacht und Wind?
Es ist der Vater mit seinem Kind;
Er hat den Knaben wohl in dem Arm,
Er fasst ihn sicher, er hält ihn warm.

"Mein Sohn, was birgst du so bang dein Gesicht?"
"Siehst, Vater, du den Erlkönig nicht?
Den Erlenkönig mit Kron' und Schweif?"
"Mein Sohn, es ist ein Nebelstreif."

"Du liebes Kind, komm, geh mit mir!
Gar schöne Spiele spiel' ich mit dir;
Manch bunte Blumen sind an dem Strand,
Meine Mutter hat manch gülden Gewand."

"Mein Vater, mein Vater, und hörest du nicht,
Was Erlenkönig mir leise verspricht?"
"Sei ruhig, bleibe ruhig, mein Kind:
In dürren Blättern säuselt der Wind."

"Willst, feiner Knabe, du mit mir gehn?
Meine Töchter sollen dich warten schön;
Meine Töchter führen den nächtlichen Reihn
Und wiegen und tanzen und singen dich ein."

"Mein Vater, mein Vater, und siehst du nicht dort
Erlkönigs Töchter am düstern Ort?"
"Mein Sohn, mein Sohn, ich seh es genau:
Es scheinen die alten Weiden so grau."

"Ich liebe dich, mich reizt deine schöne Gestalt;
Und bist du nicht willig, so brauch ich Gewalt."
"Mein Vater, mein Vater, jetzt fasst er mich an!
Erlkönig hat mir ein Leid's getan!"--

Dem Vater grauset's, er reitet geschwind,
Er hält in den Armen das ächzende Kind,
Erreicht den Hof mit Müh und Not;
In seinen Armen das Kind war tot.

This ballad was originally the first number in Goethe's *Die Fischerin,* a light operatic work performed first in 1782. But the contents of the poem have no connection with the plot of the operetta.

The theme comes from the Danish. Goethe's friend Herder translated a Danish folk song in which King Oluf rides out to invite guests to his wedding. He is stopped by an elfin maiden, who asks him to dance with her. When he refuses, she casts a spell on him and sends him home a dying man.

Erlkönig is, as a name, a mistranslation of Danish *Ellerkone* ("elfin woman"); the error was Herder's but was adopted by Goethe. This is of no stupendous importance, for Goethe's poem maintains an identity of its own that is largely independent of the Danish source.

To be sure, the motivation for the death of the boy becomes quite different. In the *Ellerkone* an offense was committed against the elfin maiden. In Goethe's poem there is no such theme. But we must not think, as generations of American students seem to have thought, that the boy is ill. He dies through fear and through the power of his own imagination. There is, on Goethe's part, probably a protest against exaggerated rationalism here. There is not a rational and logical explanation for everything in life or death. Yet the father, the voice of reason, attempts to find such explanations. "That is no *Erlkönig,* my son; it's a wisp of mist." Or: "It's the wind rustling in the dry leaves," not the whispering of a supernatural voice luring the boy. But when the boy emits an uncanny scream, "Father, he's got hold of me! He's hurt me!" the would-be rationalistic father is no longer so certain of his own explanations; the boy's scream is so vivid and his fear seems so real that the father himself now shares the fear: *Dem Vater grauset's* (he is horrified). To get away from the weird scene and to reach the comforting reassurance of home, he spurs the horse on, arriving home by dint of great effort and strain. The boy is dead.

Four voices speak, not all equally audibly: the narrator, the father, the son, and the *Erlkönig.* Only the words of the latter are enclosed in quotation marks, which shut them off from the ears of the father while not concealing them from the audience, of course. But it is possible that at the end the father begins to hear—and see—the supernatural figure.

The uncanny element of the ballad is represented abundantly in Goethe's poem. The confusion of "elf" with "alder," which is the meaning of *Erle* (cf. *Erlenkönig,* line 7), happens to coincide with various superstitions regarding the tree, which Goethe may or may not have known. Strangely enough, the trees mentioned in the poem are willows, not alders.

Notes on the text:

    5 *was=warum:* "why."
    7 *Schweif:* "trail, train of garment." *Erlenkönig:* the longer form definitely shows the meaning "alder king."
  12 *gülden:* older form of *golden.*
  19 *Reihn=Reihen=Reigen:* "dance"; *führen den Reihn:* "start up the dance."

20 *wiegen, tanzen, singen:* the *ein* belongs with each of these.
     wiegen dich ein: "rock you to sleep."
     tanzen dich ein: "dance you to sleep."
     singen dich ein: "sing you to sleep."

Of all the creative achievements in music, certainly the accomplishments of the seventeen-year-old Schubert, who created a miniature music drama in his setting of Goethe's *Erlkönig,* rank among the finest. Schubert gives the piano an ominous bass motive that thunders along beneath persistent triplet octaves in the treble (Exx. 6-a and 6-b). Beginning with this song, the piano part becomes increasingly significant, the accompaniment invariably expected to mirror the fundamental mood of the text.

Schubert manipulates harmony and melody so that the one singer sounds like the four different characters. Vocal register, size of interval, and rhythmic figures vary with the character represented. In the changing textures, we hear the accelerated gait of the horse, the anxious father astride him, the boy in his arms. When the boy cries *Mein Vater, mein Vater,* notice the dissonant seconds in the accompaniment (Ex. 6-c). As tension mounts, see how often Schubert uses the diminished seventh chord (built on the seventh degree of the scale) simultaneously with its tonic. For one instance of this harmonic convention, see * in Ex. 6-d, bar 144.

Ex. 6

SCHUBERT: *Erlkönig*

a.

b.

Mein Va - ter, mein Va - ter,

c.

den   Hof mit Müh und Not;   in   seinen Armen das Kind war tot.

d.

The lied is *durchkomponiert* and unified through the recurrence of the triplet figure in the accompaniment. The recitative at the close (Ex. 6-d) is punctuated by two chords in the progression dominant-tonic, which to some listeners sounds superfluous. Consider, however, that here Schubert was writing in the style of the ballad composer Zumsteeg (1760-1802), who combined elements of the operatic scena with the more intimate lied. Traditionally, operatic recitatives ended with this kind of cadence on the harpsichord.

Numerous settings of *Erlkönig* existed even in Goethe's day. The poet did not like Schubert's rendition, preferring instead a version by his composer-friend Reichardt (1752-1814). Richard Wagner preferred Karl Loewe's setting (which we shall discuss later), where the piano accompaniment, although sounding like a piano transcription of orchestral music, is less demanding technically than Schubert's. Curiously, of the more than fifty-seven settings of this poem, at least a dozen are in the key that Schubert used, G minor.

Goethe's *Mignon Lieder*
(*Wilhelm Meisters Lehrjahre* [1795-96])

Wilhelm, son of a prosperous merchant, was brought up, like Goethe himself, in a house where art and literature were a normal part of life. His imagination was nourished on poetry. But he seemed destined to take a job in his father's office.

As the novel opens, Wilhelm is involved with a beautiful actress. He has an obsession for the theater in general and for this beauty in particular. But an actor tells him about the seamy side of the theater, and he learns that there are such things as backbiting and infidelity. He hears that his lady love has been deceiving him. Therefore he resolves to enter a career in business, despite his instinctive aversion to such activity. He is pleasantly surprised at his father's suggestion that he travel as an agent for the firm. This results, however, in his being exposed to the lure of the theater once more. He becomes attached to a traveling troupe, and to more than one of the female members. There is a somewhat realistic portrayal of the actor's life, reminiscent of the things Goethe learned when still a child in Frankfurt (where he was taken backstage and shown details of life that both shocked and fascinated the prodigious boy).

While with the troupe Wilhelm meets Mignon; she is a child of twelve or thirteen years of age attached to a company of traveling acrobats. The brutal master of the group exploits her shamefully. When, out of sheer exhaustion, she refuses to dance her "egg dance" at his bidding, he seizes her by the hair and is about to administer a pummeling to her face. Wilhelm intervenes and buys the girl for thirty talers. He becomes her adoptive father and protector. Mignon's gratitude develops into something dangerously deeper.

Mignon has been called the most ethereal of all Goethe's characters. Indeed, she seems less a creature of flesh and blood than an unearthly combination of strange emotions. Especially dominant is the all-absorbing, almost fierce feeling for her benefactor. Somehow a mysterious harper is associated with her.

Mignon is from a southern clime (*Kennst du das Land, wo die Zitronen blühn?*) and, in part, seems to represent Italy, or possibly the traditional German yearning for that land, but her memories of her place of origin are vague. She ultimately turns out to be the missing daughter of the harper. But the situation is more complicated than that. Her mother, who had no knowledge of her own ancestry, unwittingly fell in love with her own brother and married him. He is the harper. Mignon is the innocent result of that union. When the incestuous nature of the relationship becomes known, the parents separate, entrusting Mignon to kindly and honest people who promise to rear her. One day the child fails to return home after a day of play. When her hat is found floating on a lake nearby, everyone assumes that she has drowned. Actually, she was kidnapped by the gang of scoundrels from whom Wilhelm subsequently rescues her.

One night she has a vision of the Virgin Mary, who exacts from her a vow never to reveal her past. In return for this vow, she is to have the constant protection of the Virgin. A skeptic might well ask where that protection is while Mignon undergoes the sadistic treatment by the manager of the troupe. One also wonders how much of her past she actually could divulge, anyway.

Like Goethe, Wilhelm Meister has a series of lady loves. Mignon suffers because of this but is not demolished at first. When he becomes seriously involved with a certain woman, however, the girl pines away and dies. With or without Wilhelm, she seems "not long for this world." Goethe's Mignon poems (perhaps the best part of the novel, some may think) capture the strange, unearthly charm of Mignon, as well as the mysterious aura surrounding her and the harper. And the composer is also afforded a rare opportunity to do so in music.

Kennst du das Land

Kennst du das Land, wo die Zitronen blühn,
Im dunkeln Laub die Gold-Orangen glühn,
Ein sanfter Wind vom blauen Himmel weht,
Die Myrte still und hoch der Lorbeer steht?
Kennst du es wohl?
Dahin! dahin
Möcht' ich mit dir, o mein Geliebter, ziehn.

Kennst du das Haus? Auf Säulen ruht sein Dach.
Es glänzt der Saal, es schimmert das Gemach,
Und Marmorbilder stehn und sehn mich an:
Was hat man dir, du armes Kind, getan?
Kennst du es wohl?
Dahin! dahin
Möcht' ich mit dir, o mein Beschützer, ziehn.

Kennst du den Berg und seinen Wolkensteg?
Das Maultier sucht im Nebel seinen Weg;
In Höhlen wohnt der Drachen alte Brut;
Es stürzt der Fels und über ihn die Flut!
Kennst du ihn wohl?
Dahin! dahin
Geht unser Weg! O Vater, lass uns ziehn!

The Mignon poems reflect the strange girl's vague memories of her childhood. This poem conveys her recollections of the country and her lost home. The flora, the architecture, the intervening Alps all point to Italy. (No one apparently thought to apply the test of language. Or had the young girl forgotten her mother tongue as well?) Despite the obvious haziness of her recollection, Mignon's nostalgia is strong. For Goethe, as for most Germans of his time (and other times), Italy was a promised land for which he yearned.

Someone has said that Mignon's homeland lies "in the heart of the poet." That may well be. Wilhelm's friends guess that it was the region around Lake Maggiore, which, however, does not quite fit the description.

Although the poem—so much admired that there are approximately one hundred musical settings of it—seems to spring from genuine enough sentiments, many of its figures and expressions belong to the stock-in-trade phrases of the Anacreontic poets and amount almost to clichés. They do not seem to spoil the Goethean art, despite this. But *sanfter Wind, Myrte und Lorbeer, das schimmernd' Gemach, Höhlen und Drachen,* etc., are not original with Goethe. Some of them are even found outside of German poetry; cf. Thomson's *The Seasons:* "With the deep orange glowing through the green."

Notes on the text:

1   *Zitronen* presents another cross-cultural difficulty. "Lemons" will not do as a poetic word in English. Yet it has no comical or sour connotations in German and is just as poetic in that language as the golden oranges (line 2). It belongs, with myrtle and laurel and the blue skies, to the traditional characteristics of Italy.

1-3   The verbs *blühn, glühn,* and *weht* all depend on *wo* (line 1).

8 *Das Haus* was no ordinary dwelling but something approaching a palace.

11 *Was hat man dir, du armes Kind, getan?* ("What have they done to you, poor child?"), asked rhetorically by Mignon of and about herself, emphasizes her keen awareness that she has been deprived of a palatial home in a beauteous land. It is not clear whether she recalls her kidnapping, but she knows that she has been cruelly wrenched from her roots.

15 *Kennst du den Berg:* the mountains are presumably the Alps. The "ancient brood of dragons" may not sound like an Alpine theme to us, yet Goethe, in his description of a trip through Switzerland, said of the Saint Gotthard Pass that not much imagination was required to picture dragons lurking in the rocky clefts.

17 *der Drachen alte Brut,* while understandable as an utterance of Goethe's, is hardly the expression of a young girl of Mignon's age. But Mignon is a strange, uncanny creature.

21 *ziehn:* twice before (lines 7 and 14) we have had *möcht' ich . . . ziehn,* "I'd like to go; I fain would go." The third time, however, *lass uns ziehn:* "Let's go!" And *ziehn* is not plain, ordinary "go"; it implies a trip, a venture, a duration, sometimes a procession.

Mignon, the beautiful but pitiful waif, has inspired countless numbers of composers. Of the many settings of this poem, one of the most famous in the German language, none besides that of Hugo Wolf (see p. 282) has achieved anything resembling popularity. One of the four Mignon songs by Schubert, *Kennst du das Land* is the only one for which he made but a single setting. We doubt that he was satisfied with his initial effort, yet he did not return to it. He concerned himself with this poem in 1815, at about the same time that he wrote the first versions of the other Mignon songs. Perhaps because they exist in several different settings, the other lieder show more maturity than *Kennst du das Land.*

The first two stanzas are sung to the same music (Ex. 48-a, p. 283): a chordal, thin-textured opening is succeeded by a conventional eighteenth-century triplet figure that underlines *ein sanfter Wind.* The vocal melody, first doubled in the treble of the accompaniment, proceeds to gain its independence. It is neither tuneful nor dramatic, although the line is closer to an arioso setting, predominantly stepwise with only occasional leaps. *Kennst du es wohl* (Ex. 48-c) is in recitative. The music returns to the triplet movement, continuing here in a rising chromatic scale that highlights *Dahin.* Except that it opens in the parallel minor, the third stanza follows the pattern of the others with slight modifications, duplicating these stanzas from *Kennst du ihn wohl* to the end.

In comparing this setting of the poem with the more celebrated one by Hugo Wolf, we must concede that on this occasion Schubert was out of his element. As Wolf speculated later, he probably had not read the complete *Wilhelm Meister,* and set the poem without understanding the context in which it was written.

Nur wer die Sehnsucht kennt

Nur wer die Sehnsucht kennt,
Weiss, was ich leide!
Allein und abgetrennt
Von aller Freude,
Seh' ich ans Firmament
Nach jener Seite.
Ach! der mich liebt und kennt
Ist in der Weite.
Es schwindelt mir, es brennt
Mein Eingeweide.
Nur wer die Sehnsucht kennt,
Weiss, was ich leide!

There are settings of this text by a great number of composers, including Reichardt, Zelter, Beethoven (four settings), Schubert (six settings), Schumann, Karl Loewe, Tchaikovsky, Hugo Wolf, and less important composers such as B. Klein, Konradin Kreutzer, C. Evers, A. Reisenauer, R. von Keudell, E. Moor, M. Kretschmar, E. O. Nodnagel, Josephine Lang, and F. Hiller.

In the first draft of *Wilhelm Meister,* Mignon sings this song alone. In the final version Wilhelm hears Mignon and the harper sing it as "an irregular duet." As Wilhelm listens, his mood is one of *Sehnsucht* for another girl (one who had saved his life after he was severely beaten by robbers). It is also an expression of Goethe's own *Sehnsucht.*

Who is the one *der mich liebt und kennt?* It is not at all clear. Does Mignon mean her own lost father? She has no knowledge of who the harper is and cannot, therefore, know that he is not *in der Weite* but quite nearby. On the other hand, it might be objected that there is no necessary connection between the contents of a song and the biography of the singer; yet to say this is to fail to know Goethe.

The rhyme *leide* and *Freude,* while not standard German, is accepted as such in German verse. For Goethe, who never completely lost his Frankfurt accent, the words would rhyme. Note that the entire poem has essentially only two rhymes—*kennt, -trennt, -ment, kennt, brennt, kennt* and *leide, Freude, Seite, Weite, -weide, leide*—although pedants might, untenably, assert that *Seite, Weite* is a separate rhyme.

Notes on the text:

    4   *von aller Freude:* Mignon apparently overlooks her growing love for Wilhelm in saying that she has been separated from all joy; yet, after all, she has little *Freude* from her unrequited love for her benefactor.

  5-6 *Seh' ich ans Firmament/Nach jener Seite:* she looks toward Italy.

 9-10 *es brennt/Mein Eingeweide:* the word *Eingeweide* makes a strong, violent impression on those who speak English. We hardly expect a word like "intestines" or "viscera" in a poem about yearning. But there is a venerable tradition that makes the intestines the seat of the emotions; cf. also the biblical "her bowels yearned," etc. The heart is our figure, but that is also an internal organ and could be regarded as just as unpleasant as viscera in some cultures. The burning passion of longing is what Mignon conveys. Music can convey that passion probably better than words.

Again Schubert's conception of Mignon must be measured against Wolf's understanding of the child (see p. 279). Once more Wolf comes out in front. Although this setting of the *Lied der Mignon* shows more insight than *Kennst du das Land,* it does not measure up to Schubert's best work.

The mood is appropriately sad, and the *Sehnsucht* is properly underlaid even to the slight sob (see * in Ex. 47-a). A six-bar piano introduction anticipates the beginning of the vocal melody. The texture in the accompaniment is more varied than in the other Mignon song; Schubert presents a modified *Kinderland* figure (cf. p. 34) that starts at *Allein* (bar 15). A feeling of listlessness continues into the new material at *Es schwindelt mir,* where the piano is more agitated. Text and music of the opening two lines are repeated at the conclusion. The composer exercised his musician's rights and reversed the sequence of the opening bars so that the piano postlude concludes the song exactly as it was opened. The singer's melody leaves a lingering sound in the air; and it is a rare listener who, shortly after hearing it, does not find himself humming it.

Schubert's choice of A minor sustains a feeling of uneasiness or malaise, not tragedy. Tragedy seems to sound best in D minor, at least in the so-called tragic works of Gluck, Mozart, Beethoven, and Brahms.

Heiss mich nicht reden

Heiss mich nicht reden, heiss mich schweigen!
Denn mein Geheimnis ist mir Pflicht;
Ich möchte dir mein ganzes Innre zeigen,
Allein das Schicksal will es nicht.

Zur rechten Zeit vertreibt der Sonne Lauf
Die finstre Nacht, und sie muss sich erhellen;
Der harte Fels schliesst seinen Busen auf,
Missgönnt der Erde nicht die tiefverborgnen Quellen.

Ein jeder sucht im Arm des Freundes Ruh,
Dort kann die Brust in Klagen sich ergiessen;
Allein ein Schwur drückt mir die Lippen zu.
Und nur ein Gott vermag sie aufzuschliessen.

"Don't tell me to speak; tell me to be silent." *Denn mein Geheimnis ist mir Pflicht.* Why is her secret her duty? Because she has sworn to the Blessed Virgin, who has appeared to her in a dream, not to reveal anything of her past. She would like to divulge what she is keeping secret, but she cannot.

At the proper time the "dark night" of her secret will be revealed by the sun. She compares that secret to the dark night (line 6), the hard mountain rock (line 7), and the hidden springs of the earth (line 8).

Everyone likes to confide in a friend and pour out his troubles. But Mignon cannot, for an oath seals her lips, and only a god may open them.

Notes on the text:

1 The person addressed may be Wilhelm or theoretically anyone questioning Mignon about her past.
4 *Allein:* "but" (cf. English use of "only"); similarly line 11.
5 *vertreibt:* present used in a future sense.
11 *ein Schwur:* the vow made in Mignon's dream.
12 *vermag:* "is able, can."

Schubert had set this poem earlier, but this last setting of 1826, like that of *Nur wer die Sehnsucht kennt,* is superior to the previous version. The format here is also similar to the pattern Schubert employs for *Nur wer die Sehnsucht kennt.* A four-bar introduction for the pianist antici-pates the singer's opening melody, which unfortunately is not particularly endearing. Its rhythmic design shows a resemblance to the rhythmic motive of the Funeral March from Beethoven's "Eroica" Symphony, No. 3.

Throughout most of this lied, the treble of the accompaniment doubles the singer's line. The essentially lyrical melody changes to recitative at bar 31, where the composer emphasizes Mignon's resolve that only a god could make her disclose her secret. Until this point, although the music appears to change with the text, Schubert has really used only one basic melody, adapting it to successive stanzas.

So lasst mich scheinen

So lasst mich scheinen, bis ich werde;
Zieht mir das weisse Kleid nicht aus!
Ich eile von der schönen Erde
Hinab in jenes feste Haus.

Dort ruh'ich eine kleine Stille,
Dann öffnet sich der frische Blick;
Ich lasse dann die reine Hülle,
Den Gürtel und den Kranz zurück.

Und jene himmlischen Gestalten,
Sie fragen nicht nach Mann und Weib,
Und keine Kleider, keine Falten
Umgeben den verklärten Leib.

Zwar lebt' ich ohne Sorg und Mühe,
Doch fühlt' ich tiefen Schmerz genung;
Vor Kummer altert ich zu frühe,
Macht mich auf ewig wieder jung!

Mignon appears in a white angel costume at a children's birthday party, where she distributes gifts to the little guests. She wears a golden sash, with a crown and wings of gold. In one hand she carries a lily, in the other the basket of presents. As she enters, the hostess announces, "Here comes the angel," and the children, while recognizing her (*Es ist Mignon!*), are seized by a strange feeling that she may somehow really be an angel, and they hesitate to approach her. When one asks, "Are you an angel?" she replies, "I wish I were."

Mignon is loath to change back into her everyday attire, which is boyish clothing. And her song expresses not merely a fervent wish to keep her white dress but also a realization that, young as she is, she is soon to leave this life and assume the role of angel for which she feels destined.

Notes on the text:

1 *So* can be understood only in the light of the explanation in the novel. "Like this," i.e., "like an angel; in this garb."
bis ich werde: "until I become one [an angel]."

3 *eile:* "hasten"; shows her belief that she will soon die. Yet she finds the earth *schön.*

4 *Hinab in jenes feste Haus:* "down into that solid house [the grave]"; *jenes:* "the one you all know about."

5-8 These lines express her belief that she will be transformed after a brief spell in the grave and be taken to heaven, leaving the garments and the robe of flesh behind.

10 Her concept of angels is that they are not distinguished according to sex.

12 *verklärten:* "transfigured."

13 *ohne Sorg' und Mühe:* "without care and trouble" seems a peculiar way to refer to a life that has been full of both. But Mignon

means that she has been cared for, after her harrowing experiences with the troupe, by good friends who have provided for her material needs. Her *Schmerz* (line 14) and *Kummer* (15) are of deeper origin.

14   *tiefen Schmerz:* may refer to her sense of a lost past but more probably to her unrequited love for Wilhelm.
genung: an earlier form of *genug*.

16   *Macht mich auf ewig wieder jung.* This imperative is not addressed to earthly people, as was line 1, but rather to the powers of heaven. She begs them to rejuvenate her eternally (by taking her to heaven); and the need for such rejuvenation is explained in the preceding line, which tells us that she aged before her time because of grief.

The composer is more successful with this poem. Again Schubert has written a modified strophic setting, altering the musical material to suit the meaning of the text. Similar to the other two Mignon songs, the four-bar introduction presents the melody first, the singer then entering over a repeat of the music played earlier by the pianist in a somewhat less dense texture. Schubert treats *frische Blick* (bar 18) to a lovely modulation to D major, which, on repetition for the second stanza, becomes D minor, underlaying the *tiefen Schmerz* (bar 38). The harmonic richness of the underpinning in much of this lied far exceeds that found in *Heiss mich nicht reden*. For this reason, perhaps, the song proves more significant.

Notice the way Schubert relates the voice and piano. At the conclusion of each stanza, the piano echoes the vocal melody. After the last stanza, the piano's final statement acquires the additional ornament of the turn heard earlier in the voice part (at bars 18 and 38). A tiny motive serves to unify the work. It is separated into two segments, which together comprise the opening pitches of the vocal melody. The first hardly moves at all, revolving around the tonic note; the second proceeds upward in a scalewise pattern. (The "-nen" of *scheinen* begins this second part. Unfortunately, it is an example of poor text underlay.) At the close of the song, the echo in the piano part extends this scale figure one note higher, a finishing touch for a song that still wears well after repeated hearing.

It is difficult to speak of *Ganymed* without mentioning its *Gegenstück*, or counterpart, *Prometheus*, and neither can be understood too well without a brief reference to *Sturm und Drang*. One can sum it up briefly, if inexactly, by saying that it was a revolution in literature, philosophy, life.

Ganymed

Wie im Morgenglanze
Du rings mich anglühst,
Frühling, Geliebter!
Mit tausendfacher Liebeswonne
Sich an mein Herz drängt
Deiner ewigen Wärme
Heilig Gefühl,
Unendliche Schöne!

Dass ich dich fassen möcht'
In diesen Arm!

Ach, an deinem Busen
Lieg'ich, schmachte,
Und deine Blumen, dein Gras
Drängen sich an mein Herz.
Du kühlst den brennenden
Durst meines Busens,
Lieblicher Morgenwind!
Ruft drein die Nachtigall
Liebend nach mir aus dem Nebeltal.

Ich komm', ich komme!
Wohin? Ach, wohin?

Hinauf! Hinauf strebt's.
Es schweben die Wolken
Abwärts, die Wolken
Neigen sich der sehnenden Liebe.
Mir! Mir!
In euerm Schosse
Aufwärts!
Umfangend umfangen!
Aufwärts an deinen Busen,
Alliebender Vater!

There was a fundamental difference in the conception of human nature as opposed to that held by the preceding age (*Aufklärung*, rationalism, age of reason). That age had conceived of man as a rational being. *Sturm und Drang* called him an emotional creature. Rationalism, in its most extreme form, had overemphasized logic and the law of cause and effect; it had neglected, if not denied, the other side of human nature: imagination, intuition, the irrational.

Sturm und Drang regarded human nature as incalculable. It clamored for freedom from all restraints—in law, in politics, in literature, in art, in morality—and from all authority. The unbridled expression of emotions and the complete freedom of the individual to unfold his creative

Prometheus

Bedecke deinen Himmel, Zeus,
Mit Wolkendunst
Und übe, dem Knaben gleich,
Der Disteln köpft,
An Eichen dich und Bergeshöhn;
Musst mir meine Erde
Doch lassen stehn
Und meine Hütte, die du nicht gebaut,
Und meinen Herd,
Um dessen Glut
Du mich beneidest.

Ich kenne nichts Ärmeres
Unter der Sonn als euch, Götter!
Ihr nähret kümmerlich
Von Opfersteuern
Und Gebetshauch
Eure Majestät
Und darbtet, wären
Nicht Kinder und Bettler
Hoffnungsvolle Toren.

Da ich ein Kind war,
Nicht wusste, wo aus noch ein,
Kehrt' ich mein verirrtes Auge
Zur Sonne, als wenn drüber wär'
Ein Ohr, zu hören meine Klage,
Ein Herz, wie meins,
Sich des Bedrängten zu erbarmen.

Wer half mir
Wider der Titanen Übermut?
Wer rettete vom Tode mich,
Von Sklaverei?
Hast du nicht alles selbst vollendet,
Heilig glühend Herz?
Und glühtest jung und gut,
Betrogen, Rettungsdank
Dem Schlafenden da droben?

Ich dich ehren? Wofür?
Hast du die Schmerzen gelindert
Je des Beladenen?
Hast du die Tränen gestillet
Je des Geängstigten?
Hat nicht mich zum Manne geschmiedet
Die allmächtige Zeit
Und das ewige Schicksal,
Meine Herrn und deine?

Wähntest du etwa,
Ich sollte das Leben hassen,
In Wüsten fliehen,
Weil nicht alle
Blütenträume reiften?

Hier sitz'ich, forme Menschen
Nach meinem Bilde,
Ein Geschlecht, das mir gleich sei,
Zu leiden, zu weinen,
Zu geniessen und zu freuen sich,
Und dein nicht zu achten,
Wie ich!

talents were main "tenets" of this essentially tenetless creed. In the drama this led to much ranting and raving on the stage, also to the preference for a hero who was the opponent of established order. Each author, plus numerous non-authors, claimed the title "genius." The refinements and amenities of civilization were spurned in theory (often by people who had a comfortable home to come back to every night).

Prometheus shows one theological aspect of *Sturm und Drang:* defiance of the gods and vision of a humanity able to stand on its own feet and work out its own salvation. Prometheus had defied Zeus and had brought fire to mankind; he had also taught men various useful arts. As punishment for his defiance he was chained to a rock in the Caucasus and made to endure unspeakable, lasting pain (an eagle ate his liver every day, and that vital organ was renewed every night).

Ganymed, while still *Sturm und Drang,* is almost the opposite of *Prometheus.* (It should be noted that the two poems were written within a short time of each other, probably the same year.) Ganymede, to use the English spelling, was a handsome youth carried off by the gods to serve as their cupbearer. He is thus, in a sense, the symbol of man's subservience to the gods. Yet he also lived among them virtually as an equal and enjoyed considerable honor.

To Goethe he symbolizes pantheism. Nature in all its forms is regarded by pantheists as identical with God. (Cynics ask whether the germs of dread disease are also a part of God.) Many of the *Sturm und Drang* adherents rejected the notion of a God outside the world. Instead of envisaging Him as working from without as the creator of nature, they claimed that He worked from within as the "universal principle." It is the outsider God that is rejected in *Prometheus*. In *Ganymed* the Almighty is seen as having many manifestations: *Frühling* (spring), line 3; infinite beauty, the morning breeze, the clouds, the all-loving father, the all-pervading spirit. God has many names, but the name is considered irrelevant; feeling is everything. Faust says the same thing to Gretchen in the so-called catechism scene, in which she tries to find out his religious beliefs. *Glaubst du an Gott?* ("Do you believe in God?") is her embarrassingly direct question. Faust avoids a direct answer by offering various synonyms: *Glück, Herz, Liebe*—"I have no name for it; feeling is all that counts." *Gefühl ist alles* became a slogan of the *Sturm und Drang*.

The absence of rhyme and the freedom of the meter are noticeable in *Ganymed* and are in keeping with the principles of *Sturm und Drang* poetry.

A composer attempting a setting of this poem has undertaken a formidable task, both for reasons of meter and mood. We have settings of *Ganymed* by Schubert, Loewe, Hugo Wolf, Reichardt, M. Hauptmann, R. Stöhr, E. Istel, W. Mauke, J. Reiter, and others, ranging from the famous to the obscure.

Notes on the text:

5   poetical word order (*drängt* should, strictly speaking, begin the line).

6   *Deiner:* genitive. The familiar form (*dein*) is employed because the deity is always addressed in that form. Is this inconsistent in a pantheist? He is addressing all creation, theoretically; yet it is true that he is here specifically speaking to spring, as one manifestation of the pantheistic deity.

8   *Schöne:* here the equivalent of the noun *Schönheit*.

18 *ruft:* the subject is *Nachtigall*.

26 *Mir! Mir!* is identified with *Liebe,* as if in apposition.
27 *In eurem Schosse:* the plural form of the possessive is used because the clouds are addressed; it is, once more, the familiar form.
31 *Alliebender Vater:* not the personal God, since pantheism precludes that; rather the all-pervading spirit, the universal principle. But it must be admitted that "all-loving father" is an extremely personal designation for something as vague as a principle. Note that *all* plus *liebender* does not yield *"allliebender,"* since the system of German orthography does not allow three "l"s together.

Schubert opens *Ganymed* with several bars for the piano that include features found in his instrumental music. He offers a lilting melody in the treble seemingly separated into symmetrical phrases that cadence in expected patterns. At bar 7 he breaks this pattern, extending the phrase to three bars in length. At bar 8, where the piano begins to repeat its opening phrases, we expect the voice to enter. Schubert delays it, however, until the following bar; this overlap transports the listener further along into the song. (See Ex. 7-a.) At *Mit tausend* Schubert changes the vocal line completely but retains a variant of the introductory accompanimental figures to support it. At *unendliche Schöne* he underlines the meaning of the text by bringing the music to a beautifully broad climax in a modulation to a key far removed from the tonic. Again he begins a new figure (bar 32) in both voice and piano, following it with more new material at *Du kühlst. Ganymed,* although hardly as episodic as *Prometheus,* is still a sectional song that contains within its compass a virtual lexicon of accompanimental figures. Furthermore, the composer has also included numerous examples of *Tonmalerei.* Notice the trills underlining *Morgenwind* and the figuration (right out of Beethoven's "Waldstein" Sonata) that succeeds it; observe also the new texture under *Ich komme* and the typically lush cadential figure with a built-in ritard at *alliebender Vater.* See its recurrence in one of the loveliest melismata in any Schubert song at the conclusion of this lied (Ex. 7-b). This highly idiomatic vocal passage balances the essentially pianistic opening.

To those familiar with only such songs as *Hark, Hark, the Lark* and *Die Forelle,* the composer of *Prometheus, An Schwager Kronos,* and *Grenzen der Menschheit* is virtually unknown. *Prometheus* offers vigorous music of revolt. Schubert helps the hero shake his fist angrily at Zeus in this song that is perhaps more of an operatic scene than a lied.

Ex. 7

SCHUBERT: *Ganymed*

After a striking rhythmic motive predominantly in octaves, a vocal recitative sounds over a tremolo in the accompaniment. Several successive recitatives are linked by the recurrence of the opening rhythmic motive in the piano. A quasi-hymnlike section begins at *Ihr nähret kümmerlich* and moves into Schubert's favorite *Kinderland* music. (Cf. *Heidenröslein*, p. 34. Incidentally, this figuration may represent Schubert's idea of a child's first steps.)

Angry dissonances pierce the texture at the recitative *Wer half mir?*

These short phrases reach a climax at *da droben*. New material characterized by alternating octaves and dissonant chords introduces still another
recitative which, with its fast harmonic rhythm, moves into the climax
of the song (at the Vigoroso). Here Prometheus, visibly moved, defies Zeus
and declares he will form men in his own image. In this lied, recitative
merges into arioso in anticipation of Wagner's style of *Sprechgesang*. Far
from his usual lyricism, Schubert triumphs here in another style: melodic
declamation.

An Schwager Kronos

A note by Goethe seems to indicate that this was written during an
actual ride in a coach or at least had its origin in such a ride, one which
gave Goethe the notion of comparing our journey through life to a trip
in a stagecoach.

Spute dich, Kronos!
Fort den rasselnden Trott!
Bergab gleitet der Weg;
Ekles Schwindeln zögert
Mir vor die Stirne dein Zaudern.
Frisch, holpert es gleich,
Über Stock und Steine den Trott
Rasch ins Leben hinein!

Nun schon wieder
Den eratmenden Schritt
Mühsam Berg hinauf!
Auf denn, nicht träge denn,
Strebend und hoffend hinan!

Weit, hoch, herrlich
Rings den Blick ins Leben hinein,
Vom Gebirg zum Gebirg
Schwebet der ewige Geist,
Ewigen Lebens ahndevoll.

Seitwärts des Überdachs Schatten
Zieht dich an
Und ein Frischung verheissender Blick
Auf der Schwelle des Mädchens da.
Labe dich!--Mir auch, Mädchen,
Diesen schäumenden Trank,
Diesen frischen Gesundheitsblick!

Ab denn, rascher hinab!
Sieh, die Sonne sinkt!
Eh' sie sinkt, eh' mich Greisen
Ergreift im Moore Nebelduft,
Entzahnte Kiefer schnattern
Und das schlotternde Gebein.

Trunknen vom letzten Strahl
Reiss mich, ein Feuermeer
Mir im schäumenden Aug',
Mich geblendeten Taumelnden
In der Hölle nächtliches Tor.

Töne, Schwager, ins Horn,
Rassle den schallenden Trab,
Dass der Orkus vernehme: wir kommen,
Dass gleich an der Türe
Der Wirt uns freundlich empfange.

But there is no implication of escape from life. This is another *Sturm und Drang* poem, and that means affirmation of life, the impulsive seizing of existence, and the urge to live it to the full. All the pleasures and enjoyments of life are to be savored, including joy in nature, society of the fair sex, and all the rest that life offers. The journey toward death is not to be taken to mean that life is something to be finished as soon as possible. Why then the acceleration of the pace at the end? Perhaps to show Goethe's belief that it is best to finish one's course before reaching a stage of mental and physical helplessness. An almost defiant attitude toward death makes him welcome the end. Goethe intends to come driving up to the gates of the underworld in grand style. The coachman will blow his horn, and the host will come to greet the new arrival. (A theme of Germanic mythology was just such a welcoming of a newly arrived hero in Valhalla.) In Goethe's *Egmont* the hero says: "As if lashed by invisible spirits the sun-horses of time gallop by, pulling the fragile chariot of our fate," which is slightly different in emphasis but not unrelated to the present poem and its theme.

Notes on the text:

Title. *Schwager* means "brother-in-law," but used to be a designation for a coachman or postilion.

1   *Spute dich:* "hurry, speed up."
    Kronos: It seems that Goethe, despite his thorough classical back-
    ground, may have confused *Kronos,* the father of Zeus, with
    Chronos, "time." Both would have been pronounced the same
    in German.

2   *den . . . Trott:* accusative, as if the object of *fort.*

4   *zögert* is used transitively and *Schwindeln* is the object.

5   *Haudern,* not *Zaudern,* is the authentic form. *Zaudern* is evidently
    the result of a *Verschlimmbesserung* ("misimprovement") by some
    printer, proofreader, or typesetter. Goethe wrote *Haudern,* which
    in Rhenish dialects meant "to drive a cab, to hack" but also "to
    dawdle, drive slowly and indifferently" (because the driver was
    paid by the hour, perhaps). The replacement of *Haudern* by
    Zaudern partly destroys the effectiveness of *zögert* as a transitive.

6   *holpert es gleich=obgleich es holpert:* "even though it's bumpy."

7   *Trott:* as in line 2, accusative, although no verb is present; *frisch*
    acts almost as an imperative.

10   *den eratmenden Schritt:* "the panting pace." This is another ac-
    cusative without a verb to govern it; it amounts to a kind of
    "absolute" construction.

12   *auf* (like *fort* in line 2, *hinein* in 15, *hinab* in 26, etc.) has the
    force of an imperative, *sans verbe.*

18   Goethe has *ahndevoll* (archaic for *ahnungsvoll* "having a pre-
    monition, full of foreboding"), not *ahnevoll.*

24   There is time to stop on this ride for a refreshing drink.

30-32   He hopes to end the journey before he becomes a toothless,
    senile oldster, babbling away.

37-39   The defiant facing, yet acceptance, of the inevitable end has
    much the same sentiment as Dylan Thomas utters in his mag-
    nificent poem "Do not go gentle into that good night" and its
    other repeated imperative, "Rage, rage against the dying of the
    light."

With *An Schwager Kronos,* Schubert reached the second culminating
point of his achievement in lieder composition. This song was to 1816 what
Gretchen was to 1814 and what *Erlkönig* meant to 1815. A powerful singer
must project the striking vocal line; its vigorous leaps should sound above
the insistent bass octaves. Galloping along in a hammering $\frac{6}{8}$ rhythm,

An Schwager Kronos exudes confidence. The voice part is completely independent of the accompaniment.

At *frisch*, Schubert reuses a section of the opening octave figure to support a variant of the voice part. The sharply accented words *Weit, hoch,* and *herrlich* are reflected in booming bass arpeggios in octaves. Still another section of new material appears before the return of the opening music. But the composer has not yet completed his statement. In conclusion we hear a victorious horn call reminiscent of the triumph symphony of Beethoven's *Egmont*.

This song was beyond the technical capacity of singers in Schubert's day. The accompanist, too, is taxed to the limit of his abilities. In many ways, however, it is typical of Schubert's writing. The change to the major for the last section of the song is an example of his characteristic minor-major alternation. Despite its length and highly colorful harmonic palette, *An Schwager Kronos* emerges as a work far more unified than either of the two preceding songs, *Ganymed* and *Prometheus*.

In his quasi-autobiographical work *Dichtung und Wahrheit* (often translated "Truth and Fiction"), Goethe quotes the first three lines of this poem when talking about the kind of poetry which springs forth

Der Musensohn

Durch Feld und Wald zu schweifen
Mein Liedchen wegzupfeifen,
So geht's von Ort zu Ort!
Und nach dem Takte reget
Und nach dem Mass beweget
Sich alles an mir fort.

Ich kann sie kaum erwarten,
Die erste Blum' im Garten,
Die erste Blüt' am Baum.
Sie grüssen meine Lieder,
Und kommt der Winter wieder,
Sing' ich noch jenen Traum.

Ich sing ihn in der Weite,
Auf Eises Läng' und Breite,
Da blüht der Winter schön!
Auch diese Blüte schwindet,
Und neue Freude findet
Sich auf bebauten Höhn.

Denn wie ich bei der Linde
Das junge Völkchen finde,
Sogleich erreg' ich sie.
Der stumpfe Bursche bläht sich,
Das steife Mädchen dreht sich
Nach meiner Melodie.

Ihr gebt den Sohlen Flügel,
Und treibt durch Tal und Hügel
Den Liebling weit von Haus.
Ihr lieben, holden Musen,
Wann ruh' ich ihr am Busen
Auch endlich wieder aus?

almost unbidden, even against the will of the poet. The Muses' son is obviously the poet himself. A poet's activity does not, to be sure, reflect all the spheres of all the Muses, but it is related to most of them. As the poet roves through field and forest, Nature keeps time to his beat, not vice versa. Spring is the poet's favorite season, but even in winter he nurtures his dreams of spring and sees in the icy "frost blossoms" of winter the counterparts of the blossoms of spring.

The young people under the linden tree, assembled there for festivity and lovemaking, are all given stimulus and inspiration by the poet and shake off any lethargy they may have. The favorite son whom the Muses drive over hill and dale is, once more, the poet. He has, however, his own special girl and would like to suspend his poetic roving for a while and settle down with her. He asks the Muses: *Wann ruh' ich ihr am Busen mich endlich wieder aus?* We imagine that the girl herself reads the poem.

Notes on the text:

6   *an mir fort:* "past me."

10 *Sie grüssen meine Lieder* is ambiguous. It can mean "they greet my songs," but it may also mean "my songs greet them."

12 *jenen Traum:* "that dream" means the dream of spring.

13 *ihn* is still the dream.

14 *Auf Eises Läng' und Breite:* refers to skating, a favorite pastime of Goethe's in the 1770's.

19 *Linde:* In America we refer to this tree as the linden, perhaps under the influence of German immigrants. The English equiv-

alent is actually "lime," which, however, is an ambiguous name and could lead to misunderstanding because of the citrus tree so named. The *Lindenbaum* has long been associated in Germany with love, trysts, dreams. (Cf. *Am Brunnen vor dem Tore/Da steht ein Lindenbaum.*)

22   *Bursche:* "country boy, yokel."

  bläht sich: "puffs himself up, brags," but this is because of the poet's instigation.

25   *Ihr:* "you" (plural familiar) refers to the Muses, who, as semi-divinities, are addressed in the familiar form.

Unlike *Ganymed* or *An Schwager Kronos,* this poem has rhyme of a rather conventional form. It is still *Sturm und Drang* poetry, but it is later than most of Goethe's poems of that period and shows signs of incipient classical style, although more in form than in content and ideas.

Of Schubert's four Goethe settings of 1822, *Der Musensohn* is the best known. Two versions of the song exist, but the most frequently performed

Ex. 8

SCHUBERT: *Der Musensohn*

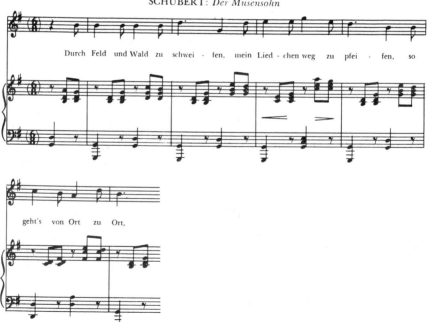

Durch Feld und Wald zu schwei - fen, mein Lied - chen weg zu pfei - fen, so

geht's von Ort zu Ort,

is the one in G major. Here is a rare example of Schubert's treatment of a dancing melody (see Ex. 8; cf. Schumann's *Das ist ein Flöten und Geigen,* p. 124).

Schubert uses all five stanzas of the poem and sets them alternately to two closely related melodies, one in G major and one in B major, concluding with the one in G. Instead of modulating from one key to the other, he plunges into the new key via the pivot note of B natural, common to both tonic chords. This alternation reminds us of Meyerbeer's use of E/A flat in the "Consecration of the Daggers" scene in *Les Huguenots,* which produced a startling effect in its time. In *Der Musensohn* we delight in the smooth transition from one key to the other; it suits the simple accompaniment and relaxed mood that Schubert sustains throughout the entire song. He uses melodic and rhythmic means to suggest recurrent poetic strophes. Surely the publishers must have been pleased with this work. Anyone could play the piano part!

Wanderers Nachtlied II

```
Über allen Gipfeln
Ist Ruh,
In allen Wipfeln
Spürest du
Kaum einen Hauch;
Die Vögelein schweigen im Walde.
Warte nur, balde
Ruhest du auch.
```

These few lines were written by Goethe on the rough-timbered wall of a hunter's hut on the Kickelhahn (or Gickelhahn) mountain, near Ilmenau, on September 6, 1780. On August 29, 1813, he returned and renewed the writing. And in August, 1831, the year before he died, he came back once more and read the poem again, apparently with deep emotion. More musical settings (almost 180) have been made of this poem than of any other by Goethe.

The mood and the situation seem to be this: a man stands on a mountain—not at the top, but not too far from the summit. He has a view of surrounding wooded mountains. It is twilight, and an air of complete tranquillity pervades the scene. Everything is peaceful. Nature seems to hold her breath; hardly a murmur can be heard in the treetops. The very birds in the forest have stopped their singing. And, to himself, the man says, "Patience, you too soon shall rest."

To Goethe in 1831, the poem surely meant something like this; he knew that his life would not last much longer. When he wrote the poem, however, he was a man scarcely past thirty. His capturing of a tranquil mood is genuine enough. But his closing, consoling admonition cannot have sprung from any belief in imminent death. Therefore it is either a contrived ending with vicarious emotion or it means something else. Perhaps the "rest" will be from one of those occasional fits of melancholy from which he suffered. Perhaps he meant that life is short for anyone, and that any person "soon" will rest. At any rate, the quiet simplicity of these verses has appealed to a great number of composers. The tempo is easy but not plodding. The mood is calm, with an almost uncanny peacefulness. There is a conventional rhyme scheme.

The word *Ruh* in line 2 sets the mood and is, in a sense, recapitulated in *ruhest* (line 8), which sees in that *Ruh* a promise for poet and reader alike.

Schubert set two poems entitled *Wanderers Nachtlied,* both by Goethe. The first one opens with the words *Der du von dem Himmel bist.* The second, beginning with the well-known words *Über allen Gipfeln ist Ruh,* is an exceptionally short song of only fourteen bars. Schubert expresses the meaning of the text with the utmost simplicity. He turns away from the element of tunefulness and uses instead an arioso statement of the text. The delicately syncopated accompaniment suggests the gently moving breeze in the treetops. All about us, everyone and everything prepares for rest.

The text and music of bars 9 and 10 are repeated immediately afterward, assuring the wanderer that he, too, will have the peace he desires. The composer has used one of his favorite keys of repose, B-flat major. Observe also that the music of bar 2 is repeated for the last two bars, thus providing additional unity in this through-composed lied.

West-östlicher Divan

This work does not represent a sudden turn toward the East on Goethe's part, for he had long been fascinated by the Orient. Some of his interest had been nourished and augmented by Herder, who, during Goethe's student days in Strasbourg, had called his attention to the great wealth of literature in Oriental lands.

A play, *Mahomet,* on the life of the prophet was based on the Koran (which Goethe read, like all the rest of the Oriental literature he studied, in translation). The play remained a fragment. We have mentioned the *Šakuntala* of the Indian author Kalidasa, which gave him an idea for the *Vorspiel auf dem Theater* in *Faust.*

In 1812, Josef von Hammer translated the *Divan* of the Persian poet Muhammed Shams ud-Din, or Mohammed, the Sun of Religion. The Persian author's pseudonym was Hafiz (usually written "Hafis" in German). His dates were 1300-1388, and he was therefore contemporary with Chaucer. Hafiz—"One remembering"—was not only a pen name but a special designation applied to those who had mastered the Koran, which meant memorizing that book. Although associated with a dervish order, Hafiz was far from being an ascetic. His monastic colleagues condemned him because of his delight in the pleasures of wine and the flesh; he reciprocated by satirizing them in some of his verses. Subsequent ages of Persian literary scholarship endeavored to explain his erotic lines as having mystical symbolic significance and thus to endow them with respectability. Goethe was most emphatic in opposing any such mystical interpretation of the poet, whom he regarded as a kindred spirit to himself. His lyrics and his love life paralleled those of Goethe himself, and he lived at a time which in Persian history resembled part of the age of Goethe, with all its military, political, and social upheaval.

Now, although Goethe's interest in the East was of almost lifelong duration, his writing of the *Divan* did come at a time of vast widening of his artistic and intellectual horizons, besides a significant alteration in his point of view, as he immersed himself in the study of the Eastern world. This was radically different from the classical Hellenic sphere which had hitherto dominated his attitude. He aimed, as he tells us, to unite East and West, past and present, Persian and German, and to let the two ways of life and thought intermingle and interact. (A *caveat:* the Orient is not a monolithic phenomenon, and it is fallacious to assume that there is a cultural, philosophical, or artistic unity that can be called Oriental. Goethe himself recognized and discussed the great differences between Persia, China, and India, for instance.)

The word *divan* means in Persian a "meeting, gathering, collection of poems, brochure, register, custom house [cf. *douane*], tribunal, bench"—a wide semantic range. Persian (not a Semitic language) borrowed the word from Arabic.

Goethe wrote the *Divan* in the summers of 1814 and 1815 while staying in the Rhine-Main region. There was, in addition to the literary inspiration of Hafiz, a woman involved, as usual. This one was practically a girl, Marianne von Willemer, the sixteen-year-old third wife of a widower who was, for a while, a friend of Goethe's. Goethe himself was in his sixties.

The lovers Hatem and Suleika are apparently Goethe and Marianne. She was the first person to read the *Divan* and allegedly the only one besides Goethe to understand it entirely. Five of its poems are actually written by her, Goethe says.

Suleika II

Ach, um deine feuchten Schwingen,
West, wie sehr ich dich beneide:
Denn du kannst ihm Kunde bringen,
Was ich in der Trennung leide!

Die Bewegung deiner Flügel
Weckt im Busen stilles Sehnen;
Blumen, Augen, Wald und Hügel
Stehn bei deinem Hauch in Tränen.

Doch dein mildes, sanftes Wehen
Kühlt die wunden Augenlider;
Ach, für Leid müsst' ich vergehen,
Hofft' ich nicht zu sehn ihn wieder.

Eile denn zu meinem Lieben,
Spreche sanft zu seinem Herzen;
Doch vermeid ihn zu betrüben
Und verbirg ihm meine Schmerzen.

Sag' ihm, aber sag's bescheiden:
Seine Liebe sei mein Leben,
Freudiges Gefühl von beiden
Wird mir seine Nähe geben.

Suleika Nameh ("The Book of Suleika") is the longest of the *namehs,* or books, in the *West-östlicher Divan.* Goethe mentions this in verse and says that his intent to trim it to match more nearly the others in length was frustrated by *Liebeswahn,* love's madness. It is felt by many that any excisions would be deplorable. Goethe took the name Suleika from the Koran. She was the wife of Potiphar and tried her utmost to seduce young Jussuph. Goethe let Suleika represent his beloved, Marianne, but he took the name of Hatem for himself. Jussuph—Joseph of the Old Testament— would have been singularly inappropriate, because the latter did not reciprocate Suleika's affections. (It is, of course, questionable whether Suleika is a completely fitting name for Marianne.)

The poem is said by Goethe to have been written by Marianne herself, on September 16, 1815, although it bears certain resemblances to his own style and expression. The last two strophes are based on an actual poem of Hafiz's.

Notes on the text:

1. *Schwingen:* poetic for "wings."
2. *West:* the West Wind (contrasting with Hafiz's East Wind in the corresponding verse).
7. *Augen:* there has been a debate of scholars whether the word should be *Auen* or *Augen.* Burdach, a leading authority treating Goethe and Hafiz, said that *Augen* goes better with *die wunden Augenlider* (line 10). On the other hand, *Auen* seems to fit better with the remaining words of the line (*Blumen, Wald, Hügel*).
9. *Doch:* yet, by contrast, the same beating of the wings (the blowing of the West Wind) that causes pain and longing also cools the beloved's burning eyelids. The wind as messenger is part of a series of devices common to Persian (and Indic) poetry. Clouds are also love messengers in that tradition.

In one of Schubert's longest songs, the West Wind is charged with carrying Suleika's replies to her lover. The song was dedicated to the soprano Anna Milder-Hauptmann, who tried numerous times to interest appropriate parties in a production of at least one of Schubert's operas. The song demands a singer with superb control and an extremely flexible voice. It resembles *Was bedeutet die Bewegung,* which Schubert called *Suleika I* to differentiate it from *Suleika II,* the song under discussion. Both sound more like operatic scenas than lieder. Although the tempo is moderate for the first three stanzas, the last two, in a reflection of the text, must be taken more rapidly.

A comparison of the poem with the lied discloses the extent of Schubert's use of text repetition. Indeed, the last musical strophe is twice the length of the last stanza of the poem. In addition, each of the musical strophes includes considerable interior text repetition. The composer highlights the words *Trennung* (bars 23 and 33), *Tränen* (bars 58 and 74), and *stilles Sehnen* (bar 46) in the vocal line. The third strophe is musically related to the first, but each of the others is different. The composer retains the following basic plan within each strophe: *a a b b*[1]. All the accompanimental figures are eminently pianistic. They show a marked resemblance to Schubert's style in his Impromptus. The treble of the accompaniment, however, seems to lie exceptionally high in comparison with that of other Schubert songs.

CHRISTIAN FRIEDRICH DANIEL SCHUBART
(1739-91)

Poet and musician, friend of Schiller (to whom he gave the idea for his revolutionary drama *Die Räuber*), Schubart suffered for his outspoken attacks on tyrannical princes, being imprisoned for ten years by Duke Karl Eugen of Württemberg. The Duke, who had made life miserable for young Schiller, lured Schubart across the border and put him in jail.

The little poem *Die Forelle*, a lightweight among German lyrics, is not one of his provocative writings or even an especially poetic one. But Schubert has made it immortal beyond its deserts.

Die Forelle

In einem Büchlein helle,
Da schoss in froher Eil
Die launische Forelle
Vorüber wie ein Pfeil.
Ich stand an dem Gestade
Und sah in süsser Ruh
Des muntern Fischleins Bade
Im klaren Büchlein zu.

Ein Fischer mit der Rute
Wohl an dem Ufer stand,
Und sah's mit kaltem Blute,
Wie sich das Fischlein wand.
· So lang dem Wasser Helle,
So dacht ich, nicht gebricht,
So fängt er die Forelle
Mit seiner Angel nicht.

Doch endlich ward dem Diebe
Die Zeit zu lang. Er macht'
Das Büchlein tückisch trübe,
Und eh' ich es gedacht,
So zuckte seine Rute,
Das Fischlein zappelt' dran,
Und ich mit regem Blute
Sah die Betrogne an.

Notes on the text:

Title. *Forelle* ("trout") is a word of Germanic origin, despite its foreign sound.

1   *helle:* the position of noun plus adjective is common enough in folk poetry, but it is unusual for the adjective to have an ending as here.
5   *Gestade:* "bank, shore" (poetic and old-fashioned; Schiller uses it at the beginning of *Wilhelm Tell*).
6   *sah:* goes with *zu* (line 8); "watched, looked at, looked on."
11   *mit kaltem Blute:* "coldly, heartlessly" (cf., but not exactly, *sangfroid*).
13   *Helle:* here a noun; "as long as clarity is not lacking" means "as long as the water remains clear."
14   *gebricht:* "is lacking" (infinitive *gebrechen*).
17   Schubert changes *plötzlich* to *endlich*.
20   *Eh' ich es gedacht (hatte):* "before I realized it."

A final strophe of blatantly didactic intent warns girls against being caught, like poor fish, by seducer-fishers. Schubert wisely omits it.

Examination of the five versions of Schubert's *Die Forelle* refutes the

oft-heard story that Schubert rarely revised his lieder once they were written. The composer wrote the original in 1816, and by 1820 had composed
four additional variants. The best-known version is the last written, a manuscript of which can be found today in the Library of Congress. Its delightfully refreshing piano accompaniment pictures the trout as it steals
gracefully through the water (Ex. 9). Although this figuration is but one
of Schubert's many water figures, it seems among the most suggestive from
an extramusical point of view. A folksy melody also adds to its accessibility.
The cellist Paumgartner, a contemporary of Schubert, so admired the tune
that he suggested its use to the composer as the basis for the variation
movement in the quintet for piano and strings, now called the "Trout"
Quintet. In that movement, the strings present the theme initially without
the piano. At the end of the movement, however, the original piano figuration from the lied reappears in the texture. For the quintet, Schubert very
sensibly changed the key from D flat of the song to A major, an easier
key for the strings to play.

Ex. 9

SCHUBERT: *Die Forelle*

The bouncy tune in the vocal part discloses the extent to which the
composer had assimilated the Austrian folk style. He allowed the voice
complete independence, while at the same time investing considerable
textural interest in the accompaniment. In this modified strophic lied, the
melody changes only at the denouement of the poem, where the trout is
caught.

MATTHIAS CLAUDIUS (1740-1815)

Claudius lived an externally uneventful life. His theological studies
were interrupted by ill health and never resumed. Back in his home village
of Wandsbeck he founded a paper, *Der Wandsbecker Bote* ("Messenger"),
to which such eminent authors as Goethe, Lessing, and Klopstock contrib-

uted. Claudius's own prose writings, under the pen name of Asmus (Song-ster?), were marked by a common-sense point of view and more than a modicum of suspicion of scholars and intellectuals, against whom he apparently felt he needed to defend the people.

Some literary historians have possibly underrated Claudius, mistaking the simplicity of his poetic style for a naïveté of emotion and thought. Yet, as one of the first to illustrate the validity of Herder's dictum that in the magic lyricism of the *Volkslied* lay the future salvation of German poetry, he struck the genuine tone of the folk song, capturing the voice of nature and reflecting the tranquillity of the peaceful environment of his North German village. To him we owe one of the most beautiful poems in the language, *Abendlied (Der Mond ist aufgegangen)*. He anticipated the romantic poets and showed a lyrical fervor, the depth of which can hardly be denied. When critics assert, as some few do, that he was not an "inspired" poet, or that the childlike quality of some of his verse is a sign of childishness, that is merely evidence of their own myopia.

Claudius ended his days in grinding poverty but not in bitterness, having learned to accept his lot philosophically and having become more religious as he became less theological.

Der Tod und das Mädchen

"Vorüber! ach, vorüber
Geh, wilder Knochenmann!
Ich bin noch jung, geh, Lieber!
Und rühre mich nicht an."

"Gib deine Hand, du schön und zart Gebild,
Bin Freund und komme nicht zu strafen.
Sei gutes Muts! Ich bin nicht wild,
Sollst sanft in meinen Armen schlafen."

There is a long tradition in most literatures, perhaps all, of poetic treatment of the theme of death, which in a sense is the ultimate theme of all poetry. Starting with the thirteenth century, if not before, German authors have dealt with the question of man's aversion to death, with final admission that the death of all creatures is not a curse but a necessity, even a blessing. The notion of ending one's earthly existence has been repugnant to all, even to those believing in a happy hereafter, but particularly to the young. And all mankind views premature death as especially tragic.

The maiden in Claudius's poem is at first shocked and horrified at realizing the approach of Death, the "wild skeleton figure." She resorts to the argument that she is too young to die. She then changes her tone and speaks flatteringly to Death (*Lieber*), beseeching him to leave her. But he is not one to be swayed by argument or blandishment. He replies, however, in kindly tones that he comes as a friend, not to punish. He denies that he is "wild" (*Ich bin nicht wild*) and assures her that she will sleep peacefully in his arms (the Thanatopsis motif). Death is assigned a long, serene line, contrasting with the shorter, frantic utterances of the maiden.

Notes on the text:

2 *Knochenmann* (literally "bone-man"): "skeleton," one popular conception of the way Death looks.
5 *schön, zart:* uninflected adjectives.
6 *bin:* omission of pronominal subject (not a feature of standard prose).
7 *gutes Muts:* in modern German the adjective would be *guten*.
8 *sollst:* as in line 6, the pronominal subject is omitted (here *du*).

Besides the aforementioned water figures, Schubert produced numerous other musical conventions, among them one relating to death. A variant of the rhythmic motive that Beethoven had used for his famous Funeral March in the "Eroica" Symphony became Schubert's "death motive" also. The opening bars of *Der Tod und das Mädchen*, played by the pianist, include this motive (Ex. 10). The maiden speaks in another rhythmic

Ex. 10

SCHUBERT: *Der Tod und das Mädchen*

setting, but the motive returns when Death offers his rejoinder. This simple musical statement provided the material for the variation movement of one of Schubert's best-known instrumental works: the "Death and the

Maiden" Quartet, written seven years later. The theme appears in the second movement of the quartet, where it was transposed to G minor to contrast with the opening movement in D minor.

An interesting counterpart to this song can be found in *Der Jüngling und der Tod,* written several months after *Der Tod und das Mädchen* to a poem by Schubert's good friend Josef von Spaun.

In a gesture of misdirected sentimentality, Andreas Schubert, a step-brother, cut the manuscript of "Death and the Maiden" into eleven pieces —nine squares and two strips—in order to distribute the parts among Schubert's friends after the composer's death.

FRIEDRICH VON SCHILLER (1759-1805)

Schiller is one of the giants of German literature, but his stature can hardly be said to rest upon his lyrical achievements. His dramatic works (*Die Räuber, Kabale und Liebe, Maria Stuart, Die Jungfrau von Orleans, Wallenstein, Die Braut von Messina,* the overrated *Wilhelm Tell,* etc.) have earned him a high place in world literature, and his historical writings, while now largely superseded in their theoretical premises, and even in some of their factual material, are examples of noble prose. Nevertheless, despite occasional spurts of lyrical genius under the "power of song," he is not one to be too productive for composers looking for texts to set as lieder. His conscious reflection and his philosophical cogitation, while important elements in many types of poetry, do not usually make for melodic utterances of lyric beauty.

Gruppe aus dem Tartarus

Horch--wie Murmeln des empörten Meeres,
Wie durch hohler Felsen Becken weint ein Bach,
Stöhnt dort dumpfigtief ein schweres, leeres
Qualerpresstes Ach!

Schmerz verzerret
Ihr Gesicht, Verzweiflung sperret
Ihren Rachen fluchend auf.
Hohl sind ihre Augen, ihre Blicke
Spähen bang nach des Cocytus Brücke,
Folgen tränend seinem Trauerlauf.

Fragen sich einander ängstlich leise,
Ob noch nicht Vollendung sei!
Ewigkeit schwingt über ihnen Kreise,
Bricht die Sense des Saturns entzwei.

In the *Iliad,* Tartarus is a place beneath the earth reserved for the rebel Titans, as far below Hades as Heaven is above; but later Greek poets used it to mean Hades.

The title indicates that Schiller has in mind only a certain number of the inhabitants of Tartarus, not all the victims. Strangely enough, they seem to nurture hope of ultimate release. We are not told what their specific punishment is. In the first strophe a horrible groaning is heard, like the roaring of an angry sea. One is vaguely reminded of Dante. Then the figure shifts to that of a brook "weeping" as it tumbles from a high cliff "through the basin" of a rock.

Having heard the groaning, the poet now sees the faces of the damned. They are distorted with pain. Despair causes the sufferers to open wide their jaws in curses. Desperately they look for a bridge over Cocytus, possibly regarding the river itself as a bridge to the world above, since it allegedly connects the world with Hades.

They still hope for an end to their terrible banishment and ask whether it is not yet there. Yet this *noch nicht* is ironically countered by *Ewigkeit;* there is no chance for them now, for eternity has begun. And Eternity smashes Saturn's scythe—time.

In the very hopelessness of this eternal suffering there is a majesty that should evoke a corresponding greatness in music. Does Schubert achieve it?

Notes on the text:

   4 *Qualerpresstes Ach:* This admirably economical construction
      means a "cry of woe wrested from torment." *Ach* is neuter, as
      customary when converting another part of speech into a noun.
   6 *Ihr Gesicht:* despite the singular number, this refers to their as-
      sembled faces. Similarly, *Rachen* (line 7) stands for plural.
  10 *Trauerlauf:* "its doleful course" is an appropriate expression, for
      Cocytus was, etymologically, a "river of wailing" (Greek *kōkúō*
      "shriek, wail"). If it is viewed as a bridge, it is a sort of bridge
      of sighs. In addition to this river of the underworld, there was a

real Cocytus on earth—in Epirus, which was supposedly connected with Hades.

12 *Vollendung:* "completion" means "the end."

13 *schwingt . . . Kreise:* "holds sway."

14 *Sense:* "scythe." It is actually not Saturn that has a scythe; he is depicted with a sickle (Father Time wields the scythe); but there is no great difference, and Saturn's scythe or sickle represents time.

Schiller may not have done his best work as a lyrical poet, but Schubert nevertheless set thirty-one of his poems, one of which, *Gruppe aus dem Tartarus,* ranks with his best lieder. Mayrhofer, Schubert's good friend, had led the composer back to Goethe and Schiller, far from the Italian influences that had been inspiring him of late. This setting projects the vigor and strength of its German text.

The turbulent piano accompaniment opens with three three-bar statements, the last occurring after the voice has entered. All are in the same pattern: a chromatically rising bass that moves beneath a single reiterated note. The tension thus created does not resolve until the voice has entered. Even there, however, the singer holds to one note in a declamatory style as the agitation continues in the accompaniment. After its monotone opening, the voice part incorporates several leaps. Notice the tritone at *weint,* bar 13, and the minor sixth at *empörten,* bar 9. A good example of *Tonmalerei* appears at bars 19-20 in the crush of minor seconds underlining *Qualerpresstes.* These seconds find their way into an inner voice in the middle section of the lied beginning at *Ach.* Then, at bar 32, beginning with *Hohl sind ihre Augen,* the melody reverts to a monotone which, ascending chromatically one measure at a time, is supported by a rich harmonic underpinning. Such frequent chord changes are unusual for Schubert, who here produces a daring display of dissonance.

In the concluding section, from the piano of *Fragen* (bar 49) through the fortissimo at *Ewigkeit* (bar 64), the music moves to a dynamic climax through a rich succession of keys. Oddly enough it ends pianissimo. This song belongs in the same category as *Grenzen der Menschheit* or *Prometheus.* It comprises several movements and a final Allegro. The composer's creative imagination is seemingly restricted by the sonority of the piano, which, although it tries, cannot equal the sound of a full orchestra.

JAKOB NIKOLAUS CRAIGHER DE JACHELUTTA
(1797-1855)

Born in the Veneto region of Northeastern Italy (where he also died after a life of varied activity), Craigher went to Vienna in 1820. Not primarily an author, and known chiefly because of Schubert's settings of three of his poems, Craigher was actually an accountant but also a translator, a traveler, and holder of a number of different jobs. He wrote poetry under the pen name of Nikolaus. His verse was collected in a volume *Poetische Betrachtungen* (1828).

Die junge Nonne

Wie braust durch die Wipfel der heulende Sturm!
Es klirren die Balken, es zittert das Haus!
Es rollet der Donner, es leuchtet der Blitz,
Und finster die Nacht, wie das Grab!

Immerhin, immerhin, so tobt' es auch jüngst noch in mir!
Es brauste das Leben, wie jetzo der Sturm,
Es bebten die Glieder, wie jetzo das Haus,
Es flammte die Liebe, wie jetzo der Blitz,
Und finster die Brust, wie das Grab.

Nun tobe, du wilder gewalt'ger Sturm,
Im Herzen ist Friede, im Herzen ist Ruh,
Des Bräutigams harret die liebende Braut,
Gereinigt in prüfender Glut,
Der ewigen Liebe getraut.

Ich harre, mein Heiland! mit sehnendem Blick!
Komm, himmlischer Bräutigam, hole die Braut,
Erlöse die Seele von irdischer Haft.

Horch, friedlich ertönet das Glöcklein vom Turm!
Es lockt mich das süsse Getön
Allmächtig zu ewigen Höhn.
Alleluja!

The young nun, or novice, is depicted rather extravagantly as having recently experienced emotional storms comparable to the raging of a thunderstorm. But those tempestuous passions have been stilled in her as she prepares to become, in traditional fashion, the "bride of Christ." Craigher's verse is, in places, reminiscent of baroque poetry in both theme and expression.

The first two strophes repeat the words *Sturm, Haus, Blitz,* and *Grab,* each providing a simile for the young nun to apply to her own life. The last two strophes use rhyme and, to a limited extent, assonance. There is a certain grandeur to Craigher's verse, although one cannot escape the impression that it is derived rather than original.

Notes on the text:

2   *Es:* here (as also in lines 3, 6, 7, 8, 19) anticipates the subject, whether singular or plural.
5   *immerhin:* "for all that; be that as it may."
6   *jetzo:* obsolete for *jetzt* "now."
9   The comparison suggests the desolation of unrequited love, which presumably had something to do with her taking the veil.
12   *Des Bräutigams:* genitive with *harret* "wait for."

The emotional anguish and passion depicted in the opening bars of the accompaniment reveal the extent to which the young actress Sophie Müller inspired the composition of this song. The raging storm outside the convent's walls and the memories it evokes as the young nun recalls her earlier life capture the listener's attention. Here is another symphonic texture for the accompanist. A raging motive in the lower bass sets the mood for the entire piece. (See Ex. 11-a.) The vocal line imitates the piano part almost verbatim before coming to rest on a repeated note (Ex. 11-b). A wide upward leap (at *der heulende,* bars 10-11, and *es zittert,*

Ex. 11

SCHUBERT: *Die junge Nonne*

a.

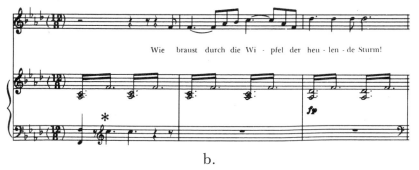

Wie braust durch die Wi - pfel der heu - len - de Sturm!

b.

bars 14-15, etc.) is a feature of the melodic profile of the vocal line. A tritone interval in the bass consistently refers to *finster* (cf. bars 22 and 24, also 43 and 45). Later, bars 31 ff., the octave displacement in the bass, supported by the continuous tremolo in the treble, adds to the agitation of the moment.

In the second statement of the motto, beginning at *Es brauste,* bars 35 ff., observe that no intervening bar for the accompanist follows. Instead, we have a telescoping of the vocal part; one statement rapidly follows on the next. In characteristic fashion, Schubert moves into major for the third stanza of the poem. The two dotted quarters of the motto (see * in Ex. 11-b) emerge as the sound of a pealing bell in the Alleluja as the young nun submits to her fate.

We note only three instances of fortissimo in the entire lied. A good accompanist must therefore keep his dynamics under control, recognizing that the storm is *outside* the window and that the girl herself is too restrained to permit her innermost thoughts to escape.

FRIEDRICH RÜCKERT (1788-1866)

Unfavorable critics have said of him, "He wrote too easily and too much," accusing him of lacking the power of concentration and careful craftsmanship that make a poet of the first rank. Perhaps he was condemned because he was a professor! A specialist in Oriental philology, he was a prolific and successful translator of poetry (Sanskrit, Persian, Arabic, Chinese, Ethiopic). Even those literary historians who have not dealt kindly with him admit that the success of his translations is to be attributed to his mastery of language and verse. His original poetry has appealed to composers because of its superior lyrical qualities.

Du bist die Ruh

Du bist die Ruh,
Der Friede mild,
Die Sehnsucht du,
Und was sie stillt.

Ich weihe dir
Voll Lust und Schmerz
Zur Wohnung hier
Mein Aug' und Herz.

Kehr ein bei mir
Und schliesse du
Still hinter dir
Die Pforten zu.

Treib andern Schmerz
Aus dieser Brust!
Voll sei dies Herz
Von deiner Lust.

Dies Augenzelt,
Von deinem Glanz
Allein erhellt,
O füll es ganz!

Notes on the text:

1-3 *Die Ruh . . . Der Friede . . . Die Sehnsucht:* the definite article with abstractions. *Sehnsucht* clashes somewhat with *Ruh* and *Friede.* His beloved is both longing and that which stills it. He dedicates his whole being to her, and he invites her to occupy his heart, his eyes, his soul.

17 *Augenzelt:* reminiscent of figures in Oriental poetry ("the tent of these eyes"), possibly owing its origin to some specific poem known to Rückert, possibly merely modeled on an Oriental theme in a general way. This may also apply to the motif of the third strophe.

One of the four Rückert poems favored by the composer, *Du bist die Ruh* is among the loveliest of the simple settings in Schubert's repertory. Of the singer it requires utmost control. The piano accompaniment is relatively uncluttered and should contribute to the mood of tranquillity. The form is that perennial German favorite: *a a b, Bar* form. At the end of the *b,* after *ganz,* the piano imitates the voice for the first time. Observe the two instances of a complete bar of silence, bars 61 and 75, perhaps a suggestion of sorrow incorporated into the piano part. The tessitura is exceptionally high. Curiously, the highest vocal notes occur at *allein erhellt,* bars 57 ff. and 70 ff., where the piano moves to the lowest part of its range and sounds full chords in place of single notes. Schubert reverses his usual progression and moves from major to minor in the third stanza before concluding finally in major.

We know of at least twenty-five other settings of the poem. Schubert himself wrote two versions, and we are uncertain which he preferred.

FRANZ VON SCHOBER (1796-1882)

Unknown in the ranks of major authors, von Schober is remembered for the fact that Schubert set a dozen of his poems to music. Von Schober was born in Malmö, Sweden, went to Vienna in 1815 to study law, became a friend of Schubert's, remained on the continent (Germany and Austria), and ended his years in Dresden, after a long life.

An die Musik

Du holde Kunst, in wieviel grauen Stunden,
Wo mich des Lebens wilder Kreis umstrickt,
Hast du mein Herz zu warmer Lieb' entzunden,
Hast mich in eine bessre Welt entrückt!

Oft hat ein Seufzer, deiner Harf' entflossen,
Ein süsser, heiliger Akkord von dir
Den Himmel bessrer Zeiten mir erschlossen,
Du holde Kunst, ich danke dir dafür!

This tribute to music praises the noble art not only for its ability to transport us in hours of gloom to a better world—a world of love, of escape from actual trouble—but also for its promise of better times to come. The sentiments are sufficiently conventional and traditional, and it is doubtful that Schober's praise best sums up the true worth of music.

Notes on the text:

1 *grau:* "gray," i.e., "somber, dreary, gloomy."
2 *umstrickt:* the auxiliary (*hat*) is omitted, as often.
3 *entzunden:* now *entzündet.*
5 *hat:* goes with *erschlossen,* line 7.

Three Schubert lieder describe his profound love of music. One is based on a poem, *An mein Klavier,* by Christian Schubart (cf. also his *Die Forelle,* p. 66) and two, *Trost im Liede* and *An die Musik,* are settings of poems by von Schober. Although Alfred Einstein believed that *Trost im Liede* best expressed Schubert's attitude toward his art, it is *An die Musik* that represents posterity's view of the composer's sentiments.

In this strophic song, introduced and concluded by several bars for the pianist, the melody appears first in the bass of the accompaniment, is taken up by the singer immediately afterward, and is extended to round off the phrase. Notice several instances where Schubert employs his favorite leap of a sixth: on *bess're Welt* in the first stanza and on *Kunst* and *danke* in the second. His choice of D major is particularly apt. This key does not sound sensual, tragic, optimistic, agitated, but instead suggests a sense of tranquillity, acceptance, and the gratefulness of the composer as custodian of his art.

LUDWIG RELLSTAB (1799-1860)

Known from reflected glory, Rellstab is remembered, if at all, as the author of the words set by Schubert in his "Serenade" and for the name-dropping in his travel sketches, for he met and wrote about Weber, Beethoven, Goethe, Arndt, Tieck, and other luminaries of his day. He shared in the enthusiasm for the cause of Greek independence, which was the great vogue of all young authors of his time, and he also supported the cause of Poland. Several of his novels, once fairly well known, have fallen into oblivion and have not been reprinted for over a century. Like Heine, and unlike most other Germans, Rellstab glorified Napoleon. This is seen especially in his novel *1812.* He has left some twenty-four volumes of mediocre writing. At times he used the pseudonym Freimund Zuschauer.

To students of music he is of some interest as the founder of the musical journal *Iris,* in which his critical articles appeared and enjoyed some esteem. Schubert set several of Rellstab's songs to music; *Aufenthalt* and *Ständchen,* both from the posthumously published cycle *Schwanengesang,* are best known.

Ständchen

Leise flehen meine Lieder
Durch die Nacht zu dir;
In den stillen Hain hernieder,
Liebchen, komm zu mir!

Flüsternd schlanke Wipfel rauschen
In des Mondes Licht;
Des Verräters feindlich Lauschen
Fürchte, Holde, nicht.

Hörst die Nachtigallen schlagen?
Ach! sie flehen dich,
Mit der Töne süssen Klagen
Flehen sie für mich.

Sie verstehn des Busens Sehnen,
Kennen Liebesschmerz,
Rühren mit den Silbertönen
Jedes weiche Herz.

Lass auch dir die Brust bewegen,
Liebchen, höre mich!
Bebend harr' ich dir entgegen!
Komm, beglücke mich!

Notes on the text:

1 The choice of *flehen* is striking. With its obvious resemblance to *fliehen* and *fliegen* it inescapably causes us to associate it with those verbs; one might expect his songs to "fly through the air." Instead, they "plead through the night," and there is imparted to *flehen,* in a manner that cannot be easily reproduced in English,

the transferred function of a verb of motion. *Flehen* is repeated twice, in more orthodox context, in the third strophe.

3   *den stillen Hain:* "the quiet grove" may mean the place from which he sings his *Ständchen,* but it may also be the symbolic grove of (non-classical) poetry.

5   *flüsternd:* an adverb with *rauschen.*

7   *Verräter:* the traitor is one who may reveal the lovers' tryst (he was a stock-in-trade character in earlier poetry). Why the sound of the serenade itself does not have the same effect is not clear, unless this is to be only a serenade in verse. Schubert has fortunately not let it remain so.

9   The nightingales are not only the songbirds of the night but also a symbol of German lyric poets. The use of *flehen* to refer to the song of the nightingale as well as to the poet's own songs (line 1) affirms this identity. Note the resemblance to Eichendorff's themes: night, moonlight, nightingales.

10   *flehen:* here transitive; "implore."

11   *der Töne:* genitive (a more prosaic and less effective equivalent would be *mit den süssen Klagen der Töne*).
     Klagen: "complaints," the song of the nightingale being traditionally plaintive.

15   *Silbertönen:* the rhyme of *Sehnen* and *-tönen* is legitimate in German verse.

19   *harr'* . . . *entgegen:* "wait for" (with anticipation that she will not fail to come to him).

The metrical scheme is simple, with no aberrant feet, and there are no unrhymed lines, but the result is not monotonous. Schubert repeats, for musical reasons, lines 6, 8, 14, 16, and 20.

We find numerous compositions entitled *Ständchen.* It would be difficult to name a single composer of lieder who has not written at least one. *Ständchen,* which is usually translated into English as "Serenade," may derive its name from the age-old story of the serenading lover who sings beneath his true love's window while accompanying himself on a lute or guitar.

Schubert's "Serenade" is one of his best-known songs. The composer set the five stanzas of the poem in an *a a b* form, returning once again to the old German *Bar* form.

a = stanzas 1 and 2 $\Big\}$
a = stanzas 3 and 4 $\Big\}$ same music
b = stanza 5

The "plucked guitar" accompaniment in the opening bars must sound detached in order to imitate realistically the sound of the guitar. The opening harmonic progression, I-VI-II-V-I, is fairly commonplace. Slightly sophisticated for a folk song, however, is the echoing phrase in the piano part immediately after *dir* and *mir*. Notice how well Schubert relates the two sections of the melody in *a*. Compare *Leise flehen* with *Flüsternd schlanke*. This technique of concealed relationships appealed also to Brahms, who used it often.

Unlike the opening stanza, the second stanza has no intervening bars for solo piano; the vocal phrases follow one after the other. At the conclusion of this stanza (at *nicht*), however, Schubert doubles the number of bars in the piano interlude before the return of the original melody starts the third stanza. The third and fourth stanzas follow the same pattern, except that in order to heighten the emotional tension before the final stanza, Schubert omits an interlude and continues without interruption to the conclusion of the piece. Notice the many instances of neumatic text setting (several notes to one syllable), contrary to the syllabic setting we usually find. Perhaps the composer changed his style here to mirror the caressing lilt of a love song.

WILHELM MÜLLER (1794-1827)

Müller's short lifetime fell in an age when people were hungry for songs, and he provided them with the lyrics for a great number, some of which have retained their popularity. But it is extremely dubious that he would even be remembered today were it not for Schubert's settings. For Müller's verse was largely derived, secondhand, emulative. Enthusiasm for Byron led him to imitate Byron's own enthusiasms, as well as his poetry; hence his interest in the cause of Greek freedom (reflected in *Lieder der Griechen*, 1821-24). It would be a distortion to claim that either his involvement or his poetry were on the same plane as those of Byron, yet there were many other imitators of the British poet, and Müller is far from being the least gifted in that crowd of echoers. His poetry does capture some of the spirit of folk song, and it seems to have struck a responsive chord in the people of his own day. But the very factors that assured its acceptance may have been the opposite of poetic worth. Many of his lines are hollow, jingling utterances of spurious merit and diluted sentiments that smack of shallowness, though hardly of insincerity. Once or twice he soars to lyric heights, and the contrast with most of his verse is then all the crasser. Never does he reach the quality of Eichendorff or Goethe.

Still, it would be unfair to deny him all merit. Heine praised Müller and admitted his debt to him, but Heine was not likely (any more than Goethe was) to praise anyone who could have rivaled him. When it is said, as it has been, that Heine wrote the greatest modern sea poetry in the German language, some may think that he was an innovator. But it was to two cycles of sea poems by Müller that Heine owed the literary inspiration for his own. That he surpassed Müller does not detract from Müller's priority.

Perhaps we should be grateful to Müller for having inspired both Heine and Schubert. Gratitude need not take the form of unwarranted praise, however, and we should not be too surprised to find a history of German literature that never mentions his name.

The poet himself called this *Wanderschaft*. Müller, certainly with an awareness of the pun on his own name (*Das Wandern ist des Müllers Lust*), accounts in this transparent poem for the traditional fondness of the miller

Das Wandern

Das Wandern ist des Müllers Lust,
Das Wandern!
Das muss ein schlechter Müller sein,
Dem niemals fiel das Wandern ein,
Das Wandern.

Vom Wasser haben wir's gelernt,
Vom Wasser!
Das hat nicht Rast bei Tag und Nacht,
Ist stets auf Wanderschaft bedacht,
Das Wasser.

Das sehn wir auch den Rädern ab,
Den Rädern!
Die gar nicht gerne stille stehn,
Die sich mein Tag nicht müde drehn,
Die Räder.

Die Steine selbst, so schwer sie sind,
Die Steine!
Sie tanzen mit den muntern Reihn
Und wollen gar noch schneller sein,
Die Steine.

O Wandern, Wandern, meine Lust,
O Wandern!
Herr Meister und Frau Meisterin
Lasst mich in Frieden weiterziehn
Und wandern.

for roving, wandering. He has learned it from the mill itself and its main constituents: the water, which wanders day and night without rest; the mill wheels, which turn incessantly; and even the heavy millstones, which execute their nimble dance and would go still faster if they could. And the miller who sings the song is not the master, but an employee or apprentice, for he begs his master and the master's wife to let him take to the road and fulfill his longing and his passion for wandering.

In this opening strophic song from *Die schöne Müllerin*, the principal means of unification is the music of the water, pictured in the accompaniment figure of three and a half bars (Ex. 12-a) that Schubert uses to introduce each of the stanzas and to connect them. The composer retains the same figuration with slightly changed harmonies throughout the entire lied. A syllabic text setting with emphasis always on the repetition of the most significant words of the phrase (*Wandern, Wasser,* etc.) preserves the element of folksiness. Observe that not only does this word fall on the first note or accented beat of the measure, but it is also sung to a note that is longer than any other note in the phrase. Later, in the conclusion of the text, it is again repeated.

Schubert's rhythmic control is very much in evidence as the words bounce along, sounding all the while like onward rushing water. The composer's concentration on water figures might well be the object of psychological research. An abundance of different figurations representing the sound of water turns up in countless numbers of songs, among them: *Am Meer, Auf dem Wasser zu singen, Der Jüngling an der Quelle, Der Müller und der Bach, Des Baches Wiegenlied, Die Forelle, Gefrorne Tränen, Meeres Stille,* and *Mein.* We have included in our musical illustrations some other water figures: Ex. 12-b is from *Wohin,* the second song from *Die schöne Müllerin,* and reflects the bubbling brook; Ex. 12-c from *Auf dem Wasser zu singen,* set in a barcarole rhythmic figuration, imitates the sound of rippling water as the boat moves gently forward.

Ex. 12

SCHUBERT: *Das Wandern*

a.

SCHUBERT: *Wohin?*

b.

SCHUBERT: *Auf dem Wasser zu singen*

c.

HEINRICH HEINE (1797-1856)

Almost everyone who knows Heine's works thinks of him as one of those poets who died young. And it is difficult to escape that impression, even when one realizes that he actually lived to the age of sixty, for his poetry, even his latest, remained youthful. The son of a Jewish merchant in the Rhineland, he was unsuccessful as an apprentice in one or two businesses in which his family hoped he would prosper. He also failed in his own business, for which his wealthy and indulgent uncle Salomon, a Hamburg millionaire and self-made man, had provided the capital, as he subsequently did for Heine the law student. After studies at the universities of Bonn, Berlin, and Göttingen (at all of which places he devoted far more attention to literature and philosophy than to law), he finally received his degree. Mistakenly hoping for better opportunities in the law, particularly for a state position, Heine underwent pseudo-conversion to Lutheranism. He failed to receive an appointment, but now he became more seriously concerned with his own ancestry and heritage. (See *The Rabbi of Bacherach* [fragment of a novel] and *Hebrew Melodies* [lyrical poetry]).

Heine fell hopelessly in love with Salomon's elder daughter, Amalie, who, after initial encouragement, rebuffed him. Some time later he felt the same tender emotion for her sister Therese, with equal success. These two unhappy love affairs provided the stimulus for a wealth of lyrical poems, some of them exquisite, others slightly contrived. His lyrics show a thorough grounding in the German *Volkslied*, but none of them is rough or unpolished.

Travels in England and Italy, as well as inside Germany, resulted in some of the best travel literature in any language, sometimes marred, sometimes enhanced, by an incurable urge to ridicule excessive sentimentality, especially his own. This same trait is found in many of his poems, in which a harsh, but usually clever, final line smashes to bits a lyrically established and artistically developed mood.

In 1831, Heine left Germany for Paris, mainly for political reasons, but wrote for German periodicals—with considerable alteration of his work by the blue pencil of the German censor. He was one of the few Germans retaining enthusiasm for Napoleon, who had instituted many reforms in Heine's native province and who had meant liberation of the Jews from many injustices, however tyrannical he was elsewhere.

During the last eight years of his life, Heine was confined to bed with a paralytic affliction now regarded by some doctors as of metabolic origin; this had plagued him most of his life, although his physician had apparently never considered it serious until the final stages. Heine became blind in one eye and had to raise the lid of the other with his fingers in order to be able to see while writing his poems—on large pieces of brown paper begged by his sweetheart from the butcher. Despite the slow torture of writing, he now wrote some of his most lyrical, as well as his most humorous, poetry. He even joked stoically about his "mattress grave" (*Matratzengruft*). During these last years he was tended by a German girl living in Paris, the last of several "loves," affectionately called by Heine the *Mouche*.

Heine was long the subject of much acrimonious debate. Some called him a poseur, lacking respect for life and religion, for fatherland and literature, capitalizing on the cheap exploitation of a facile but super-ficial talent; others enthusiastically acclaimed him as a fighter for liberal thought and politics, a sufferer bearing the woes of mankind, a superb poet creating unsurpassed literary beauty.

In the present century, and especially since World War II (hardly during the period 1933-45!), the publication of Heine's works has increased enormously, and the number of editions of his writings surpasses that of any other German poet. Studies and writings about Heine are still copious, if not all inspired. It is safe to say that he is the one German lyric poet with the greatest world reputation, not excluding the mighty Goethe. Translations of Heine's poetry exist in a great number of languages, al-though none of them can begin to convey the essence of the original.

Heine himself showed some superior ability as a translator in render-ing Byron's poetry into German. But such success is not usual. (Heine also resembled Byron in many ways in his life and works.) He is the German poet who has most strongly appealed to composers, and there are over four thousand settings of his poems by Schubert, Schumann, Hugo Wolf, Robert Franz, Edvard Grieg, F. Himmel, Moszkowski, Thalberg, R. Herr-mann, E. Lassen, Meyerbeer, Loewe, Liszt, Mendelssohn, Brahms, and a host of others.

The Heine Poems in *Schwanengesang*

Der Atlas

Ich unglückseliger Atlas! Eine Welt,
Die ganze Welt der Schmerzen muss ich tragen.
Ich trage Unerträgliches, und brechen
Will mir das Herz im Leibe.

Du stolzes Herz, du hast es ja gewollt!
Du wolltest glücklich sein, unendlich glücklich,
Oder unendlich elend, stolzes Herz,
Und jetzo bist du elend.

In Heinrich Heine's *Buch der Lieder,* from which these poems are taken, many lyrics begin with the word *ich* (far fewer with *du*). For these are personal poems, with the first person outweighing the second. To Heine his loves, his griefs, his triumphs, and his failures are all of cosmic importance. His intended implication seems to be that no one on earth ever loved or suffered as much. He bears not only the sorrows of Heinrich Heine, but pretends to bear those of the whole world, hence the choice of the figure Atlas. Not that he thought much of the rest of the world. He must bear a world of suffering; he bears the unbearable—a kind of verbal paradox of which he was extremely fond—and his heart is about to break.

Then he turns to that heart and addresses it, which is, obviously, the same as addressing himself. "It was your wish! You wanted to be infinitely happy" (because the love Heine bore for the beautiful but unattainable Amalie would have, if reciprocated, resulted in perfect bliss, he thinks). But the other side of the coin is infinite misery, if he suffers rejection—which he did.

Notes on the text:

> 5 *stolzes Herz:* at once criticizes and compliments the heart, his emotional nature: proud heart! overweening pride, daring pride, admirable pride, stubborn pride.

8 *Und jetzo bist du elend:* "and now you are miserable," and Heine is infinitely proud of his Atlaslike power to bear that misery. *Jetzo* is an archaic variant of *jetzt.*

This poem is not as smooth as most of Heine's lyrics. Unlike the majority of his poems, it lacks rhyme.

The six Heine songs of *Schwanengesang* are remarkable works, showing Schubert at the height of his development. Coming close on the completion of *Die Winterreise,* the proofs of which Schubert was busy correcting shortly before he died, many of the songs reveal new stylistic features, particularly in harmony and sonority.

Schubert had originally intended a separate cycle of Rellstab songs to be dedicated to his friends of the Schubertiads—Josef von Spaun, Moritz von Schwind, Johann Mayrhofer, Franz von Schober, and others—who performed his works in the homes of the Viennese middle class. The Heine songs were to comprise another group. When Schubert died, however, his brother Ferdinand, now the sole possessor of all the unpublished manuscripts, presented a number of songs to the publisher Tobias Haslinger. The latter decided on the sentimental title *Schwanengesang* ("Swansong"), and collected six Rellstab songs in one volume. In another he collected one Rellstab, six Heine songs, and a final unrelated one entitled *Die Taubenpost,* to a poem by Seidl. Although of uneven quality, this set, in addition to the Heine songs, includes the famous setting of Rellstab's *Ständchen* (mentioned above). The composer himself gave the Heine songs titles, repeated sections of the text wherever he felt it essential for musical unity, and blended text and tone in a highly successful manner.

Schubert projects the emotional overtones of *Der Atlas* by the peculiar sonority of a tremolo that appears in forty of the fifty-five bars in the piece. A sharp rhythmic motive (see * in Ex. 13) in the bass of the accompaniment anticipates the entry of the voice. (Compare the opening notes of the vocal part with the opening bass octaves in the piano prelude.) The text is reflected at several points: a wide leap at *die ganze Welt* (bar 12); the monotone at *ich trage Uner[trägliches]* (bar 15) followed by chromaticisms that underline *brechen will mir das Herz;* repetition of *unendlich* supported by one of the longer notes in the vocal part (bars 29, 31, and 33); and finally the A flat, the highest note in the song, that is sung to *Schmerzen* (bar 50). Using the same technique that he does in *Ständchen,* Schubert achieves unification of the contrasting parts (*a* and *b*) of this

Ex. 13

SCHUBERT: *Der Atlas*

Ich un - glück=sel - ger At - las,

ternary-form lied through melodic parallels. Notice that at the opening of the second section (*b*), *Du stolzes Herz* (bar 23), the bass octaves of the accompaniment (B–D sharp–A sharp) duplicate in transposition the bass line (G–B flat–F sharp) of the opening bars of the piece. We must allow that the opening is minor and the new section major, but again this movement from minor to major is typically Schubertian. The composer reintroduces the opening lines of the poem and repeats the text of each of the last two phrases.

Ihr Bild

Ich stand in dunkeln Träumen
Und starrt' ihr Bildnis an,
Und das geliebte Antlitz
Heimlich zu leben begann.

Um ihre Lippen zog sich
Ein Lächeln wunderbar,
Und wie von Wehmutstränen
Erglänzte ihr Augenpaar.

Auch meine Tränen flossen
Mir von den Wangen herab.
Und ach! ich kann es nicht glauben,
Dass ich dich verloren hab!

The motif of the weeping picture is known elsewhere. A striking resemblance to Heine's poem is found in the play *Julius von Tarent,* by H. A. Leisewitz. A man goes to his room, sees the likeness of his beloved illumined by a few moonbeams, and then notices that the face has a mournful expression and that bright tears fall from the eyes.

It is the loss of the same girl who caused the expression of infinite grief in *Der Atlas* that Heine bemoans here. Perhaps the miraculous weeping of the eyes in the picture means that Heine's love had some sort of blessing of fate. Yet the very first line tells us that he was *in dunkeln Träumen,* and dreams are a favorite device of his for introducing the impossible, the satiric, the strange. At the very least, however, he lets himself imagine that his beloved really did return his affection. And his own tears are not imaginary.

The forthright statement of the poetry is reflected here in the stark simplicity of the accompaniment. *Ihr Bild* offers one of the few examples of a vocal line doubled throughout the entire piece. Indeed, the opening bars present the theme doubled in octaves. Except for occasional movement in an inner voice, the texture is absolutely transparent. Our interest must focus instead on the predominantly stepwise vocal melody, the ternary pattern (*a b a*[1]) of the three stanzas, and the apparently effortless musical framework of the poem. Schubert has avoided text repetition, restricting himself absolutely to the lines of the poet. In his customary manner, he modulates to a key a third distant from the tonic (bars 15 ff.); he mirrors the concept of *wunderbar* (bar 17) and *Augenpaar* (bar 21) with a sigh in the piano accompaniment.

For some listeners this song is a disappointment. For others, it shows how Schubert can restrict to a bare minimum the musical elaborations of a poem.

Das Fischermädchen

Du schönes Fischermädchen,
Treibe den Kahn ans Land;
Komm zu mir und setze dich nieder,
Wir kosen Hand in Hand.

Leg an mein Herz dein Köpfchen
Und fürchte dich nicht zu sehr;
Vertraust du dich doch sorglos
Täglich dem wilden Meer!

Mein Herz gleicht ganz dem Meere,
Hat Sturm und Ebb und Flut,
Und manche schöne Perle
In seiner Tiefe ruht.

Heine spent a vacation on the seashore at Cuxhaven, at the expense of his rich uncle Salomon, and the North Sea was a revelation to him. The *Fischermädchen* is evidently a casual acquaintance; Heine always managed to find female companionship to assuage his aching heart. Whether this one is real or fictitious does not matter too much. One suspects that she was real.

He invites her to lean her pretty little head against his breast and not to be afraid; he reminds her that, after all, she risks her life at sea every day. He finds his own heart to be very much like a wild sea. It beats with ebb tide and flow, and it even reaches flood-tide proportions in moments of great emotional stress. He means less the physical heart than the symbolic, but he was pretty physical, too.

What does Heine mean by the pearls that reside in the depths of his heart? Pearls ordinarily represent tears. If so, he may mean that the heart is the source of pearly tears, which would continue the simile of his heart's resembling the sea, the source of actual pearls.

An uncommonly repetitive rhythmic figure characterizes the brief piano prelude that recurs as a postlude. The $\frac{6}{8}$ meter provides an additional element of folksiness. Both together contribute to the generally cheerful picture of *Das Fischermädchen*. In a standard approach to the three strophes, Schubert set them in an *a b a¹* pattern, but reversed his usual alternation of colors, moving here from an opening in major to the middle section in minor. *Das Fischermädchen* is the least extraordinary of the lieder in this cycle.

On the distant horizon looms the city. The city with its towers is no doubt Hamburg (Hamburg's coat of arms shows three towers). It was here that he met, loved, and lost Amalie, his beautiful cousin.

A temporary return to Hamburg reawakens memories. He approaches by boat. It is evening, and the mist of twilight enshrouds the city with a

Die Stadt

Am fernen Horizonte
Erscheint, wie ein Nebelbild,
Die Stadt mit ihren Türmen
In Abenddämmrung gehüllt.

Ein feuchter Windzug kräuselt
Die graue Wasserbahn;
Mit traurigem Takte rudert
Der Schiffer in meinem Kahn.

Die Sonne hebt sich noch einmal
Leuchtend vom Boden empor
Und zeigt mir jene Stelle,
Wo ich das Liebste verlor.

nostalgic gloom, matching the emotions aroused in Heine. Once more nature captures his interest, as the sun temporarily reappears and illumines with its last rays the very spot where he wooed and lost his beloved. The loss of that one little girl paid incalculable dividends to Heine, for she seems to have prompted scores of poems. Cynics have claimed that he continued to exploit the theme of his broken heart long after it had healed. Others forgive him because of his superb verse—not the best of which is found in this poem.

Using the same technique as he had already tried in *Der Atlas,* Schubert borrowed an orchestral sonority for *Die Stadt:* a tremolo in combination with a diminished seventh chord. (See * in Ex. 14.) Seven years earlier, in 1821, Weber had startled Berlin theatergoers with such coloristic musical effects to describe Samiel, the evil spirit in *Der Freischütz.*

Ex. 14

SCHUBERT: *Die Stadt*

The figuration appears in the opening piano prelude of *Die Stadt;* it cushions the entire middle section (the second stanza of the poem); and it recurs in the closing postlude as well. A dotted rhythmic figure (See ** in Ex. 14), whose shape derives from the text accents, characterizes the vocal line of this mysterious, impressionistic song, where the dynamics alternate between pianissimo and piano. The only fortissimo appears at *Liebste* (bar 34), on the highest pitch, at the climax of the song. Notice the text reflection at *Boden* (bar 30) and the quasi-recitative style of the melodic line throughout.

Am Meer

Das Meer erglänzte weit hinaus
Im letzten Abendscheine;
Wir sassen am einsamen Fischerhaus,
Wir sassen stumm und alleine.

Der Nebel stieg, das Wasser schwoll,
Die Möwe flog hin und wieder;
Aus deinen Augen liebevoll
Fielen die Tränen nieder.

Ich sah sie fallen auf deine Hand,
Und bin auf's Knie gesunken;
Ich habe von deiner weissen Hand
Die Tränen fortgetrunken.

Seit jener Stunde verzehrt sich mein Leib,
Die Seele stirbt vor Sehnen;
Mich hat das unglücksel'ge Weib
Vergiftet mit ihren Tränen.

We find Heine on the shore of the North Sea once more. The verses begin with a tranquil mood; the sea gleams in the setting sun, and a loving couple sit in promising solitude beside a lonely fisher hut. The mist, the water, the sea gulls are all stock-in-trade devices of the poet. Amorous tears fall from the girl's eyes. And now we encounter one of Heine's devastating effects, the practice called *Stimmungsbrechung* ("mood-breaking"). This negating or ridiculing, in the final lines, of a mood produced earlier in the poem was apparently employed when the poet found himself mouthing familiar words and associations that he had used too many times before, or when he found himself taking life too seriously, becoming overinvolved in an emotion which, however genuine, sounded trite when put into words. The supreme irony, perhaps, is that the very feeling and expression at which he poked fun were usually sincere. Heine, like many other people, combined both sentimentality and cynicism in his character.

As the girl's tears fall from her eyes upon her hand, Heine pretends to drop to his knees and lap them up. Ever since then, he says, he has been sick and suffering in body and soul. "The confounded woman has poisoned me with her tears!"

Heine was unable here to resist the impish urge to smash a beautifully set mood with the crude ax of devastating wit, as if he were always aware of the ridiculous element of reality that is so close to even our most sacred feelings and serious beliefs. He is embarrassed at his own participation in them. He is, perhaps, too sincere, rather than insincere.

Schubert began this song with a dissonance, perhaps to underline the essential loneliness of the text. He fashioned the four stanzas of the poem into a modified strophic lied and sectionalized the piece by means of changing figurations in the accompaniment. He selected a chordal texture for the first stanza, a tremolo followed by the same chordal texture for the second stanza. Retaining the chordal texture for the third, he duplicated the pattern of the second stanza in the final one. Thus we have *a ba a ba,* in terms of musical style.

Notice the singer's leap of a fifth at *stieg* (bar 13) and the swell in the accompaniment at *schwoll* (bar 15). Schubert usually preferred the key of C major for his epic works. Here, however, he alternated between C major and C minor in this short but dramatic song. The poet's cynicism went relatively unnoticed by the composer, who believed *vergiftet* required a dissonance (bar 42). Observe that in this song none of the previously mentioned water figures appears. Even in the sounds he uses for the imitation of nature, Schubert has changed his style.

Schubert rearranged the order of all of the Heine poems. The transposed sequence of *Am Meer* and *Die Stadt* is distressing, because we should first be at sea, and only later view the city in the distance.

The motif of the "double" is widespread in literature and folk belief. Everyone has supposedly at least one. According to one superstition, there are six doubles for each person on earth, constituting with him a magic seven.

Sometimes the figure of the *Doppelgänger* is symbolic of schizophrenia. Heine is not concerned with that here. He uses the device as a means of

Der Doppelgänger

Still ist die Nacht, es ruhen die Gassen,
In diesem Hause wohnte mein Schatz;
Sie hat schon längst die Stadt verlassen,
Doch steht noch das Haus auf demselben Platz.

Da steht auch ein Mensch und starrt in die Höhe,
Und ringt die Hände vor Schmerzensgewalt;
Mir graut es, wenn ich sein Antlitz sehe--
Der Mond zeigt mir meine eigne Gestalt.

Du Doppelgänger, du bleicher Geselle!
Was äffst du nach mein Liebesleid,
Das mich gequält auf dieser Stelle
So manche Nacht, in alter Zeit?

depicting the dire consequences of his unhappy love. He visits the scenes of yesteryear, the house where the lovely Amalie was wooed and where she rejected him. And he imagines he sees his own double standing before that house, staring and wringing its hands in pain. Amalie is no longer there, but the old site is, and the specter of Heine's grief is, too. And he pretends to shudder at the ghastly look on his own pale face as he catches a glimpse of the young man in the moonlight. The theme of painful revival of ancient grief on return to the scenes of old is frequently encountered in German folk poetry, and is often exploited by Heine. Here his pretense of seeing a double affords him the opportunity of addressing the image of his own tortured pain of love, as he directs a rhetorical question to his fancied *Doppelgänger* and to the world of his readers.

Notes on the text:

1 *Still ist die Nacht:* a line of lyrical calm ushers in a tranquil mood.

3-4 Superficially a more prosaic utterance, this statement nevertheless expresses the paradox that the environment can remain—and, somehow, the experience in that environment—even after the participants have all gone.

5-6 These lines introduce the intruder.
auch: in addition to the house, the scene, and also in addition to Heine?

7-8 *Mir graut es:* the pretended horror at the ghostlike double.
9-12 These lines emphasize the lasting grief that still haunts Heine.
      in alter Zeit: "in olden times" is a chronological hyperbole; it was
      not very long ago.

Here Schubert surpasses many of his own extraordinary achievements.
He changes the music to suit the text and unifies the three stanzas by
means of a motto theme consisting of four chords, repeated in an ostinato
throughout the entire piece (Ex. 15-a). This theme undergoes slight modifications as the music slowly and inexorably builds to a climax (Ex. 15-b).

Ex. 15

SCHUBERT: *Der Doppelgänger*

Another feature of *Der Doppelgänger* is the use of an inner pedal on
F sharp in all but five bars of the lied. Schubert omits the note for the
first time at *Gestalt*, bar 40. The combination of the sustained F sharp
with the recurrent ostinato effectively portrays the agitation of the principal character.

Most of the lines of the text are set in monotone, with pitch changes reserved for the final lines and with wide leaps and ornaments restricted to a few specific words. For example, notice the octave drop at *Schmerzensgewalt* (bar 32) and the written-out turn on *alter Zeit* (bar 54). Rhythmic interest centers on the voice, not the figurations of the accompaniment, which Schubert here uses to provide harmonic coloring. Observe the piano's cautious echo of the voice at *Schatz* (bar 12) and *Platz* (bar 22), the dissonance at *Gestalt* (bar 40), and at the final stanza, the gradual move into D-sharp minor via the pivot note of F sharp (bar 47).

Could it be that Schubert made such extensive use of altered chords in these concluding bars to reflect the transformations in the physical image of the phantom double?

IV

The New Style
of Piano Accompaniment

SCHUMANN (1810-56)

Before Schumann composed a single lied, he had written the vast majority of piano pieces which brought him fame. For example, *Papillons, Davidsbündlertänze, Toccata, Carnaval, Fantasiestücke, Etudes symphoniques, Kinderscenen, Kreisleriana, Fantasia in C, Arabeske, Humoreske, Novelletten, Nachtstücke,* and the three sonatas all appeared before 1840, the famous song year that witnessed his marriage to Clara Wieck. Their courtship had been stormy, and only after litigation with Friedrich Wieck, his future father-in-law—who had been his piano teacher—did the wedding take place. The joy of newly found happiness inspired numerous songs, most of which appeared in cycles.

Unlike Schubert, whose orientation was primarily vocal, Schumann was first and foremost a pianist and composer of piano music. The accidental injury to his fourth finger, which occurred while he was a piano student of Wieck's, proved beneficial to posterity. The young musician recognized early in his career that this physical handicap would impede his digital facility and therefore began to concentrate more of his efforts on composition. Again different from Schubert, who was by nature easygoing and carefree, Schumann was excessively compulsive. After having developed and mastered a distinct style in piano music, he decided to embark on the path of vocal music. Figures may often prove false, but for whatever they are worth: when Schumann decided to compose lieder, he produced 168 in one year!

As a pianist, it was only natural that he should concern himself with the significance of the accompaniment. For this reason, preludes, interludes, and postludes are an integral part of most of his songs. Indeed, the cycles often conclude with rather extensive codas for solo piano.

As the son of a prominent bookseller and translator, Schumann showed far more discrimination in his choice of texts than did Schubert. He was better educated, better read, more sophisticated, more traveled, and far more articulate. Robert Schumann was also a writer on music and a critic. The extent of his influence has not yet been accurately acknowledged.

Schumann set the poetry of Goethe, Schiller, Mörike, Eichendorff, Kerner, Rückert, Chamisso, Mosen, and Hoffmann von Fallersleben among German poets, and Byron, Burns, Moore, and Hans Christian Andersen in translation. But of all the poets whose works he set, the man who is most closely associated with Schumann's music is Heinrich Heine. The *Liederkreis*, Op. 24, several ballads and romances, and the *Dichterliebe*, Op. 48, are all settings of Heine poems. As a group each differs from the other. As individual songs, the wide variety of vocal styles and piano figurations are testimony of his remarkable creative powers. For the first time, the piano achieves equality with the voice, sometimes even dominating it. But always the voice and the piano parts are interrelated, one growing out of the other in a reciprocal arrangement. This does not imply that the pianist doubles the vocal line or that the sole function of the keyboard instrument is to provide chordal support for the voice. The two sonorous elements have been brought together in a kind of wedded bliss. To separate them or to hear them separately is not only unthinkable, it is impossible.

In short, the listener is far less likely to come away from a recital whistling a song by Schumann. His melodies are not folksy or tuneful. They are long-line melodies often fragmented between the piano and the voice. Schumann releases the song from its origin in the bosom of the people. He places it on a pedestal where it becomes the art song, a highly sophisticated, intimate vocal genre.

Schumann did not regard himself as a humble musician. He selected his works with care. He did not hesitate to affix titles where none had existed previously, or to change a word or two for metric purposes, or to rearrange word order for musical reasons in order to achieve his desired goal. If Schumann was a character, or *ein Original*, as the Germans would call him, then certainly Heine was another. Together they were responsible, albeit unwittingly, for the *Dichterliebe*—one of the masterpieces of nineteenth-century music—a discussion of which follows.

HEINE

Dichterliebe

This was not Heine's title. The poems in this group are all taken from the slender collection called by Heine *Lyrisches Intermezzo* (because in the first printing they were inserted between the two tragedies *Almansor* and *William Ratcliff*). The date of these poems, sixty-five in number, was 1822-23. Heine acknowledged in a letter to Wilhelm Müller (of *Die schöne Müllerin*) his debt to that poet in matters of form and "sound." Heine attempts in these poems to create out of the old forms of the *Volkslied* a new poetry, adopting something of the style and expression of the folk song, but avoiding the "clumsiness and unevenness" often found in that genre.

The old unrequited love for Amalie is still the inspiration for his utterance. It seems that his love for her was genuine, and there is evidence that his grief was not a mere literary pose. In fact, it seems to have been his unhappy love for Amalie that really made him develop as a poet. He wrote the *Lyrisches Intermezzo* during his late student years in Berlin (at the age of twenty-five or so).

(1)   Im wunderschönen Monat Mai

Im wunderschönen Monat Mai,
Als alle Knospen sprangen,
Da ist in meinem Herzen
Die Liebe aufgegangen.

Im wunderschönen Monat Mai,
Als alle Vögel sangen,
Da hab ich ihr gestanden
Mein Sehnen und Verlangen.

(2)   Aus meinen Tränen spriessen

Aus meinen Tränen spriessen
Viel blühende Blumen hervor,
Und meine Seufzer werden
Ein Nachtigallenchor.

Und wenn du mich lieb hast, Kindchen,
Schenk ich dir die Blumen all,
Und vor deinem Fenster soll klingen
Das Lied der Nachtigall.

(3) Die Rose, die Lilie, die Taube

Die Rose, die Lilie, die Taube, die Sonne,
Die liebt' ich einst alle in Liebeswonne.
Ich lieb' sie nicht mehr, ich liebe alleine
Die Kleine, die Feine, die Reine, die Eine;
Sie selber, aller Liebe Wonne
Ist Rose und Lilie und Taube und Sonne.

(4) Wenn ich in deine Augen seh'

Wenn ich in deine Augen seh',
So schwindet all mein Leid und Weh;
Doch wenn ich küsse deinen Mund,
So werd'ich ganz und gar gesund.

Wenn ich mich lehn'an deine Brust,
Kommt's über mich wie Himmelslust;
Doch wenn du sprichst: Ich liebe dich!
So muss ich weinen bitterlich.

(5) Ich will meine Seele tauchen

Ich will meine Seele tauchen
In den Kelch der Lilie hinein;
Die Lilie soll klingend hauchen
Ein Lied von der Liebsten mein.

Das Lied soll schauern und beben,
Wie der Kuss von ihrem Mund,
Den sie mir einst gegeben
In wunderbar süsser Stund.

(6) Im Rhein, im heiligen Strome

Im Rhein, im heiligen Strome,
Da spiegelt sich in den Welln,
Mit seinem grossen Dome,
Das grosse heilige Köln.

Im Dom da steht ein Bildnis,
Auf goldenem Leder gemalt;
In meines Lebens Wildnis
Hat's freundlich hinein gestrahlt.

Es schweben Blumen und Englein
Um unsre liebe Frau;
Die Augen, die Lippen, die Wänglein,
Die gleichen der Liebsten genau.

(7) Ich grolle nicht

Ich grolle nicht, und wenn das Herz auch bricht,
Ewig verlornes Lieb! Ich grolle nicht.
Wie du auch strahlst in Diamantenpracht,
Es fällt kein Strahl in deines Herzens Nacht.

Das weiss ich längst. Ich sah dich ja im Traume,
Und sah die Nacht in deines Herzens Raume,
Und sah die Schlang, die dir am Herzen frisst,
Ich sah, mein Lieb, wie sehr du elend bist.

(8) Und wüssten's die Blumen, die kleinen

Und wüssten's die Blumen, die kleinen,
Wie tief verwundet mein Herz,
Sie würden mit mir weinen,
Zu heilen meinen Schmerz.

Und wüssten's die Nachtigallen,
Wie ich so traurig und krank,
Sie liessen fröhlich erschallen
Erquickenden Gesang.

Und wüssten sie mein Wehe,
Die goldenen Sternelein,
Sie kämen aus ihrer Höhe,
Und sprächen Trost mir ein.

Sie alle können's nicht wissen,
Nur eine kennt meinen Schmerz;
Sie hat ja selbst zerrissen,
Zerrissen mir das Herz.

(9) Das ist ein Flöten und Geigen

Das ist ein Flöten und Geigen,
Trompeten schmettern darein;
Da tanzt wohl den Hochzeitsreigen
Die Herzallerliebste mein.

Das ist ein Klingen und Dröhnen,
Ein Pauken und ein Schalmein;
Dazwischen schluchzen und stöhnen
Die lieblichen Engelein.

(10) Hör ich das Liedchen klingen

Hör ich das Liedchen klingen,
Das einst die Liebste sang,
So will mir die Brust zerspringen
Von wildem Schmerzendrang.

Es treibt mich ein dunkles Sehnen
Hinaus zur Waldeshöh,
Dort löst sich auf in Tränen
Mein übergrosses Weh.

(11) Ein Jüngling liebt ein Mädchen

Ein Jüngling liebt ein Mädchen,
Die hat einen andern erwählt;
Der andre liebt eine andre,
Und hat sich mit dieser vermählt.

Das Mädchen nimmt aus Ärger
Den ersten besten Mann,
Der ihr in den Weg gelaufen;
Der Jüngling ist übel dran.

Es ist eine alte Geschichte,
Doch bleibt sie immer neu;
Und wem sie just passieret,
Dem bricht das Herz entzwei.

(12) <u>Am</u> <u>leuchtenden</u> <u>Sommermorgen</u>

Am leuchtenden Sommermorgen
Geh ich im Garten herum.
Es flüstern und sprechen die Blumen,
Ich aber wandle stumm.

Es flüstern und sprechen die Blumen,
Und schaun mitleidig mich an:
"Sei unsrer Schwester nicht böse,
Du trauriger, blasser Mann!"

(13) <u>Ich</u> <u>hab'</u> <u>im</u> <u>Traum</u> <u>geweinet</u>

Ich hab' im Traum geweinet,
Mir träumte, du lägest im Grab.
Ich wachte auf, und die Träne
Floss noch von der Wange herab.

Ich hab' im Traum geweinet,
Mir träumt', du verliessest mich.
Ich wachte auf, und ich weinte
Noch lange bitterlich.

Ich hab' im Traum geweinet,
Mir träumte, du wärst mir noch gut.
Ich wachte auf, und noch immer
Strömt meine Tränenflut.

(14) <u>Allnächtlich</u> <u>im</u> <u>Traume</u>

Allnächtlich im Traume seh' ich dich,
Und sehe dich freundlich grüssen,
Und laut aufweinend stürz' ich mich
Zu deinen süssen Füssen.

Du siehest mich an wehmütiglich
Und schüttelst das blonde Köpfchen;
Aus deinen Augen schleichen sich
Die Perlentränentröpfchen.

Du sagst mir heimlich ein leises Wort,
Und gibst mir den Strauss von Zypressen.
Ich wache auf, und der Strauss ist fort,
Und's Wort hab' ich vergessen.

(15) <u>Aus alten Märchen winkt es</u>

Aus alten Märchen winkt es
Hervor mit weisser Hand,
Da singt es und da klingt es
Von einem Zauberland;

Wo bunte Blumen blühen
Im goldnen Abendlicht,
Und lieblich duftend glühen,
Mit bräutlichem Gesicht;

Und grüne Bäume singen
Uralte Melodein,
Die Lüfte heimlich klingen,
Und Vögel schmettern drein;

Und Nebelbilder steigen
Wohl aus der Erd' hervor,
Und tanzen luft'gen Reigen
Im wunderlichen Chor;

Und blaue Funken brennen
An jedem Blatt und Reis,
Und rote Lichter rennen
Im irren, wirren Kreis;

Und laute Quellen brechen
Aus wildem Marmorstein,
Und seltsam in den Bächen
Strahlt fort der Widerschein.

Ach, könnt' ich dorthin kommen,
Und dort mein Herz erfreun,
Und aller Qual entnommen,
Und frei und selig sein!

Ach! jenes Land der Wonne,
Das seh' ich oft im Traum,
Doch kommt die Morgensonne,
Zerfliesst's wie eitel Schaum.

(16) <u>Die alten, bösen Lieder</u>

Die alten, bösen Lieder,
Die Träume bös' und arg,
Die lasst uns jetzt begraben,
Holt einen grossen Sarg.

Hinein leg' ich gar manches,
Doch sag' ich noch nicht was;
Der Sarg muss sein noch grösser
Wie's Heidelberger Fass.

Und holt eine Totenbahre,
Und Bretter fest und dick;
Auch muss sie sein noch länger,
Als wie zu Mainz die Brück.

Und holt mir auch zwölf Riesen,
Die müssen noch stärker sein,
Als wie der starke Christoph,
Im Dom zu Köln am Rhein.

Die sollen den Sarg forttragen,
Und senken in's Meer hinab;
Denn solchem grossen Sarge
Gebührt ein grosses Grab.

Wisst ihr, warum der Sarg wohl
So gross und schwer mag sein?
Ich senkt' auch meine Liebe
Und meinen Schmerz hinein.

1. *Im wunderschönen Monat Mai (Lyrisches Intermezzo,* No. 1)

Resounding with the echoes of a hundred other poems on the month of May, this one nevertheless has its own special tone and the personal touch of Heine's "bittersweet" verse. Just as all the buds are sprouting in spring, so too does love blossom in his heart—a conventional enough figure. Just as all the birds of May pour out the fullness of their song, so too does Heine pour forth his. But, unlike theirs, his is not a song of joy. It is one of confession of longing and desire. And the tone of the last two lines is essentially pessimistic, because that *Sehnen und Verlangen* sounds as if it can never be stilled.

The rhyme scheme is *a b c b, a b d b;* that is, there is only one rhyme: *b b b b.* Economical utilization of a few resources achieves an effect that is far from monotonous. Note the repetition of *Im, Als, Da* in the first three lines of each strophe.

2. *Aus meinen Tränen spriessen* (*Lyrisches Intermezzo,* No. 2)

The figure of flowers blossoming forth from tears is not one of Heine's invention but is a familiar theme of the folk song. The chorus of his sighs turns into a chorus of nightingales. Nightingales have been symbolic of lyric poets from at least the time of Gottfried von Strassburg (thirteenth century). A medieval tradition in Germany said that they stopped singing when love was fulfilled. Heine's own "sighs" result in a *Nachtigallenchor,* and that "chorus of nightingales" is a mass of lyrical poetry.

Notes on the text:

5 *wenn du mich lieb hast:* "if you love me"—a vain hope.
6 *die Blumen* means these poems. Figuratively, he bestows these flowers on her anyway.

3. *Die Rose, die Lilie, die Taube* (*Lyrisches Intermezzo,* No. 3)

This poem has been called empty tinkling by some and defended as lyrically excellent by others, evidence that the evaluation of poetry is not an exact science. It seems to say that instead of being enamored of all the sundry elements of nature (the rose, the lily, the dove, the sun) about which he once raved, in traditional poetic fashion, the poet is now to concentrate his affection wholly on one single beauty. For she herself is viewed as the quintessence of all those elements. Line 1 seems to match line 4 thus: *Rose: Kleine, Lilie: Feine, Taube: Reine, Sonne: Eine;* and the poet sees her as possessing the attributes of the tiny rose, the gentle lily, the pure dove, the solitary sun. The fourfold rhyme of line 4 with *alleine* of line 3 must be more than a prosodic trick. It seems to symbolize or to underline the union in one adored person of all the desirable qualities of those phenomena of nature which Heine once deemed worthy of individual adoration. He may also be figuratively bidding adieu to all the other ladies he once loved; but that might be too much to expect of Heine, save as an extravagant poetic promise.

Notes on the text:

 5 *Wonne:* the more authentic reading here is *Bronne,* an archaic and poetic word meaning "fount, source."

4. *Wenn ich in deine Augen seh'* (*Lyrisches Intermezzo*, No. 4)

As early as Walther von der Vogelweide (the greatest medieval lyric poet in the German language), in the twelfth and thirteenth centuries, the image of a kiss as a cure for love's suffering is found, even with the adjective *gesund,* as here (line 4). Folk song, too, has this theme. Looking into his beloved's eyes makes all pain and sorrow disappear. Kissing her lips makes him well again. Leaning his head on her breast brings a heavenly ecstasy. But as soon as she says *Ich liebe dich,* the poet must weep bitter tears. Why must he cry? Optimistically, because the admission of her love from her own lips, something hoped for but not really deemed possible, would overwhelm him. But that doesn't make a man weep bitterly, not even Heinrich Heine. Is it because he knows her words are insincere? Or because even this admission could not yield any lasting love?

5. *Ich will meine Seele tauchen* (*Lyrisches Intermezzo*, No. 7)

In the preceding poem in the *Lyrisches Intermezzo,* Heine confronted his beloved and she reacted, at least to his mind's eye. Here there is no face-to-face encounter envisaged, only memory and imagination. The only expression of his love is through his poem, which is whispered to him, he pretends, by the lily, the symbol of purification. And the poem is conceived of as trembling and vibrating, like the kiss he once had from her lips.

6. *Im Rhein, im heiligen Strome* (*Lyrisches Intermezzo*, No. 11)

The Cologne Cathedral *(der Kölner Dom)* is perhaps the most magnificent Gothic structure in Germany. The work of art to which he refers is by Stephan Lochner (Cologne school of painting, mid-fifteenth century).

It is a painting in three sections, the center one dominated by the Virgin Mary and the Three Wise Men (*Drei Könige*), whose bones are said to be enshrined there. The two side sections of the painting are occupied by other figures not particularly pertinent to the present poem. The painting was not on leather, as Heine says, but on wood. Yet Heine was quite familiar with Cologne and the Cathedral in particular. His birthplace, Düsseldorf, is not far away. He mentions elsewhere that he fell in love with the beautiful Madonna in a picture in Cologne. The beauty of the Cologne Madonna rests, for Heine, in her resemblance to his beloved, as the almost blasphemous ending reveals.

Notes on the text:

1 Heine has *im schönen Strome*. Replacing *schönen* by *heiligen* does not enhance the verse, particularly since line 4 has the same adjective.

9 The background was a flowery gold tapestry held aloft by angels.

7. *Ich grolle nicht (Lyrisches Intermezzo*, No. 18)

This is one of the most powerful poems resulting from Heine's love for Amalie. The words *Ich grolle nicht* have overtones and undertones that cannot be rendered in any English translation. Heine's device of the dream is involved again. "I saw ou in a dream and saw the night that engulfed your heart, and I saw the serpent eating at your very heart—the serpent of remorse, chagrin, and frustration. I saw, my love, how wretched you are, too." We almost need the next poem in the *Lyrisches Intermezzo* to be able to interpret this one. It begins as a continuation of the last line of this poem: *Ja, du bist elend, und ich grolle nicht* (recapitulating line 1 of the present poem). "You and I are both destined to be wretched. You face life with a proud but twisted smile." It may be the death of poetry, as some critics assert, to consider any biographical facts behind a work of literature. But for Heine, as for Goethe, literature was a very personal creation, and we are considerably enlightened if we know the events in his life that brought forth a given poem. After Amalie had rejected Heine, she was herself spurned by the man she loved, and endured the chagrin of seeing him marry another woman. Then she became the wife of a Mr. John Friedländer, a businessman of solid promise, about whom Heine had sarcastic things to say, as can be imagined.

Notes on the text:

1   *Ich grolle nicht:* approximately "I bear no grudge," but only approximately.
    und wenn . . . auch: "even though."
3   *Diamantenpracht:* "diamond [-studded] splendor." Amalie's father (Heine's uncle, Salomon Heine) was well-to-do and she lacked nothing material.
    du strahlst: the verb contains the word "ray," which is then repeated in the noun *Strahl* (line 4). "However radiant you are in all your diamond-studded splendor, not a ray falls into the dark night of your heart."
8   *mein Lieb:* as in line 2, *Lieb* as a neuter noun (seems to be the equivalent of *Liebchen,* hence the gender).

8. *Und wüssten's die Blumen, die kleinen (Lyrisches Intermezzo,* No. 22)

In this poem, Heine indulges in his hyperbole once more. If the flowers, the nightingales, the stars knew how deeply wounded his heart is, they would put forth their utmost effort to console him. His grief would tax the ability of all the forces of nature, were they to attempt consolation, but they cannot know. Only one knows his pain; she who caused it, she who broke his heart. Heine pretends once more that his emotional woes are of cosmic importance, as in *Der Atlas.*

Notes on the text:

1   *die Blumen, die kleinen:* folk-song word order.
2   In dependent constructions of this sort, nineteenth-century German often omitted the verb "be" (as here) or "have." It is no longer a feature of German style.
6   The same omission of the verb "be" as in line 2.

9. *Das ist ein Flöten und Geigen* (*Lyrisches Intermezzo*, No. 20)

When Amalie is married, her father apparently hires the most lavish hall and a big band. That is the source of all the noise. But the marriage itself, from the point of view (or hearing) of the rejected suitor, is a blaring, blatant affair that screams to high heaven. And amid the noise of the instruments, the angels are sobbing and moaning, as if heaven itself realized that this is a great wrong. In German folk songs, angels are occasionally depicted as sighing over disappointed lovers; sometimes they console them and sing them to rest.

Notes on the text:

> 2 *schmettern:* "blare, blast."
>   *darein* conveys the notion of intruding or interrupting (the trumpets interrupt the fluting and fiddling).
> 3 *Hochzeitsreigen:* "the wedding dance" (the object of *tanzt*).
> 6 *Schalmeien:* "playing the *Schalmei* ['shawm']," an ancient, oboe-like reed instrument).
> 8 Heine has *guten* (instead of *lieblichen*; the reason for the change is probably metrical).

10. *Hör' ich das Liedchen klingen* (*Lyrisches Intermezzo*, No. 40)

This poem has the qualities of a folk song, and the theme is well known in such songs. The hearing of a song once sung by a now lost love evokes tremendous grief. The consolation of the forest as a place of refuge is a familiar idea in German folk poetry, although by no means limited to that poetry. Once more, Heine's woe is not merely *gross* but *übergross*; his sufferings are often portrayed as of cosmic proportions. But crying helps.

Notes on the text:

> 4 Heine has *vor* (not *von*); the difference is not great, except that *vor* is idiomatically preferable.

5   *dunkles Sehnen:* some obscure, mysterious longing drives him, not the longing for his beloved.

    11. *Ein Jüngling liebt ein Mädchen (Lyrisches Intermezzo,* No. 39)

There has been much disputation, learned and other, about the possible source of this poem. Max Müller, the famous Oxford philologist and son of Wilhelm Müller—in "Coincidences," an article in the *Fortnightly Review,* July, 1898—claims that a poem by the Indian poet Bhartṛhari is the probable source. That poem reads, in prosaic English translation:

    She of whom I'm always thinking is estranged from me;
    She, in turn, desires another man; that man is devoted to another,
    And some other girl pins her hopes on me;
    Fie on her, on him, on Love, on that girl, and on me!

The question is whether we have borrowing or coincidence. Müller thinks the similarity is too great for coincidence. But similar lines occur in Arabic poetry, in Greek, in Horace, and elsewhere. If Heine did have a source, the Sanskrit poet is the most likely one. Heine pursued Indic studies, although not with great scholarly devotion. His interest was first aroused by A. W. Schlegel, at the University of Bonn, and Professor Franz Bopp, at the University of Berlin, caused that interest to deepen. Heine did not study the Sanskrit language (the classical language of ancient India), but, like Goethe, read translations of Sanskrit literature. He mentions that Schlegel revealed to him the secrets of Indian metrics. It is conceivable that Schlegel or Bopp translated the little poem for Heine, but there is no proof.
    The primary source for Heine's poem was, obviously, his own experience. The *Jüngling* is Heine himself, the girl Amalie. She loved "another," who jilted her for another woman, and she married *aus Ärger* (for spite) the first likely man to come along; that was Mr. Friedländer, called elsewhere by Heine "the stupidest of the stupid." (See also notes on No. 7.) In a letter to a friend named Straube, Heine wrote, *"Es ist eine alte Geschichte* ("It's an old story"), the exact words of line 9, in bewailing the whole situation. It *is* an old story—obviously as old as the Sanskrit one—but it is not trite to the ones to whom it occurs.

Notes on the text:

> 2   *die:* "she" (not "who," although the sense is not too different).
> 6   *den ersten besten Mann:* "the first available man."
> 8   *übel dran:* "badly off; in a bad way."
> 11-12   Heine reacts as if it had happened only to one person, instead of five.

12. *Am leuchtenden Sommermorgen (Lyrisches Intermezzo, No. 45)*

The contrast between the bright summer morning and the sad, pale young man is nothing unusual. The talking flowers, attempting to comfort a suffering love, are a theme of folk song. The young man remains silent. As he walks through the garden, the flowers intercede for their "sister" (reminiscences of *Du bist wie eine Blume*). She too is a flower—but one from whom no comfort comes.

Notes on the text:

> 4   *Ich aber, ich wandle stumm:* altered by Schumann to *Ich aber wandle stumm.*
> 6   *schaun* (Schumann: *schauen*) . . . *mich an:* "look at me."
> 7   *böse:* "angry."

13. *Ich hab' im Traum geweinet (Lyrisches Intermezzo, No. 55)*

Strophe 1: He dreams he has lost her through death; hence his tears.
Strophe 2: He dreams she has left him; hence his tears (of bitterness).
Strophe 3: He dreams she is still with him and loves him; the tears still flow. The same sentiment is expressed in song No. 4, lines 7 and 8: "But when you say 'I love you,' I must cry bitterly." Fruition is as bad as frustration, it seems.

14. *Allnächtlich im Traume* (*Lyrisches Intermezzo*, No. 56)

From strophe to strophe there is an intensification of his pain. Strophe 1: In dreams, she bestows a kindly greeting on him. He cries. By now we are accustomed to his tears, even when his beloved shows him favor. In strophe 2, his beloved weeps herself, and he pretends that she is sad because nothing can come of their love. In strophe 3, she gives him a cypress wreath (symbolic of the death of love?) and speaks a secret word. The "secret word" was a device of romantic poetry (and prose). Heine claimed not to be a part of the romantic movement and wrote about it most sarcastically. Be that as it may, the author Novalis has in his romantic novel *Heinrich von Ofterdingen* a scene in which the girl gives her beloved a kiss, and, with labial agility, simultaneously whispers a secret word which causes his whole being to tremble. He is about to repeat the word when he hears the voice of his grandfather awaking him from the dream—for that is what it was—and the young man cannot recall the word. He says he would give his life to know it, which is difficult to understand. Heine loses both the word and the wreath.

Notes on the text:

   5   Heine has *siehst;* Schumann alters it to *siehest* for metrical reasons (but without justification).

  12   *Und das Wort:* altered by Schumann to *Und's Wort.*

15. *Aus alten Märchen winkt es* (*Lyrisches Intermezzo,* No. 43)

There is great variation here from Heine's original. Heine has as strophe 2:

> Wo grosse Blumen schmachten
> Im goldnen Abendlicht
> Und zärtlich sich betrachten
> Mit bräutlichem Gesicht.

Heine's third strophe is:

> Wo alle Bäume sprechen
> Und singen, wie ein Chor,
> Und laute Quellen brechen
> Wie Tanzmusik hervor.

His fourth strophe reads:

> Und Liebesweisen tönen,
> Wie du sie nie gehört,
> Bis wundersüsses Sehnen
> Dich wundersüss betört!

The fifth and sixth strophes of the *Dichterliebe* version are lacking in the "definitive" edition of Heine's *Lyrisches Intermezzo*. Schumann's seventh strophe is No. 5 in Heine; Schumann's eighth strophe is No. 6. There have apparently been a number of versions of this poem.

Flowers that sing and talk are a common device in romantic German poetry (as they are in Indian poetry). The situations depicted in all but the last strophe are in a make-believe land. That is the only setting in which his happiness can persist. It dissolves like sea-foam when he awakes.

16. *Die alten, bösen Lieder (Lyrisches Intermezzo,* No. 65)

This is the final poem of Heine's *Lyrisches Intermezzo,* as well as of the *Dichterliebe*. Heine's idea for the poem is said to have come from a New Year's song, or end-of-year chant, with the theme "Ring out the old, ring in the new; the year is dying, let him die." The poet says, "Let's bury *die alten, bösen Lieder*" and all the bad dreams he has had. He seems to mean more than his unhappy experience in love. The "many things" which he is to put into the coffin—the nature of which he refuses to reveal—are mysterious. On a banal plane, we might suspect some New Year's resolutions about getting rid of old bad habits, but that would not be like Heine. A few years later he would have meant something political, but not at this stage of his career.

Notes on the text:

8 The *Heidelberger Fass* in the famous castle at Heidelberg is a gigantic cask with a capacity of fifty thousand gallons of wine. It is so enormous that a dance floor has been built on it, and the *Tun* is still one of the great tourist attractions (or traps) of the town. Still, it would not be big enough to serve as a coffin for all the bad things Heine would bury.

12 There have been several bridges at Mainz since Heine's day, but any bridge across the Rhine at that point would be a large structure, tremendously long for a coffin, at any rate.

15-16 *der starke Christoph*: There is a statue of St. Christopher in the Cologne Cathedral that is about ten feet tall, but looks taller. Heine asks for a dozen giants of that size to serve as pallbearers to carry the coffin he envisages. He does not scrimp in such computations. It took Atlas to bear his sufferings (indeed, he regarded himself as Atlas).

21-24 It is anticlimactic enough for Heine to ask, "Do you know why?" and then to answer, "Because I have placed all my love and grief in that coffin." But this may be a new attitude. Is he putting an end to the love that has caused so much woe and has been such a hopeless cause? As the final poem of the *Intermezzo*, this brings to a close his sixty-five lyrical "Amalie poems." They are the "old bad songs," not because they are inferior products of his muse, but because they incorporate an experience which is now past and which has worn him out with grief and suffering. But they are sixty-five exquisite expressions of that experience.

The *Dichterliebe* is one of the few song cycles in which a composer has attained the most complete synthesis of text and tone. In view of Schumann's predilection for collections of piano pieces, each with its own title and all grouped under a communal caption, it is not surprising that he conceived of his song groups similarly. The vast majority of Schumann's songs were published in cycles. The *Dichterliebe* was composed between May (cf. the first song in the cycle) and June of 1840. Earlier in the same year Schumann had written the *Liederkreis*, Op. 24, also to Heine's poems; *Myrten*, Op. 25, containing a mixed assortment of poems; the *Liederkreis*, Op. 39, to Eichendorff's poetry; and *Frauenliebe und -leben*, Op. 42, to

Chamisso's poems. Each cycle is different primarily because of the diversification of the subjects covered in the poetry and the various moods reflected therein.

Schumann, much more than Schubert, concerned himself with moods and sentiments, with people's innermost feelings. Only occasionally does he communicate with nature. Because Schumann regarded himself as a poet (cf. *Der Dichter spricht,* No. 13 in *Kinderscenen*), he carefully attended to text underlay, coordinating musical and textual accents. He does not show the same concern for specific words as Schubert, preferring instead to translate the mood of the poem into his lied. That he occasionally missed Heine's cynicism is probably true. Schumann was too literal and took words at their face value. He himself, however, selected, rearranged, and provided titles for the songs of *Dichterliebe,* so that from his point of view, he could justifiably exercise poetic license and interpret these poems as he saw fit.

Most of the lieder are short: each contains one basic accompanimental figuration. Except for No. 1, most are through-composed or modified strophic forms (Nos. 5, 7, and 8), although the listener may not grasp the form after one performance. Seven of the sixteen begin with a short piano prelude. Almost all conclude with a piano postlude, some of which are fairly extensive, particularly the one that concludes the entire set. The vocalist uses any number of different melodic styles, from free declamation and recitative to arioso and outright lyricism. The burden of responsibility for setting the scene, however, rests in large part with the pianist. The vocal melody seems to grow out of the accompaniment's figures. The piano often finishes off a vocal phrase and presents a musical commentary on the text. Nevertheless, the piano sonority is not obtrusive or irritatingly aggressive.

We imagine that Schumann had an overall harmonic scheme for the cycle. Beginning in F-sharp minor, he moves through Nos. 6 and 7 toward keys with fewer sharps. He then proceeds to the flat keys but returns to the sharp keys, closing with a lied in C-sharp minor. The final measures of this song are in D-flat major (enharmonically equivalent to C-sharp major), whose tonic chord could very readily lead us back to the opening *Im wunderschönen Monat Mai.* In effect, what Schumann has written is another *Liederkreis,* a cycle that can be sung over and over again, the ending taking us back to the opening.

1. *Im wünderschönen Monat Mai*

This song has an improvisational quality suggested by the free-flowing accompanimental figures of the piano. Compare the three variants of the same figure: the beginning of Ex. 16-a appears in the introductory bars; the conclusion of Ex. 16-a supports the opening bars of the text, using the same material with modifications at *; Ex. 16-b shows the conclusion of the entire lied. Here the composer has highlighted the final word *verlangen* ("longing") by ending on an unresolved dominant seventh chord. Even the uninitiated listener will sense that the song is somehow incomplete. He is left unsatisfied, still longing. Schumann actually avoids the tonic chord throughout the entire song. Although the two stanzas are not set together beneath the vocal part, as is customarily done, this lied is strophic, the only truly strophic setting of the entire cycle.

Ex. 16

SCHUMANN: *Im wonderschönen Monat Mai*

a.

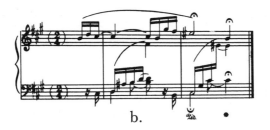

b.

2. *Aus meinen Tränen spriessen*

This ternary song (*a b a¹*) relates to the first song harmonically. It is in A major, the relative major of F-sharp minor. It opens on a monotone, as do many of these songs. The piano concludes the vocal phrase and resolves to the tonic after *hervor, Nachtigallenchor,* and *Nachtigall.* The descending eighth-note line in the accompaniment, set against the monotone opening, emphasizes the mood of the lied.

3. *Die Rose, die Lilie, die Taube*

This patter song, with perpetual sixteenth notes alternating between the bass and treble of the accompaniment (see Ex. 17), hardly allows a singer time to breathe. Although Schumann generally prefers a syllabic text setting for his lieder, this one seems particularly rapid, more in the Italian singing style of Rossini's Figaro in *The Barber of Seville.* Notice that the singer's opening A is the same note the pianist used in concluding the previous song. An extended tonic pedal in the last six bars contrasts with the activity of the sixteenth notes.

Ex. 17

SCHUMANN: *Die Rose, die Lilie*

Die Ro - se, die Li - lie, die Tau - be, die Son - ne,

4. *Wenn ich in deine Augen seh'*

Observe Schumann's use of vocal declamation (Ex. 18-a). The opening monotone setting for the voice is followed by repeated tonic chords that echo the vocal statement. Notice the tender harmonic coloring at *wenn du sprichst* (Ex. 18-b) as Schumann uses the lush, but tonally ambiguous, diminished seventh chord. Heine may have been cynical in this statement, but Schumann obviously took him seriously.

Ex. 18

SCHUMANN: *Wenn ich in deinen Augen seh'*

Wenn ich in dei - ne Au - gen seh', so schwin - det all mein Leid und Weh;

a.

doch wenn du sprichst: ich lie - be dich!

b.

5. *Ich will meine Seele tauchen*

A densely flowing piano accompaniment cushions the singer's melody. Doubling often appears inconspicuously in an inner voice of the pianist's figuration. In this modified strophic lied, only the vocalist's final bar is altered. The piano postlude includes a figure very reminiscent of the *Arabeske,* Op. 18.

6. *Im Rhein, im heiligen Strome*

One of the only declamatory songs of this cycle, *Im Rhein* recalls the texture of *Auf einer Burg* (the cathedral song in the *Liederkreis*, Op. 39; see p. 162) as well as the fourth movement of Schumann's "Rhenish" Symphony. Notice, for example, the churchly Phrygian mode at *heilige Köln*. The vocal melody is fragmented, the piano continuing (see * in Ex. 19) where the vocalist leaves off. Actually, pianist and singer take turns declaiming the melodic line. Careful listening reveals that the piano is descending in a scalewise pattern, from middle C to low A beginning at bar 4 (to bar 9).

Ex. 19

SCHUMANN: *Im Rhein*

Observe the same descent in the piano postlude. The composer's preference for thirds after *gemalt* (bar 21) anticipates Wagner's use of the same interval to describe the flowing river in the *Ring*. The piano interlude following *gestrahlt* (bar 27) presents meandering modulations, but the real controlling element of the lied is the recurrent rhythmic motive: ♩. ♪ ♩. The voice ends curiously on a leading tone (D sharp), whose resolution is delayed two measures until the octave on low E sounds in the accompaniment.

7. *Ich grolle nicht*

For his epic songs, Schubert favored C major. Schumann here uses the same key for this impassioned utterance where persistently repeated chords in the accompaniment set the mood of this modified strophic lied. The long note on *längst* (bar 17) not only reflects the text at that point; it also serves as an inverted pedal against the movement in the bass. At the climax of the poem, Schumann employs two sequences (Ex. 20), each of which retains the same note for nine and twelve syllables, respectively. The familiar descending scale appears also in this song.

Ex. 20

SCHUMANN: *Ich grolle nicht*

bricht.   Ich sah   dich ja   im Trau - me,   und sah die Nacht in deines Herzens

Rau - me,   und sah die Schlang', die dir am Her - zen   frisst,

8. *Und wüssten's die Blumen, die kleinen*

Another modified strophic song in a key (A minor) that complements the C major of No. 7, *Und wüssten's die Blumen* opens with a descending scale pattern that grows right out of the rich accompaniment. An incessant tremolando figure continues relentlessly until abruptly terminated by a ferocious piano postlude. This virtuoso conclusion contains an arpeggiated figure, a dotted rhythmic motive, and a sustained note, which together provide the needed agitation. The sense of wrenching loose reflected in the close might well derive from Schumann's taking the word *zerrissen* (bar 29) too literally.

9. *Das ist ein Flöten und Geigen*

Here is one of the few examples in this cycle where the piano accompaniment must imitate the sounds of other instruments: flute, fiddle, trumpet, drums, and shawms. The dancelike figures of this modified strophic song extend into the piano postlude that recalls *Florestan* of the *Carnaval*. The piano part of *Das ist ein Flöten und Geigen* could stand as a solo piece. Despite the vocalist's immediate repetition of the first four bars of the piano prelude (at the beginning of Ex. 21), the listener does not get the impression he does from Italian opera: namely, that the singer is cued into his part by the orchestral prelude. We notice that Schumann conceals his musical seams remarkably well.

Ex. 21

SCHUMANN. *Das ist ein Flöten*

Das   ist   ein   Flö - ten und Gei - - gen,

10. *Hör' ich das Liedchen klingen*

Again a piano prelude introduces the lied, this time with a melody in the bass. Unlike the treatment in No. 9, here, when the voice enters over a repetition of the same material, the vocal line acts as a foil to the accompanimental figuration, presenting a distinct melody of its own. The syncopation in the opening bars might represent tear drops, with a "sob" at *auf in Tränen*, bar 17. This *durchkomponiert* lied concludes with a typical Schumannesque texture: multi-leveled activity consisting of a walking bass line, dotted rhythm in one inner voice and the top voice, and a syncopated chromatic scale in another middle voice. Schumann enters the postlude by reusing the music of the piano introduction.

11. *Ein Jüngling liebt ein Mädchen*

This folklike tale is set to a rather sophisticated accompaniment. The piano imitates the sound of a plucked and strummed guitar. Off-beat accents and sharp modulations underline the significant words of the text (for example, *wem sie just passieret*, bar 29). Schumann preferred a through-composed setting for this poem, using melodic and rhythmic sequences in place of a recurrent melody to unify it.

12. *Am leuchtenden Sommermorgen*

The arpeggiated figure in the accompaniment is the type that influenced Brahms in his Intermezzi. Notice the diversified harmonic progressions in both the piano interludes and the postlude, where the composer employs the altered sixth chords. In this modified strophic song, subtle harmonic changes conceal the formal outlines.

13. *Ich hab' im Traum geweinet*

The composer here alternates sections of unaccompanied recitative with chords on the piano in his characteristic dotted rhythm (Ex. 22). Notice the monotone featured in the vocal recitatives. The dramatic silences in the piano postlude may obscure the meter and the flow until the long-awaited final cadence. For the climax of the song, at *Ich wachte auf*, bar 28, Schumann writes some of the highest notes in the vocal part; he then continues with a rising chromatic passage in the inner voice and a D-flat pedal (both in the bass) to heighten the expression of the text.

Ex. 22

SCHUMANN: *Ich hab' im Traum*

Ich hab' im Traum ge - wei - net,

14. *Allnächtlich im Traume*

In another modified strophic setting, the first two stanzas are almost identical and the third opens like the previous ones. The singer's line proceeds in tiny phrases (Ex. 26-b) basically of only three notes. Since *Allnächtlich* means "every night," Schumann, unlike Mendelssohn (Ex. 26-a, p. 181), duplicates the motive immediately. The melody is occasionally fragmented so that the accompanist's upper note sometimes completes the melodic pattern started by the vocalist (see bar 6, last beat). Schumann has changed the meter twice to accommodate the text. Indeed, most of the rhythmic activity here is in the voice part.

15. *Aus alten Märchen winkt es*

One of Schumann's favorite folk tunes was the eighteenth-century *Grossvatertanz*. He used it at the conclusion of *Papillons* and also in *Carnaval*, in the "March of the Davidsbündler against the Philistines," whom he characterizes, through his use of this tune, as old-fashioned. The rhythmic profiles of this dance appear here in *Aus alten Märchen*, perhaps because of the fairy-tale reference.

The accompanist first plays an eight-bar phrase of thick-textured material. The singer then continues with the same accompaniment in support. In a game of perpetual variation, the piano interlude includes a variant of the initial material, and the voice, beginning at *und grüne Bäume* (bar 29), inverts the original melody but retains the rhythmic shape. In this through-composed song, one of the longest in the cycle, we notice Schumann changing his accompanimental figure as the work progresses. The texture thickens after *und laute Quellen* (bar 57), and the rhythm is augmented at *Ach, könnt' ich* (bars 68 ff.), where the composer writes dotted quarters instead of quarter-plus-eighth patterns. The postlude relates closely to the introduction. In this unusual song, the *Stimmung* resembles those of the episodic finales of the *Etudes symphoniques* and *Carnaval*.

16. *Die alten, bösen Lieder*

Bold, dramatic, and virile in its presentation of the concluding music, *Die alten, bösen Lieder* is a fitting climax to the cycle. Schumann elects to close with Heine's own choice of a final poem. Piano and voice are totally independent and of equal importance. The opening octaves foreshadow the vocal part at *Die sollen den Sarg*, bar 35, with a descent on the same pitches. Although the entire lied is not as long as the penultimate song, the piano postlude here is the longest of the entire cycle. Curiously, it incorporates material from the cadenza of the first movement of Schumann's Piano Concerto, which appeared the following year, 1841, as a one-movement Fantasie. Once again, in this lied, the figuration changes as the song proceeds. The text is well reflected in the seven steps taken to bury the coffin (bars 39-42). As previously mentioned, the D-flat key of the extensive postlude and the improvisational nature of the figuration could readily lead back into the opening song.

CHAMISSO (1781-1838)

Louis Charles Adélaïde de Chamisso de Boncourt was born in Champagne, France, in 1781. In German literature he is knwon as Adelbert von Chamisso, or simply Chamisso. When he was eight or nine, the family fled to Germany. (They were of the nobility.) They settled in Berlin, where Chamisso first became a page of the Prussian Court and later joined the army, for which he had no great liking. He was long torn between two loyalties: to France and to Prussia. He always hoped that he would never be called upon to bear arms against his native land.

He was also torn between two language loyalties and hesitated for a while whether to write in French or in German. While not forgetting his native French, he became a complete master of German and even translated the works of Béranger and others.

In Berlin, Chamisso was introduced into the literary salon of Varnhagen von Ense and his wife Rahel, where he met the leading authors of Germany, among them Heine. Before Chamisso became famous himself, he and Varnhagen von Ense edited the periodical *Grüner Musenalmanach* ("Almanac of the Muses," 1804-06), in which Chamisso's first poems appeared. Before embarking on a literary career in earnest, Chamisso tried other callings. After serving in the military, he went back to France, hoping to obtain a professorship but in vain. From France he went to Switzerland, where he met Madame de Staël. From 1815 to 1818, he participated in a Russian scientific voyage around the world, keeping careful notes. He became well known as a botanist; on his return to Germany he was appointed keeper of the botanical gardens of Berlin, a position he never relinquished.

In 1831, his collected poems appeared. His lyrics do not sound like those of a French aristocrat. He depicts the simplest joys and sorrows in an overly sentimental fashion. There is no "mood-breaking" or irony, such as we find in Heine. Yet he only partly achieves the naturalness of the *Volkslied*. In his narrative poems he deserts his simplicity of utterance and tends toward the bizarre and even the gruesome (*Die Giftmischerin, Die Löwenbraut*). One poem based on reminiscences of his childhood home in France. however, has become a favorite:

> Ich träum' als Kind mich zurücke
> Und schüttle mein greises Haupt.
> Wie sucht ihr mich heim, ihr Bilder,
> Die lang' ich vergessen geglaubt!

The work for which he is best known is his *Strange Story of Peter Schlemihl*. He makes quite believable the story of a man who sells not his soul but his shadow to the devil. This is a story that may be allegorical of his own life. Peter trades his shadow for the inexhaustible purse of Fortunatus; from it he can take all the gold coins he wants. The loss of this apparently insignificant appurtenance—his shadow—causes him incalculable difficulties. He is scorned, mistreated, abandoned. The mysterious gray gentleman from whom he got the purse in the first place reappears and offers to return his shadow; the price this time will be his soul. But Peter proves to be less of a *Schlemihl* this time and throws away the purse. He then providentially finds seven-league boots and wanders through the world, regaining his peace of mind.

Some say that the shadow symbolizes Chamisso's native country and nationality and the loss of his shadow the tragedy of homelessness. The poet himself did suffer, to some extent, from his exile and his dual loyalty, despite his generally satisfying experience in Prussia. One's native land, something taken for granted, is grasped in all its real value only when one loses it, say such interpreters. This is a debatable interpretation. After all,

Chamisso was a child when he left France. Even occasional trips to the old homeland would hardly be enough to cause such ancient wounds to bleed again. *Peter Schlemihls wundersame Geschichte* does not necessarily have to symbolize anything specific. It is a good tale.

Frauenliebe und -leben

Chamisso had nine poems in this group. Schumann omitted the ninth, also the third strophe of No. 6. In this cycle of poems, Schumann perhaps sees more beauty than Chamisso imparted to them. The poet attempts empathy with a woman, as Goethe did, for example, in *Gretchen am Spinnrade*. This was not seen in any of Heine's poems. When Heine says *ich,* he means Heinrich Heine. He can write about women, but it is hard to picture Heine speaking as a woman.

(1)

```
Seit ich ihn gesehen,
Glaub' ich blind zu sein;
Wo ich hin nur blicke,
Seh' ich ihn allein;
Wie im wachen Traume
Schwebt sein Bild mir vor,
Taucht aus tiefstem Dunkel,
Heller nur empor.

Sonst ist licht- und farblos
Alles um mich her,
Nach der Schwestern Spiele
Nicht begehr' ich mehr,
Möchte lieber weinen,
Still im Kämmerlein
Seit ich ihn gesehen,
Glaub' ich blind zu sein.
```

(2)

```
Er, der Herrlichste von allen,
Wie so milde, wie so gut!
Holde Lippen, klares Auge,
Heller Sinn und fester Mut.
```

So wie dort in blauer Tiefe,
Hell und herrlich, jener Stern,
Also er an meinem Himmel,
Hell und herrlich, hehr und fern.

Wandle, wandle deine Bahnen,
Nur betrachten deinen Schein,
Nur in Demut ihn betrachten,
Selig nur und traurig sein!

Höre nicht mein stilles Beten,
Deinem Glücke nur geweiht;
Darfst mich niedre Magd nicht kennen,
Hoher Stern der Herrlichkeit!

Nur die Würdigste von allen
Darf beglücken deine Wahl,
Und ich will die Hohe segnen,
Segnen viele tausendmal.

Will mich freuen dann und weinen,
Selig, selig bin ich dann;
Sollte mir das Herz auch brechen,
Brich, O Herz, was liegt daran?

(3)

Ich kann's nicht fassen, nicht glauben,
Es hat ein Traum mich berückt;
Wie hätt' er doch unter allen
Mich Arme erhöht und beglückt?

Mir war's, er habe gesprochen:
"Ich bin auf ewig dein,"
Mir war's--ich träume noch immer,
Es kann ja nimmer so sein.

O lass im Traume mich sterben,
Gewieget an seiner Brust,
Den seligen Tod mich schlürfen
In Tränen unendlicher Lust.

(4)

Du Ring an meinem Finger,
Mein goldenes Ringelein,
Ich drücke dich fromm an die Lippen,
Dich fromm an das Herze mein.

Ich hatt'ihn ausgeträumet,
Der Kindheit friedlich schönen Traum,
Ich fand allein mich, verloren
Im öden, unendlichen Raum.

Du Ring an meinem Finger
Da hast du mich erst belehrt,
Hast meinem Blick erschlossen
Des Lebens unendlichen, tiefen Wert.

Ich will ihm dienen, ihm leben,
Ihm angehören ganz,
Hin selber mich geben und finden
Verklärt mich in seinem Glanz.

Du Ring an meinem Finger,
Mein goldenes Ringelein,
Ich drücke dich fromm an die Lippen,
Dich fromm an das Herze mein.

(5)

Helft mir, ihr Schwestern,
Freundlich mich schmücken,
Dient der Glücklichen heute mir.
Windet geschäftig
Mir um die Stirne
Noch der blühenden Myrte Zier.

Als ich befriedigt,
Freudigen Herzens,
Sonst dem Geliebten im Arme lag,
Immer noch rief er,
Sehnsucht im Herzen,
Ungeduldig den heutigen Tag.

Helft mir, ihr Schwestern,
Helft mir verscheuchen
Eine törichte Bangigkeit,
Dass ich mit klarem
Aug'ihn empfange,
Ihn, die Quelle der Freudigkeit.

Bist, mein Geliebter,
Du mir erschienen,
Giebst du mir, Sonne, deinen Schein?
Lass mich in Andacht,
Lass mich in Demut,
Lass mich verneigen dem Herren mein.

Streuet ihm, Schwestern,
Streuet ihm Blumen,
Bringet ihm knospende Rosen dar,
Aber euch, Schwestern,
Grüss ich mit Wehmut,
Freudig scheidend aus eurer Schar.

(6)

Süsser Freund, du blickest
Mich verwundert an,
Kannst es nicht begreifen,
Wie ich weinen kann;
Lass der feuchten Perlen
Ungewohnte Zier
Freudighell erzittern
In dem Auge mir.

Wie so bang mein Busen,
Wie so wonnevoll!
Wüsst' ich nur mit Worten,
Wie ich's sagen soll;
Komm und birg dein Antlitz
Hier an meiner Brust,
Will in's Ohr dir flüstern
Alle meine Lust.

Weisst du nun die Tränen,
Die ich weinen kann,
Sollst du nicht sie sehen,
Du geliebter Mann?
Bleib' an meinem Herzen,
Fühle dessen Schlag,
Dass ich fest und fester
Nur dich drücken mag.

Hier an meinem Bette
Hat die Wiege Raum,
Wo sie still verberge
Meinen holden Traum;
Kommen wird der Morgen,
Wo der Traum erwacht
Und daraus dein Bildnis
Mir entgegen lacht.

(7)

An meinem Herzen, an meiner Brust,
Du meine Wonne, du meine Lust!
Das Glück ist die Liebe, die Lieb'ist das Glück,
Ich hab's gesagt und nehm's nicht zurück.
Hab'überschwenglich mich geschätzt
Bin überglücklich aber jetzt.
Nur die da säugt, nur die da liebt
Das Kind, dem sie die Nahrung giebt;
Nur eine Mutter weiss allein
Was lieben heisst und glücklich sein.
O, wie bedaur' ich doch den Mann,
Der Mutterglück nicht fühlen kann!
Du lieber, lieber Engel, du
Du schauest mich an und lächelst dazu!
An meinem Herzen, an meiner Brust,
Du meine Wonne, du meine Lust!

(8)

Nun hast du mir den ersten Schmerz getan,
Der aber traf.
Du schläfst, du harter, unbarmherz'ger Mann,
Den Todesschlaf.

Es blicket die Verlassne vor sich hin,
Die Welt ist leer.
Geliebet hab'ich und gelebt, ich bin
Nicht lebend mehr.

Ich zieh'mich in mein Innres still zurück,
Der Schleier fällt,
Da hab'ich dich und mein verlor'nes Glück,
Du meine Welt!

1.

Ever since she has seen this magnificent male creature, the girl is completely dazzled. She is, in fact, no longer a girl, and the childish games she used to play with her sisters have lost all their allure. She would rather stay in her room and cry.

Notes on the text:

1   *gesehen (habe):* omission of the auxiliary.
3   *wo ich hin nur blicke:* "wherever I look."
13   *möchte = ich möchte.*

2.

Her adulation of the man increases. She places him on a pedestal of perfection and worships him from afar. She cannot imagine that he would ever deign to look at her. The object of his love must be a loftier creature, matching with her superlative qualifications (*die Würdigste von allen* [feminine]) his own unsurpassed excellence (*der Herrlichste von allen* [masculine]). She will not, she claims, begrudge that woman—slightly reminiscent of Heine's *ich grolle nicht,* although not completely parallel—who may be chosen as his loved one. To be sure, her heart may break, but that is the fate of one who falls in love with a paragon.

Notes on the text:

8   *hoch und fern:* altered by Schumann to *hehr und fern,* a debatable improvement.
10-12   These lines are elliptical, or syntactically stranded. In English they may be rescued by some introductory expression as "Let me" or "I would."
18   For *soll* Schumann has *darf.*
19-20   The repetition of *segnen* is rejected by Schumann, who also takes the liberty of repeating the first strophe at the end of the poem, to round out the composition, apparently, for the alteration is hardly justified poetically; nor is the additional repetition of *Wie so milde, wie so gut* as the final line of this song.

3.

Despite these pious protestations of self-sacrificing resignation, she finds, to her utter amazement, that he loves her. She pretends that she is dreaming, and she would be willing to die in the bliss of that dream.

Notes on the text:

5 and 7   *Mir war's:* "it seemed to me."

11   Where Chamisso has *seligsten,* Schumann prefers *seligen,* conceivably to avoid an excess of sibilant sounds, but nevertheless with a radical alteration of point of view.
schlürfen: this verb applies to the act of drinking, usually with gusto and sound effects. Its appropriateness here, if any, may be seen in the implication that such a death (as if a drink) would be eagerly welcomed, as is further borne out by the word *Lust* in the following line.

4.

By now they are engaged, and the ring becomes almost a religious symbol. She kisses it devoutly (*fromm* "piously"), as if it were the bishop's ring, perhaps. But she also presses it to her heart, as a sign that the experience is not only pious but also emotional. Still, her devotion is little short of abject: "I'll wait on him hand and foot; I'll belong to him alone." This is rather blatant sentimentality. She says she will even be "transfigured" (*verklärt*) in the radiance of his presence. She shows him more adoration than another might bestow on a deity.

Notes on the text:

4   Schumann alters the line thus: *dich fromm an die Lippen, an das Herze mein.*

6   Schumann changes the line to: *Der Kindheit friedlichen schönen Traum.*

12   Once again, Schumann increases the number of syllables: *Des Lebens unendlichen, tiefen Wert.*

13   For *Ich werde* Schumann has *Ich will*, a "modal" alteration not prompted by musical or metrical considerations. If *will* connotes greater determination than the relatively colorless *werde* of the original, it is quite likely that the poet intended to convey a degree of submissiveness on the lady's part.

Note the grammatical distinction between the two occurrences of *ihm* in this line. The first is dative because *dienen* requires that case. The second *ihm* is semantically determined ("I'll live *for* him").

5.

The wedding day arrives, and she asks her sisters to help her put on her nuptial finery, not forgetting the myrtle wreath on her brow, symbolic of lasting love. We are told that the man has also longed for this day with some impatience. Yet she is frightened and cannot hide her foolish fears. She begs her sisters to help her dispel the cloud of fear so that she may face with fittingly serene countenance the brilliance of the groom, her Sun. She takes leave of her sisters on a bittersweet note of farewell. No longer will she be their playmate or share their home, for she is entering, with mingled joy and sorrow, her new life as a married woman.

Notes on the text:

8   *freudigen Herzens:* genitive of manner or of attendant circumstance ("with a joyful heart"), hence an adverbial use of that case.

9   Schumann adds a syllable: *sonst dem Geliebten* (*sonst* here means "formerly").

12   Rejecting the contraction *heut'gen*, Schumann has *heutigen*.
     Tag is the object of *rief* in line 10.

21   Schumann alters, or rearranges, the line thus: *Giebst du mir, Sonne, diesen Schein.*

24 Schuman has: *Lass mich verneigen dem Herren mein.*
   Herren is now *Herrn* (dative singular).

6.

Despite the idealized notion of love that she evinces, she finds out one day that she is to become a mother. Schumann omits eight lines of Chamisso's third strophe which reflect "mother-and-daughter talk." The cradle is, of course, a sufficiently broad hint.

Notes on the text:

   7-8   Schuman has: *Freudighell erzittern/In dem Auge mir.* Here the composer is giving the poet a lesson, for there is no metrical or syllabic change. Such corrections are far less justified than those demanded by the music.
   25   *Weisst:* here means "do you know the reason for, do you understand?"
   32   After this line (end of the strophe) Schumann repeats *fest und fester.*

          After the final strophe of this poem, Schumann repeats *dein Bildnis,* thereby imparting to the words a prominence scarcely intended by the woman—or Chamisso.

7.

The maternal glow outshines all previously known radiance. The fulsome worship of a glorious male is seemingly forgotten as the new mother, with a naïve arrogance, pities men, for they can never experience the joy that a mother knows. This almost replaces entirely the humility of her love for the man before their marriage, for he is included in those whom she pities, being no doubt the first of them.

The obvious change in poetic tempo is in keeping with the new kind of joy which the young mother feels, and her repetition of trite sayings is equally apropos.

Notes on the text:

4 Schumann has *Ich hab's gesagt.*
5 Chamisso has *überglücklich* here and in the following line. Schumann changed the first to *überschwenglich* "exuberantly," a gratuitous amendment of dubious validity.
13-14 Schumann reverses the order of these two lines.

8.

Life has moved on at a rapid pace. We hear not a word of the father, yet we must conclude that he has been a kind and understanding husband, even indulgent, to his overly sentimental wife, for she says that he has never caused her any grief until this moment, when he deals her the unmerciful blow of dying. She berates him, as if his death were an act of desertion: "Hard, pitiless man, you sleep the sleep of death!"

To all intents and purposes, her life comes to an end also. Retreat into herself is a sort of death. Schumann is no doubt right in regarding this as the end of the song cycle, for the ninth poem breaks the unity. It is a coda, in which the woman calls her grandchild (*Tochter meiner Tochter*) to her for advice and blessing, after which the old matriarch is ready to go to her own eternal rest.

Uneven in poetic quality, ranging from banal to inspired lines, this cycle of poems in Chamisso's acquired tongue appealed to the genius of Karl Loewe as well as to that of Schumann. If there is an exaltation of the whole group to a more uniform quality, that is the achievement of the composer. If there is any tendency to slip into a mawkish sentimentality, that must be the fault of the poet.

Notes on the text:

2 *Der* is a demonstrative, not a relative pronoun. "But that blow really struck home."
7 The words *Geliebet . . . und gelebt* (cf. *Frauenliebe und -leben*)

recapitulate her own story and imply that her life has really come
to its end.

11   Schumann alters *vergang'nes* to *verlor'nes*.

In *Frauenliebe und -leben,* Schumann has created a far more sub-
stantial musical composition than would seem likely from a reading of
the poetry alone. The set is unified primarily by the extramusical associa-
tion of the poem, but also through melodic recurrence. As Beethoven had
done in *An die ferne Geliebte,* Schumann brings back the musical material
of the first song in the piano postlude of the last one. Characteristic features
include Schumann's preference for a relatively independent vocal line,
either cushioned by a thick-textured accompanimental figure or supported
by full-bodied chords, and a piano postlude that typically concludes each
song. Exceptionally here, Nos. 4 to 8 include more than one figuration
in each song; several songs (Nos. 1, 3, 6, and 8) are more declamatory than
lyrical, even quasi-recitative in vocal style; and many songs include deceptive cadences the composer has used for musical articulations that do not
relate to the text. Text reflection is held to a minimum, perhaps because
of the inferiority of the poetry.

This cycle differs from the *Dichterliebe* in its lack of unusual piano
figurations in the accompaniment, the absence of any truly remarkable
vocal melodies, relatively few harmonic excursions, and, finally, the equal
distribution of modified strophic and through-composed settings. Also,
these are among the few songs to which Schumann did not affix titles. Of
course Chamisso was not Heine, but even so the poetry acquired better
music than it deserved.

1.

Two practically identical strophes here reveal the composer's problem
in the use of this repetitive musical form. Notice that at *tiefstem* (bar 12)
the melody dips appropriately. Unfortunately, the setting of *ihn* at the
same point in the next stanza makes no sense at all. The concluding
material of the piano postlude of this song reappears at the conclusion of
the entire cycle.

2.

Er, der Herrlichste von allen offers a good example of the way in which musical rhythm derives from the text. Schumann balances this rhythmically active vocal part with a suitably even-tempered chordal accompaniment. He attains glorification of the lover in one sweeping arpeggio which then drops suddenly down a seventh (Ex. 23-a). The vocal phrase provides the material for the piano interlude later on (Ex. 23-b). Notice

Ex. 23

SCHUMANN: *Er, der Herrlichste*

a.

b.

the interweaving vocal/piano motive at *Holde Lippen,* bar 5. Later the composer continues to link the two performers as the pianist plays the principal motive (derived from Ex. 23-b) three times in a sequence that moves from one register to the next (bars 54 ff.). Finally, the singer enters on the fourth statement of the motive in a return to the opening material of the lied. Observe Schumann's control of tension: to heighten the drama, he repeats the phrase *hoher Stern,* extending the vocal line and thus eliminating the customary piano interlude before the next strophe. This rather long song comprises seven sections: *a a*¹ *b a*² *c d a*³. With *a*³, we return to the text of *a,* but the accompaniment in the first few bars is different.

3.

Here the vocal line is of prime importance. The singer begins on a monotone and maintains a declamatory style throughout. The song is in ternary form with a coda, exceptionally here shared by pianist and singer. Each section begins with the same rhythmic profile, even though the pitches differ (cf. *Mir war's* and *O lass*). Observe that in the *b* section *(Mir war's)* the legato accompaniment contrasts with the staccato chords of the *a* section.

4.

The three strophes of this lied are so closely knit that only in retrospect can we recognize the separate sections. In the vocal melody, the composer makes characteristic use of an ascending scale (between *Finger* and *Ringelein*). His thick-textured accompaniment could stand on its own as a piano piece. The singer's highest pitch appears at *ganz,* bar 28, the climax of the song.

5.

Combining a joyous, folklike melody with an ambitious piano accompaniment, Schumann reveals still another approach to an essentially strophic lied. Each of the last two stanzas is sung to a variant of the original melody of the opening strophe. The pattern of the interior phrase structure also contributes to the principle of unity in variety. The three strophes and their phrases might be diagramed as follows:

Strophes	*Phrases*
a	a a b c
a¹	a a d e
a²	a f g h + postlude

6.

Süsser Freund, du blickest mich verwundert an is a declamatory song where the lack of tunefulness contrasts sharply with the lyricism of the previous song. The articulations in this example of ternary form are precisely drawn. Nevertheless, the composer manages to interrelate the sections most effectively by use of the three-note motive that begins the vocal line in bar 2. To heighten the drama at the end, Schumann delays (by three bars) the resolution of the vocal line.

7.

Here another modified strophic song offers a rapid, arpeggiated accompanimental figure that supports a lyrical vocal line. Schumann seems to have alternated between declamatory and lyrical settings in this cycle. After three statements of the principal melody, the fourth strophe incorporates a new texture in the accompaniment. In the codetta, we hear echoes of the Fantasia in C, Op. 17.

8.

This final song opens in D minor. A starkly dramatic accompaniment supports the singer's recitative. After the first two phrases, Schumann injects an element of harmonic ambiguity that prepares the way for the final extensive piano postlude in B-flat major. Here he returns to the music of the opening lied, incorporating both vocal and piano melodies.

EICHENDORFF (1788-1857)

Freiherr (Baron) Joseph von Eichendorff hailed from Silesia and was born at Lubowitz Palace into a family of Catholic nobility. This was near Ratibor (now Racibórz, Poland), on a hill overlooking the Oder river. Culturally, this was a meeting place of the Slavic and Germanic worlds.

Joseph and his brother Wilhelm were taught by private tutors; as a child the former was prodigious and showed talent for writing. Much has been made of the poetic nature of his environment, and biographers have seen a connection between the mysterious elements of nature and mood which he absorbed in Lubowitz and the qualities of his later poetry and novels. But reading in his father's extensive library could have been just as decisive in his literary development.

After studying at the Gymnasium in Breslau (now Wrocław, Poland), the brothers were sent, although not immediately, to the University of Halle, but their studies were interrupted when the French took that town. Some time later we find Joseph at the University of Heidelberg. This was a decisive step for his development as a "romanticist." He met the leaders of that movement there: Achim von Arnim and Clemens Brentano, who were collecting folk songs for *Des Knaben Wunderhorn.*

Prussia was defeated by Napoleon, and Eichendorff went to Vienna in the hopes of finding work. Here he met, among others, Friedrich Schlegel, who was regarded as the chief theoretician of romanticism. He began work on his first novel, *Ahnung und Gegenwart,* which immediately gave him a position of prominence among the romanticists, although it never enjoyed a wide reading public—undeservedly it seems, for it is an imaginative and beautiful work. But his novelette *Aus dem Leben eines Taugenichts* ("Memoirs of a Good-for-nothing") is a little masterpiece. It often reads more like poetry than prose. The story itself is of slight consequence, although the hero is said to be Eichendorff's anti-self. Eichendorff had settled down to a relatively quiet life in government service (following, however, hectic years of military service, war, pestilence, and bankruptcy) in Breslau, Danzig, Königsberg, and Berlin. The hero of *Taugenichts* is a young musician who leaves his father's mill and roams the world, fiddle in hand. He has a temporary job as gardener at a beautiful palace, falls in love with a charming "countess," who turns out to be no such thing, is forcibly taken to Italy by two strange characters pretending to be artists, becomes involved in a series of complicated misunderstandings, and finally returns to the palace, where everything is straightened out and all ends happily—for Eichendorff was an optimistic romanticist. Out of the meager substance of this slender tale he produced an amazing book. His poetic urge, his love of wandering, his yearning for Italy (never fulfilled), his love of nature all are poured into the work. A dozen of his best poems are included in the *Taugenichts.*

Mendelssohn was a friend of the poet's and set some of his verse to music. On Mendelssohn's tombstone are inscribed two lines from Eichendorff, selected by the composer himself.

Some romanticists turned away from contemporary life and devoted themselves to moonlight, the Middle Ages, ancient times, the Orient, legends, sagas, daydreams; and Eichendorff showed an interest in most of these, but he also wrote political articles on constitutionalism, liberalism, and similar topics. He did not subscribe to the doctrine of "romantic irony" or *Stimmungsbrechung* (contrast Heine!). His literary significance rests largely on his lyrical poems. He has one foot in the dreamworld of romanticism, but the other is on solid practical ground. He spoke, of the poet's serious responsibility as a citizen and human being.

Eichendorff's was a rare gift, for he succeeded in blending the music and the magic of the *Volkslied*. His metrical schemes are natural and uncontrived. He is perhaps at his best when "singing" of the forest, the happy wanderer, the moon, nature, the seasons of the year. At times there are reminiscences of Mignon, particularly in his longing for Italy. He often anticipates Heine, who had high praise for Eichendorff's lyrical poetry. Many of Heine's poems start like Eichendorff's, although they often end quite differently. Such favorite turns of expression as *Ich weiss nicht, wie mir geschah; mir ist, als ob; ich wollt'; ich möchte* are sprinkled throughout the poems of both. Wilhelm Müller also followed Eichendorff in his predilection for the wanderer theme. Eichendorff's lyrics invite musical composition, and that invitation was seized by many.

Schumann's *Liederkreis*, Op. 39

Schumann's *Liederkreis* ("Song Cycle") is made up of poems taken out of context from Eichendorff's works. Most of them have a context in a novel or story, but that is usually irrelevant to the composer's purpose.

(1) In der Fremde

Aus der Heimat hinter den Blitzen rot
Da kommen die Wolken her.
Aber Vater und Mutter sind lange tot,
Es kennt mich dort keiner mehr.
Wie bald, ach wie bald kommt die stille Zeit,
Da ruhe ich auch; und über mir
Rauscht die schöne Waldeinsamkeit,
Und keiner kennt mich mehr hier?

(2)   Intermezzo

Dein Bildnis wunderselig
Hab' ich im Herzensgrund,
Das sieht so frisch und fröhlich
Mich an zu jeder Stund'.

Mein Herz still in sich singet
Ein altes, schönes Lied,
Das in die Luft sich schwinget
Und zu dir eilig zieht.

(3)   Waldesgespräch

Es ist schon spät, es ist schon kalt,
Was reitst du einsam durch den Wald?
Der Wald ist lang, du bist allein,
Du schöne Braut! ich führ' dich heim!

"Gross ist der Männer Trug und List,
Vor Schmerz mein Herz gebrochen ist,
Wohl irrt das Waldhorn her und hin,
O flieh! Du weisst nicht, wer ich bin."

So reich geschmückt ist Ross und Weib,
So wunderschön der junge Leib;
Jetzt kenn ich dich--Gott steh' mir bei!
Du bist die Hexe Lorelei.

"Du kennst mich wohl--von hohem Stein
Schaut still mein Schloss tief in den Rhein.
Es ist schon spät, es ist schon kalt,
Kommst nimmermehr aus diesem Wald!"

(4)   Die Stille

Es weiss und rät es doch keiner,
Wie mir so wohl ist, so wohl!
Ach, wüsst' es nur einer, nur einer,
Kein Mensch es sonst wissen soll!

So still ist's nicht draussen im Schnee,
So stumm und verschwiegen sind
Die Sterne nicht in der Höh',
Als meine Gedanken sind.

Ich wünscht', ich wär' ein Vöglein
Und zöge über das Meer,
Wohl über das Meer und weiter,
Bis dass ich im Himmel wär'!

Es weiss und rät es doch keiner,
Wie mir so wohl ist, so wohl!
Ach, wüsst' es nur einer, nur einer,
Kein Mensch es sonst wissen soll!

(5) Mondnacht

Es war, als hätt' der Himmel,
Die Erde still geküsst,
Dass sie im Blütenschimmer
Von ihm nur träumen müsst'.

Die Luft ging durch die Felder,
Die Ähren wogten sacht,
Es rauschten leis' die Wälder,
So sternklar war die Nacht.

Und meine Seele spannte
Weit ihre Flügel aus,
Flog durch die stillen Lande,
Als flöge sie nach Haus'.

(6) Schöne Fremde

Es rauschen die Wipfel und schauern,
Als machten zu dieser Stund'
Um die halb versunkenen Mauern
Die alten Götter die Rund'.

Hier hinter den Myrtenbäumen
In heimlich dämmernder Pracht,
Was sprichst du wirr, wie in Träumen,
Zu mir, phantastische Nacht?

Es funkeln auf mich alle Sterne
Mit glühendem Liebesblick,
Es redet trunken die Ferne
Wie von künftigem grossen Glück!

(7)   <u>Auf</u> <u>einer</u> <u>Burg</u>

Eingeschlafen auf der Lauer
Oben ist der alte Ritter;
Drüben gehen Regenschauer,
Und der Wald rauscht durch das Gitter.

Eingewachsen Bart und Haare,
Und versteinert Brust und Krause,
Sitzt er viele hundert Jahre
Oben in der stillen Klause.

Draussen ist es still und friedlich,
Alle sind ins Tal gezogen,
Waldesvögel einsam singen
In den leeren Fensterbogen.

Eine Hochzeit führt da unten
Auf dem Rhein im Sonnenscheine,
Musikanten spielen munter,
Und die schöne Braut, die weinet.

(8)   <u>In</u> <u>der</u> <u>Fremde</u>

Ich hör' die Bächlein rauschen
Im Walde her und hin,
Im Walde, in dem Rauschen
Ich weiss nicht, wo ich bin.

Die Nachtigallen schlagen
Hier in der Einsamkeit,
Als wollten sie was sagen
Von der alten, schönen Zeit.

Die Mondesschimmer fliegen,
Als säh ich unter mir
Das Schloss im Tale liegen,
Und ist doch so weit von hier!

Als müsste in dem Garten
Voll Rosen weiss und rot,
Meine Liebste auf mich warten,
Und ist doch so lange tot.

(9) Wehmut

Ich kann wohl manchmal singen,
Als ob ich fröhlich sei,
Doch heimlich Tränen dringen,
Da wird das Herz mir frei.

Es lassen Nachtigallen,
Spielt draussen Frühlingsluft,
Der Sehnsucht Lied erschallen
Aus ihres Kerkers Gruft.

Da lauschen alle Herzen,
Und alles ist erfreut,
Doch keiner fühlt die Schmerzen,
Im Lied das tiefe Leid.

(10) Zwielicht

Dämmrung will die Flügel spreiten,
Schaurig rühren sich die Bäume,
Wolken ziehn wie schwere Träume--
Was will dieses Graun bedeuten?

Hast ein Reh du lieb vor andern,
Lass es nicht alleine grasen,
Jäger ziehn im Wald und blasen,
Stimmen hin und wieder wandern.

Hast du einen Freund hienieden,
Trau ihm nicht zu dieser Stunde,
Freundlich wohl mit Aug' und Munde,
Sinnt er Krieg im tück'schen Frieden.

Was heut gehet müde unter,
Hebt sich morgen neugeboren.
Manches geht in Nacht verloren--
Hüte dich, sei wach und munter!

(11) Im Walde

Es zog eine Hochzeit den Berg entlang,
Ich hörte die Vögel schlagen,
Da blitzten viel Reiter, das Waldhorn klang,
Das war ein lustiges Jagen!

Und eh'ich's gedacht, war alles verhallt,
Die Nacht bedecket die Runde;
Nur von den Bergen noch rauschet der Wald,
Und mich schauert's im Herzensgrunde.

(12) Frühlingsnacht

Überm Garten durch die Lüfte
Hört ich Wandervögel ziehn,
Das bedeutet Frühlingsdüfte,
Unten fängt's schon an zu blühn.

Jauchzen möcht' ich, möchte weinen,
Ist mir's doch, als könnt's nicht sein!
Alte Wunder wieder scheinen
Mit dem Mondesglanz herein.

Und der Mond, die Sterne sagen's,
Und im Traume rauscht's der Hain,
Und die Nachtigallen schlagen's:
Sie ist deine, sie ist dein!

1. *In der Fremde*

In der Fremde is the concluding poem in a group called *Totenopfer* ("Sacrifices to the Dead"). The theme here is nostalgia—longing for a place and a time. He is homesick for a homeland that is no more. His "home thoughts from abroad" are directed to times and people long gone. He expects his own death to come soon, and he sees himself buried in the peace of sylvan solitude (*Waldeinsamkeit* says it better), where none will know or remember him.

Notes on the text:

1 *hinter den Blitzen rot:* the word order is reminiscent of the *Volkslied.*

4 *dort:* in his homeland.

5 Schumann has *Wie bald, ach wie bald.*

7 Schumann alters *rauschet* to *rauscht.*

8 Schumann changes *kennt mich auch hier* to *kennt mich mehr hier,* a gratuitous alteration. *Hier:* in his present abode. *Kennt,* like all the verbs in this second strophe, is present tense for future time.

2. *Andenken*

Schumann calls this poem *Intermezzo,* the reason for which is not clear. It is part of a group entitled *Sängerleben* ("Singer's Life"). It has many of the characteristics of a folk song. Separated from his sweetheart, he keeps her likeness in his heart. His heart sings a song softly to itself, a song which is borne on the breeze to the place where his beloved is (Indian motif once more).

Notes on the text:

1 The word order is common in folk song; cf. *hinter den Blitzen rot* in the first poem of the cycle.
5 The verb in final position is also an archaic order; not, however, in lines 7 and 8.

3. *Waldesgespräch*

Sometimes this poem is called *Die Lorelei,* but that title takes away all the suspense. The song is incorporated into Eichendorff's novel *Ahnung und Gegenwart,* although that connection is not relevant as far as Schumann's setting is concerned.

Not every version of the Lorelei legend presents her as a Rhine maiden. In some she is a woodland figure. Here she seems to be a forest *Nixe,* although she says that she has left her castle on the lofty crag above the Rhine. What has caused her to leave her home is somewhat mysterious. When the young man offers to escort her home, calling her "lovely bride," for she is so attired, she warns him to flee before it is too late. She shows pity for him, despite the fact that she has been wronged by men's deceit and treachery. "You don't know who I am," she adds; but he does. She can only be the Lorelei ("God help me"). She admits the identity. Now, however, it is too late; he will never be able to leave the forest. An unusual touch, but one found elsewhere in Eichendorff's writings, is the compassion shown a victim by the siren. There is something of the mood of the *Erlkönig* here.

Notes on the text:

1 Eichendorff has *es wird schon kalt,* contrasting with the third line
of the last strophe: *es ist schon kalt.* Schumann has *ist* in both instances. In line 1 of Eichendorff's poem, there is still a chance to
escape the cold (of death)—"It's getting cold"—but in the second
occurrence we have a much more ominous line, with the implication that there is now no way to escape.

2 *Was:* "why."

4. *Die Stille*

Here the *ich* is a girl. No one knows her secret; no one knows how
happy she is—but she wishes one particular man (*einer,* masculine) knew
it, and no other. Her thoughts are tranquil and placid, more so than the
silent snow or the lofty stars. A strophe omitted by Schumann says that
she wishes it were morning: two larks would soar aloft, overtaking each
other in flight, and her heart would follow them. The final strophe repeats
one of the oft-expressed wishes of the romanticists—to be able to fly like
birds. It is the age-old wish of mankind (Daedalus and Icarus, Euphorion).
But this girl would fly beyond the sea and still farther, until she reached
heaven itself.

In Eichendorff's collected poems, *Die Stille* is part of a group called
Frühling und Liebe ("Spring and Love"). It was sung in the novel *Ahnung
und Gegenwart,* but by a man! In the *Taugenichts,* the wandering fiddler
sings four lines with sentiments very similar (beginning *Wenn ich ein
Vöglein wär'*). There have been numerous settings of *Die Stille.*

Notes on the text:

1 The first *Es* is an introductory word; the second is the object
of *weiss* and *rät.*

4 Instead of *soll,* Schumann has *sollt'* ("should" instead of "shall").

5. *Mondnacht*

This well-known poem (*Es war, als hätt' der Himmel*) has been set to music over forty times. It is part of a group designated by Eichendorff as "Spiritual Poems." Romantic transcendental longing is the theme. The *Mondnacht* induces in the poet a religious kind of nostalgia, a longing for a better life beyond this, to which the soul will return home (*als flöge sie nach Haus'*). The "love affair between Heaven and Earth" is a mystical theme. The poem is regarded by the author as a hymn.

Notes on the text:

4   Eichendorff has *nun*, replaced by *nur* in Schumann's text.
6   *Ähren:* ears of grain (not corn).
    sacht: poetic and dialectic for *sanft.*
11 *Lande:* poetic for *Länder.*

6. *Schöne Fremde*

This is one of a group called *Wanderlieder,* but it is also incorporated into the novel *Dichter und ihre Gesellen,* where it ill fits. The theme is *Wanderlust,* yearning. The setting could be Italy or Greece—the ruined walls, the ancient gods, the myrtle trees. If we had *Zitronen* and *Orangen* we would have another Mignon poem, although the point of view is obviously quite different. The notion of a night that speaks to humans is another romantic idea. Here the message is mysterious.

Notes on the text:

1   *Es* (as in lines 9 and 11) is an introductory, anticipatory particle.
9-12 Not only the night itself but the stars and the distance communicate with the poet—or the *ich* of the poem (represented only by the accusative *mich*).
11 *trunken:* although rendered "ecstatically, in ecstasy" by translators, the word means "intoxicated, drunken(ly)."

7. *Auf einer Burg*

This poem is reminiscent of the legend of Barbarossa, who sits at a stone table under the Kyffhäuser mountain; he has been there for centuries and will arise, it is said, in times of need. (Several opportunities have been given him, but he has not yet appeared.) What the connection may be between legend and the present poem is unclear. Romanticism was exceedingly fond of castles, especially those in ruins. The birds singing into glassless windows is also a romantic touch.

The wedding procession down by the Rhine reminds one of another poem by Eichendorff called *Die weinende Braut* ("The Weeping Bride"); she cries because her real lover has deserted her and the man she is marrying is not one she loves. But what that may have to do with the present poem—or what the wedding in the sunlight has to do with the ruined castle in the rain—is obscure indeed. The Lorelei in *Waldesgespräch* was also clad in a bridal gown and complained of the treachery of men. The present poem has many of the features of a ballad, but there is no obvious narrative.

8. *In der Fremde*

This is the last in a group of poems designated as *Wanderlieder.* The rippling of the brooks and the song of the nightingales confuse the wanderer. He forgets where he is. The nightingales, in romantic fashion, seem to be trying to tell him something, singing about happier times long since vanished. In the shimmering magic of the moonlight he seems to be able to see the castle in the valley below, although he knows that it is too far away. It also seems as if his sweetheart were waiting for him in the rose garden, but she died long ago. This romantic merging of past and present, of near and far, with the accompanying sweet melancholy of nostalgic mood, is in keeping with the point of view of the romantic "school," which blended all categories and genres.

The easy melodiousness of Eichendorff's verse could well lead to an overly cheerful musical interpretation; and it seems that Schumann may have fallen into that trap, for his lilting rhythm and frivolous melody do not match the Eichendorff mood in this poem—until the end, when it is obvious that no lighthearted mood can accompany a line like "Yet she died so long ago."

Notes on the text:

1 *Ich hör' die Bächlein rauschen* is obviously reminiscent of the famous line in *Die schöne Müllerin* (but it differs in both tense and number).

2 *her und hin:* a reversal of the more usual *hin und her* (as if one were to say in English "fro and to" for "to and fro"). It is difficult to believe that Eichendorff chose this order to effect a rhyme for *bin.*

3 *Rauschen* does not, strictly speaking, qualify as a rhyme for *rauschen* in line 1, because identity is ruled out: a rhyme requires initial difference plus final sameness.

5 *schlagen:* "sing, warble" (of birds; the meaning probably developed from the sense of "beat, pulsate, throb").

8 *von alter, schöner Zeit:* a favorite expression of one group of romantic poets. Schumann has *Von der alten, schönen Zeit,* which is decidedly inferior.

9 *Mondenschimmer:* plural!

13 *in den Garten:* the accusative *den* is perplexing ("into the garden"?). Schumann changes it to *dem,* and for once he appears to be justified, unless Eichendorff had some subtle intent, in "spectral syntax."

14 *Rosen weiss und rot:* archaic word order, with uninflected adjectives, favored by the *Volkslied.*

16 Eichendorff has *Und ist doch lange tot,* which Schumann alters to *Und ist doch so lange tot;* but he then repeats it twice in Eichendorff's original form: *Und ist doch lange tot.* The repetition, quite apart from the change in wording, may have been necessary to accommodate the somber mood introduced after the (unwarrantedly) lighthearted setting of the rest of the poem.

9. *Wehmut*

This *Wehmut,* in Eichendorff's works under the heading *Sängerleben,* is the first of two poems with that title. It is a sort of variation on the *pagliaccio* theme. The poet, like the nightingale, often sings to relieve his grief. All who listen are delighted by the beauty of his poetry, but none can feel the pain that is inherent in the song—and which is presumably the cause of that song's birth.

Notes on the text:

1 *wohl:* "true enough, quite so, admittedly."
5 Eichendorff has *So* as the first word of the line; Schumann replaces it with the "anticipatory" *Es.*
  Lassen belongs with *erschallen* two lines farther on ("let resound").
6 The word order (verb first) indicates a conditional (or temporal) clause: "When . . ."
8 For Eichendorff's *Käfigs* ("cage"), Schumann has *Kerkers* ("prison").
10 *alles:* although neuter, this word often means "everyone," as here.

10. *Zwielicht*

Twilight is another favorite theme of romanticism. This poem is part of the *Wanderlieder,* but it is also included in the novel *Ahnung und Gegenwart,* although the poem antedates the novel by four years.

The setting: night begins to fall; it is already dark in the valleys. The hunt seems over, save for an occasional hunter still clinging to the cliffs, which are illumined by the last rays of the setting sun. In the novel, Friedrich stands leaning on his rifle, far away from his companions. Then he hears, at some distance, singing in the forest.

The hour of twilight is not to be trusted; the very trees shudder, and the ominous clouds drift by like "heavy dreams." There is peculiar concern for a special deer (as if killing them in general were all right). The singer warns, "Do not even trust a friend; take care, it is the treacherous twilight hour!" We almost have the impression that nobody, however well meaning, is responsible for his own actions at this magic, perilous time.

Notes on the text:

1   *will:* "is about to."
4   *Graun:* the word means "shuddering," but there are overtones, perhaps, of *grau,* "gray," which is not etymologically related but can easily be associated with *Graun* in the popular mind.
13   Eichendorff's line *Was heut' müde gehet unter* is changed by Schumann to *Was heut' gehet müde unter,* which is no serious revision.

11. *Im Walde*

Eichendorff often used the theme of a wedding party in his poems. Here it is juxtaposed to a hunt. The sudden contrast of the terror of on-coming night is made more vivid by the shift to the present tense.

Notes on the text:

3   *das Waldhorn:* one of the most frequently mentioned devices in Eichendorff's novels and poems, being especially prominent in the *Taugenichts.*
6-8   The verbs are now all present tense.
8   Eichendorff has *mich schauert,* a perfectly legitimate impersonal construction with no expressed subject; Schumann found it necessary to alter it to *schauert's,* thereby providing the "missing" subject pronoun.

12. *Frühlingsnacht*

Eichendorff crowds into this song of a spring night a plethora of romantic symbols and devices—migrant birds, spring breezes, wondrous experiences of old times, moonlight, dreams, nightingales, longing. Spring nights are not terrifying; they are peculiarly "romantic," but the mood is bittersweet. This is a very musical poem, although it is perhaps not great poetry; it may be said to "sing itself."

Notes on the text:

1 Eichendorff's *Übern,* perfectly proper, is changed to *Überm.*
8 Eichendorff has *Mondesglanz,* which Schumann alters to *Monden-glanz.*

At the end of the song, Schumann repeats line 3.

The twelve songs of Schumann's *Liederkreis,* Op. 39, include some of the loveliest he has ever written. Unlike the *Dichterliebe,* no single story or poetic idea links these poems. Indeed, along with the *Liederkreis,* Op. 24, these songs illustrate instead the freedom with which Schumann combined a variety of different poems and packaged them under one title. Some of the titles are Eichendorff's and others are Schumann's own.

The *Liederkreis* offers a fair sample of the numerous ways in which Schumann approached the composition of lieder. Except for Nos. 3, 5, and 10, all are short, and each features but one figuration throughout. The vocal melody, whether or not it is doubled in the accompaniment, seems to grow out of the piano figuration. Most often the vocal melodies are stepwise, and, unlike the *Dichterliebe,* there are few instances of monotonic openings. The *Liederkreis* differs from the *Dichterliebe* in still other ways: none of the songs—not even the concluding one—has an extensive piano postlude; except for the three cited earlier, none begins with a piano prelude; most of the poems selected describe a scene, a season, or a time of day; relatively few make reference to personal sentiments.

Schumann appears to have followed a harmonic scheme for the twelve songs in that he opens in F-sharp minor, concludes in F-sharp major, and centers much of his music around two focuses, E and A (major or minor), with occasional forays into tonal areas a third removed (G and B). Two-thirds of the songs make use of the focal tonalities: Nos. 2 and 11 are in A major, Nos. 7 and 8 in A minor; Nos. 3, 5, and 9 are in E major, with No. 10 in E minor. Besides these parallel major/minor relationships, there are relative major/minor relations: No. 4 in G major is the relative of No. 10 in E minor; No. 1 in F-sharp minor is the relative of Nos. 2 and 11 in A major. The connections between adjacent songs proceed in this way:

No. 1		No. 2		No. 3
F-sharp minor	(relative min. of →)	A major	(subdominant of →)	E major

(parallel mj. to	No. 4		No. 5	
the rel. min. of →)	G major	(third relationship →)	E major	

	No. 6		No. 7	
(subdominant of →)	B major	(supertonic mj. of →)	A minor	(same as

No. 8		No. 9		
→) A minor	(subdominant min. of →)	E major	(parallel mj. of	

No. 10		No. 11		No. 12
→) E minor	(dominant min. of →)	A major	(third relationship)	F-sharp major

Each song is self-contained and could therefore be sung separately. One, however, concludes on an unresolved dominant, leaving the listeners waiting impatiently for the resolution in the following song. Among the most popular Schumann songs is *Mondnacht*, No. 5, which is often sung alone, completely removed from the context of the cycle.

1. *In der Fremde*

On its first publication, this *Liederkreis* opened with another song, *Der frohe Wandersmann. In der Fremde,* now No. 1, appeared with the cycle for the first time in 1850, when No. 8 (with the same title) was already part of the set. This information may explain why the cycle contains two songs with the same title.

This song presents features typical of Schumann's lieder: a stepwise lyrical melody seems to grow out of the accompanimental figure; the piano's repeated arpeggios are closely spaced; and their recurrence unifies this through-composed song. Often the piano echoes or anticipates the vocal melody (see bar 10). The damper pedal is essential to the general sonority. A flowing, leisurely tempo allows the singer sufficient time to enunciate the syllabically set text. The form is free; the material from the opening does not return at the conclusion. Additional unity derives from Schumann's employment of alternating variants of his initial phrase. Although the subject matter has much in common with folk material, this lied sounds nothing like a folk song.

2. *Intermezzo*

Schumann was apparently very fond of this melody. He used it again as the slow movement of the String Quartet in A, Op. 43, No. 3 (1842), and also in the Piano Trio in F, Op. 80 (1847). The syncopated accompaniment, which from bars 6 to 17 does not sound a single note on the beat, also features a countermelody beginning in bar 3 (Ex. 24-a). Occasionally this countertheme occurs after the vocal phrase; at other times it is heard together with the voice, adding another dimension to the mood of the piece. Schumann uses traditional ternary form for *Intermezzo* and concludes with a few bars for solo piano. This piano postlude displays Schumann's linear writing at its best: observe the various levels of melodic and rhythmic activity in Ex. 24-b.

Ex. 24

SCHUMANN: *Intermezzo*

a.

b.

3. *Waldesgespräch*

When properly performed, the hunting calls in the opening bars of *Waldesgespräch* resemble numerous piano pieces by Schumann. Similar to the solo compositions, this lied contains many different figurations and can, if not well handled, sound too episodic. The woodland conversations are reflected in the various sections, where characteristic rhythms, textures, and figurations mirror the sounds of the forest. The vocal melody is alternately declamatory and lyrical, although generally moving in stepwise patterns. Because Eichendorff views the Lorelei as a huntress, as well as a witch and sorceress, the sound of the hunting horns returns at the mention of her name. At the conclusion, where the Lorelei repeats some of the hunter's words from the first stanza, she does so to a new and more dramatic melody. Notice the delightfully unexpected modulation to C major at *Heim,* bar 15. Schumann, like Schubert, often moved to keys a third apart. This kind of relationship, more than the tonic-dominant of the previous century, prevailed during the first part of the romantic period.

4. *Die Stille*

Schumann builds this "patter" parlando song (one note to each syllable in a clipped, breathless style) out of tiny two-note phrases. The rests at bars 1, 2, 4, etc., significantly mirror *die Stille* and offer an example of how Schumann avoids the usual monotony of $\frac{6}{8}$ meter. The brittle staccato accompaniment contrasts with the flowing figurations of the previous song. The ternary form (*a b a¹*) is the composer's doing. He eliminates the second strophe of the original poem and, instead, repeats the text and music of the first stanza at the end. In this song, as he did in *Waldesgespräch,* Schumann repeats the final line of the text. Also, in both lieder the piano postludes continue the principal figuration of the accompaniment.

5. *Mondnacht*

As a young man, Brahms set this poem. He was undoubtedly influenced by Schumann's earlier version. Indeed, the piano style of the introduction found its way into many of Brahms's Intermezzi. The harmonic ambiguity that characterizes the piano prelude reappears at bar 23 and again in the postlude, where the tonality finally crystallizes. The particular sonority of the prelude portrays the mysterious power of the moon over man. (Remember how the fiery red moon appears in both Strauss's *Salome* and Berg's *Wozzeck* as a symbol of death.)

The piano figuration that supports the recurrent vocal strophes contrasts sharply with the introduction. The formal pattern of the song, essentially ternary, is, however, divided musically into four sections, while there are only three poetic stanzas.

Poetic divisions		Musical divisions	
stanza 1	(4 lines of text)	*a*	(bars 1-22)
stanza 2	(4 lines of text)	a^1	(bars 28-43)
stanza 3	(2 lines of text)	*b*	(bars 44-52)
	(2 lines of text)	a^2	(bars 53-60)

Observe the recurrence of a fundamental pattern of descent: melodic motives in the prelude and also in the main body of the lied (bars 10-13, 18-21, 23-25, 30 ff.) all proceed in a downward motion and counter the continuously rising line of the voice. These motives give a sense of forward motion to the song, despite the static repeated chords.

6. *Schöne Fremde*

Schöne Fremde presents a fine example of a *Nachtstück*. A companion to *Mondnacht*, this lied, similar to those in the *Dichterliebe*, contains but one figuration throughout. In addition, Schumann employs a striking device to unify the work. In the first bar, he features a melodic fragment (A sharp–D sharp–A sharp) which is restated and then extended. At the postlude, the interval between the pitches has expanded from a fourth to a sixth. Eric Sams, in his book on Schumann's songs, is convinced that this kind of motive had hidden significance for the composer. We are content to observe merely that it serves to tighten a composition which might otherwise seem too disorganized.

The three strophes are treated to a through-composed setting.

7. *Auf einer Burg*

This declamatory, modal setting with imitative entries in the piano accompaniment recalls the similar style of *Im Rhein, im heiligen Strome* from the *Dichterliebe* and the cathedral sonority of the fourth movement of the "Rhenish" Symphony. The majesty and strength of the castle are reflected in the sturdy half notes of the piano part. Curiously, Schumann eliminates prelude and postlude here, but the clear-cut linear writing nevertheless assures the pianist that he will be heard. A rhythmic motive dominates the voice part; it appears in two-thirds of the twenty-one bars of the first stanza and characterizes the opening bars of the second as well. Notice that *Bart und Haare, Brust und Krause,* and *hundert Jahre,* all important words, do *not* share this rhythmic motive. On the contrary, these words are all set to a rising-sixth interval in equal quarter notes.

The two stanzas of this strophic song are connected by a short piano interlude. Observe that this lied is the only one to end inconclusively on a dominant triad, requiring resolution into the following *In der Fremde.*

8. *In der Fremde*

One of the few instances where Schumann evolves a water figure, this delightful *In der Fremde* is based on two alternating bars of material which persist throughout: the first has running sixteenth notes and the second a syncopated figure. In no way do these compare with Schubert's conception of water music. The voice, which enters on the last sixteenth of the opening bar, has two rhythmic motives that alternate, but not as consistently as those in the accompaniment. Although the song is cast into modified strophic form, it is not immediately obvious because Schumann combines the first two poetic stanzas into one musical strophe and sets the last two to the same music, following it with a brief codetta.

Sams comments that the melody at the opening of this lied duplicates the intervals that begin *Auf einer Burg*. True, but the rhythmic profile is so completely altered that one cannot hear the resemblance. Curiously, for the listener the overall impression of the song is a pleasurable one; the musical mood does not reflect the text.

9. *Wehmut*

It is rather strange that this painfully sad song should have been set in a major key. Yet Schumann sustains a sorrowful mood throughout. He separates three four-line stanzas into six two-line musical units. These units, or phrases, are interrelated by means of a recurrent melodic motive that appears first under *manchmal singen*. Observe the variants of this motive later on at bars 6, 10, 18, and 22 in the voice part.

10. *Zwielicht*

Schumann set both *Wehmut* and *Zwielicht* as modified strophic lieder, although the formal outlines of *Zwielicht* are far easier to hear (a a^1 a^2 a^3). Again each stanza changes only slightly in the voice part, but considerably in the accompaniment. Notice, for example, the changing harmony in the stanza beginning *Hast du einen Freund,* bar 24. The cumulative changes reach a climax in the last stanza, where Schumann employs a completely different texture for the closing section.

The meandering broken-chord design of the piano figuration appears first in the opening prelude and persists throughout each of the stanzas. The composer ends each stanza with a quasi-recitative (bars 14 and 22). The final strophe, too, concludes with a short, jerky recitative in a low range that is exceptional in Schumann's lieder.

11. *Im Walde*

The dancelike opening recalls some of the *Dichterliebe* songs as well as many of Schumann's solo piano pieces. The descending scalar motive in sixths (bars 5-6) that links the successive textual phrases sounds familiar. A sustained dominant pedal in the opening bars of the lied anchors the bass, as voice and treble of the piano part skip merrily along. Recollections of the woods, the birds, the knights, the wedding are all joyful. Surely one of the few lighthearted settings of this group, *Im Walde* reveals Schumann's brand of folksiness, more subtle and sophisticated than Schubert's.

The mood changes suddenly, and so does the tonality at *Und eh' ich's*, bar 23. Rhythmic and melodic motives, however, join the two disparate sections. Observe Schumann's repetition of the text at the close, and the manner in which he set *Herzensgrunde*, in an example of *Tonmalerei*, at the very end of the song.

12. *Frühlingsnacht*

Another night piece to join the numerous *Nachtstücke* among Schumann's works, *Frühlingsnacht* shows a freneticism unique to this cycle. The insistent triplet sixteenth-note chords anticipate Wolf's setting of *Er ist's*. Compounding the tension of the opening bars is the sequence of unresolved dominant sevenths that demand resolution. In addition, Schumann uses a rhythmic device that will become a trademark of Brahms's style: two notes (here in the voice) against three (in the accompaniment). So much happens so quickly in this lied that it is difficult to hear the overall ternary design.

Unlike the *Dichterliebe* or *Frauenliebe und -leben*, this *Liederkreis* has no extended coda. Schumann instead closes with a short six-bar codetta —into which he manages to squeeze the two basic motives of the lied: the descending scale heard in the opening bar of the accompaniment and the rising triad heard in the second bar in the voice part.

Three Songs from *Myrten*, Op. 25

Schumann intended to give Clara the twenty-six songs of *Myrten* as a wedding present. For this reason, perhaps, he selected a bouquet from among the poems of numerous writers, many of them non-Germans. Besides Rückert, Mosen, Goethe, and Heine, the collection includes Burns, Byron, and Thomas Moore.

RÜCKERT

Widmung

```
Du meine Seele, du mein Herz,
Du meine Wonn', o du mein Schmerz,
Du meine Welt, in der ich lebe,
Mein Himmel du, darein ich schwebe,
O du mein Grab, in das hinab
Ich ewig meinen Kummer gab.
Du bist die Ruh, du bist der Frieden,
Du bist vom Himmel mir beschieden.
Dass du mich liebst, macht mich mir wert,
Dein Blick hat mich vor mir verklärt,
Du hebst mich liebend über mich,
Mein guter Geist, mein bessres Ich!
```

Widmung is not Rückert's title, but Schumann's. The first song in the cycle called *Myrten* by Schumann, it is No. 4 in Rückert's *Liebesfrühling* but has no separate title of its own. It is somewhat reminiscent of the passionate verse of Heine, but there is a preponderance of metaphor rather than simile. Rückert equates his beloved, boldly and directly, with a series of phenomena, not all of which are completely appropriate in lyrical poetry; consider line 5, for example: *O du mein Grab* ("Oh thou, my grave"), a metaphor hardly likely to endear a man to a maiden. He seems to be aiming at the expression of an all-inclusive, almost pantheistic view of life and love (heart and soul, life and death, heaven—but, fortunately, not hell). Some of the metaphor is clearly extravagant. Whoever the *Du* may be, she is accorded attributes more properly belonging to a deity. There are possibly echoes of "Oriental" poetry here.

Notes on the text:

In the first strophe, even the verb "to be" is omitted as Rückert addresses his beloved.

2   Schumann alters *Wonne* to *Wonn'* and inserts a slightly disturbing *O,* a change hardly required by the meter; yet the composer obviously felt a musical need for the full vowel rather than the "reduced" *e* (schwa) of *Wonne.*

7   Here begins a different kind of expression after the direct address (apostrophe) of the first six lines. The verb "to be" is now employed in more typical metaphoric language. Note that line 7 is also the first line of an even better-known poem of Rückert's.

8   Schumann sees fit to change *Du bist der Himmel mir beschieden* to *Du bist vom Himmel mir beschieden*, a *Verschlimmbesserung* which destroys the identification of the girl with heaven itself and demotes her to a gift *from* heaven, with corresponding loss of metaphor.

10 *vor mir:* "before myself, in my own eyes."

Schumann now repeats the first four lines of the poem and ends the song with a repetition of the final line, *Mein guter Geist, mein bessres Ich.*

Although most lieder enthusiasts think of Mahler when Rückert's name is mentioned, Schumann, too, was inspired by this poet. Actually, the entire *Gedichte aus "Liebesfrühling,"* Op. 37, as well as five songs in *Myrten,* are settings of Rückert's poems. *Widmung* (the first song in *Myrten,* Op. 25) is fairly typical of Schumann's lyrical style, and it projects the kind of *Stimmung* musicians invariably associate with the composer. For example, the arpeggiated figure with which the song opens appears in numerous piano pieces (e.g., *Aufschwung*, No. 2 of the *Fantasiestücke,* and *Chopin* of the *Carnaval*) as well as in lieder. *Widmung* includes another feature generally seen in Schumann's songs: two different textures within the same lied. The composer defines the ternary form here by means of these two different accompanimental figures, one arpeggiated and the other chordal. Curiously, the articulations seem exceptionally distinct for Schumann, who ordinarily shows greater subtlety when outlining successive sections. He does not disappoint us, however, as we shall see when we scan the overall plan of the lied.

Rückert did not divide his poem into strophes, but Schumann felt the necessity of subdivisions. Tonality and melodic style are both altered in the middle section, the key changing from A flat to E major (common-tone modulation, cf. p. 61), and the vocal line becoming noticeably more conjunct. The gentle chords here are reminiscent of *Ich grolle nicht,* p. 123. A descending scale in an inner voice at bars 14-16 reinforces the sense of *Ruh,* bar 15; particular words *(Wonne, ewig, Grab,* and later *Schmerz)* receive special treatment. For musical reasons, Schumann restates the first four lines as well as the last line of the poem. From this material he constructs his a^1 before concluding with a six-bar postlude. He effectively joins the *b* and a^1 by restoring the *a* accompaniment before the conclusion of *b* in the following manner:

Text	Music	Accompaniment	Key
6 lines	*a*	arpeggiated	A flat
4½ lines	*b*	chordal	E
1½ lines		arpeggiated	A flat
4 lines (repeat)	a^1	arpeggiated	A flat
1 line (repeat of last line)		fuller chords	A flat
[piano postlude]	a^2	arpeggiated	A flat

Rhythm emerges unexpectedly as one of the principal controlling elements in the lied. Observe how the rhythmic pattern, relatively stable at the beginning of each section, becomes increasingly agitated as the music progresses, only to lose its momentum at the close. Happily, Schumann distributes the rhythmic activity equally between voice and piano. How he achieves this kind of rhythmic equilibrium eludes the casual listener but proves fascinating to the theorist.

JULIUS MOSEN (1803-67)

Mosen was one of the poets who were enthusiastically on the side of the cause of Greek freedom (like Byron) and also a supporter, at a safe distance, of Poland's struggle for liberation. He was the author of a number of dramas, now forgotten, also a ballad or two, and some lyrical poetry. His song on the death of the Tyrolean patriot Andreas Hofer *(Zu Mantua in Banden)*, sung to a folk melody in a felicitous match, is one of the best known of German songs.

Der Nussbaum

Es grünet ein Nussbaum vor dem Haus,
Duftig,
Luftig
Breitet er blättrig die Äste aus.

Viel liebliche Blüten stehen d'ran;
Linde
Winde
Kommen, sie herzlich zu umfahn.

Es flüstern je zwei zu zwei gepaart,
Neigend,
Beugend
Zierlich zum Kusse die Häuptchen zart.

Sie flüstern von einem Mägdlein, das
Dächte
Nächte
Tagelang, wüsste, ach! selber nicht was.

Sie flüstern,--wer mag verstehn so gar
Leise
Weise?
Flüstern von Bräut'gam und nächstem Jahr.

Das Mägdlein horchet, es rauscht im Baum;
Sehnend,
Wähnend,
Sinkt es lächelnd in Schlaf und Traum.

The tree is conceivably a chestnut tree, which has spectacularly beautiful blossoms. We encounter once more the theme of wind-borne messages. But there is a new point of view here: the winds whisper about a girl who pretends not to know her mind, yet they whisper so softly that their gentle song can scarcely be heard. Still, there is a message about a fiancé and some talk of "next year," which is not too obscure. The tree stands next to the house where the girl lives. Presumably she listens at her window. She seems satisfied with the message of this "singing telegram," for she falls asleep smiling, although not without a tantalizingly wistful longing.

Note that the two middle lines of each strophe consist, in Mosen's original verses, of one word each, and rhyming:

> Es grünet ein Nussbaum vor dem Haus,
> Duftig,
> Luftig
> Breitet er blättrig die Äste aus.

The metrical effect is partly lost in Schumann's music, although the loss may be more than compensated by the superiority of the composition.

Notes on the text:

4   *blättrig:* "leafily, in leafy fashion"; the whole line means "stretches out its leafy boughs."

8   *umfahn:* archaic for *umfangen* "embrace, caress."

9   *je zwei zu zwei gepaart:* a rather redundant way to say "two by two" or "in pairs."

15   Schumann has *die Nächte* (for *Nächte*).

19   Schumann has *Weis'* for *Weise,* which is tampering with Mosen's metrical scheme.

20   *von* is preferable to *vom,* found in some printings of Schumann's collection (otherwise *nächstem* is syntactically unjustified). And Schumann's altered repetition of *von nächstem Jahr* is also somewhat upsetting.

24   *es:* "she" (*das Mägdlein,* neuter).

Schumann ignores the arrangement of the text (see poem, p. 167) and focuses instead on the mood. In this fine example of an interwoven instrumental/vocal fabric, the piano introduces the vocal phrase and then concludes it. Again an arpeggiated figure prevails, the notes of the countermelody seemingly plucked from among the flowing waves of sound. Both hands share in the recurrent arpeggio, and the piano interludes feature refreshing harmonic progressions. Schumann, less adventurous when voice and piano sound together, is apparently uninhibited when writing for solo piano.

Except for the steady sixteenth-note pattern of the accompaniment, rhythmic activity is kept to a minimum. Surprisingly, the $\frac{6}{8}$ meter does not become monotonous, perhaps because of the more varied patterns in the voice and the treble. Besides the recurrent accompanimental figure, the brief opening motive at the keyboard (E–B–A–G) also serves to unify the song. The formal scheme offers more than usual interest because it is not too obvious.

Der Nussbaum begins with three statements of the same music (*a*). Each short vocal phrase is followed by two bars for piano. After *zart,* however, the harmony changes. A modulation to the supertonic is carried along with the same texture. In the following middle section (*b*), Schumann increases the tension, the voice continuing uninterruptedly for its longest

musical phrase (8 bars). With *Sie flüstern, a¹* begins, its modifications starting
after *Weis'.* Then, at bar 57, Schumann introduces a pedal point on the
tonic note G, which (except for one bar) continues to the close. He concludes
the lied with a codetta containing the tonic pedal in the bass, the arpeggiated
figure in the accompaniment, topped by a motive from the original *a.*
(Compare the music of *Schlaf und Traum* with that of *Äste aus.*)

HEINE

Die Lotosblume

Die Lotosblume ängstigt
Sich vor der Sonne Pracht,
Und mit gesenktem Haupte
Erwartet sie träumend die Nacht.

Der Mond, der ist ihr Buhle,
Er weckt sie mit seinem Licht,
Und ihm entschleiert sie freundlich
Ihr frommes Blumengesicht.

Sie blüht und glüht und leuchtet,
Und starret stumm in die Höh';
Sie duftet und weinet und zittert
Vor Liebe und Liebesweh.

This poem is No. 10 in the *Lyrisches Intermezzo* (cf. the remarks above
on the *Dichterliebe*) and, as such, is another reflection of Heine's unhappy
love for Amalie. The lotus (German *Lotos* has the Greek ending "-os") is an
Indian symbol and is very prominent in Sanskrit love poetry, as well as in
the religious poetry of India. The name is a popular botanical term for
several different plants. The Egyptian lotus was a water lily, as was the
sacred lotus of the Hindus. It symbolized in ancient India the world—
the cosmos—but also female beauty. Heine conceives of it as a night-bloom-
ing flower, timidly avoiding the violent splendor of the sun but willingly
unfolding to receive the gentler rays of her beloved, the moon. A fragrant,
delicate blossom, she trembles with love and love's sweet woe.

In another poem *(Die schlanke Wasserlilie),* Heine repeats the same
theme and even some of the words of *Die Lotosblume,* employing the same

meter and rhyme scheme as in the present poem. Later he is unable to restrain his irony, and in a poem called *Lotosblume,* the flower is an aging woman, the moon her arthritic lover, able to give her nothing but a poem. This is not precisely a repudiation of the emotion and sentiment in our song but rather an expression of nostalgic regret, with some stoical laughter at his own increasing infirmity.

Although the poet's external stimulus for *Die Lotosblume* is apparently Oriental, there is no reason for the composer to introduce Oriental features into his setting, and Schumann rightly refrains from any such attempts.

Notes on the text:

1-2 The sense carries over from one line to the next *(enjambement),* a fact which Schumann deliberately ignores in his setting ·by placing a half-measure rest after line 1. This leaves a burden of interpretation on the singer, who must make the text sound like good German. The same holds true in lesser degree for the last two lines of each strophe, although the pause is by no means as serious here. Schumann's practice throughout the poem, in fact, is to insert a rest after every line. The text requires this in only one-half of the cases.

5 *Buhle:* archaically "sweetheart, lover"; now "paramour, lover."

8 *frommes:* "devoted" (rather than "pious"; the semantic link is "devout").

The second and fourth lines of each strophe rhyme. The rhymes are masculine (the final, rhyming syllable is accented). Lines 1 and 3 do not rhyme; their last word is in each instance disyllabic, consisting of an accented syllable followed by an unstressed one. Seven of the lines end in *t,* and there is, possibly accidentally, a prominence of dental sounds throughout, which may constitute a difficulty for composer and singer alike.

Because it represents a setting of utmost tranquillity, *Die Lotosblume* (No. 7 of *Myrten*) may fail to attract listeners on first hearing. Only after repeated performances does this song reveal its beauty. Schumann coordinates rhythm, melody, harmony, and texture to achieve a nearly perfect reflection of the ambience of the poem, if not the individual words of the text. Unusually here, we notice several instances of neumatic text setting (two or three notes sung to one syllable; see "blu" of *Lotosblume*). A conjunct melodic line moves in scalewise patterns, but the pause after each phrase can distort the meaning of the words. Schumann links these phrases by means of the recurrent opening motive. For example, six of the first seven phrases begin on the identical note (the dominant) and all show a closely related rhythmic profile. The composer reserves the highest pitch of the song for *zittert,* the high point of the accelerando, after which voice and piano gradually descend together into the final cadence. Exceptionally, there is no piano postlude.

In this *durchkomponiert* lied, the music changes ever so slightly with the text, while the homorhythmic chordal accompaniment remains the same throughout all but the last two bars.

Die beiden Grenadiere

Nach Frankreich zogen zwei Grenadier',
Die waren in Russland gefangen.
Und als sie kamen ins deutsche Quartier,
Sie liessen die Köpfe hangen.

Da hörten sie beide die traurige Mär:
Dass Frankreich verloren gegangen,
Besiegt und geschlagen das tapfere Heer
Und der Kaiser, der Kaiser gefangen.

Da weinten zusammen die Grenadier'
Wohl ob der kläglichen Kunde.
Der eine sprach: "Wie weh wird mir,
Wie brennt meine alte Wunde!"

Der andere sprach: "Das Lied ist aus,
Auch ich möcht'mit dir sterben,
Doch hab'ich Weib und Kind zu Haus,
Die ohne mich verderben."

"Was schert mich Weib, was schert mich Kind,
Ich trage weit bessres Verlangen;
Lass sie betteln gehn, wenn sie hungrig sind--
Mein Kaiser, mein Kaiser gefangen!

Gewähr'mir, Bruder, eine Bitt':
Wenn ich jetzt sterben werde,
So nimm meine Leiche nach Frankreich mit,
Begrab'mich in Frankreichs Erde.

Das Ehrenkreuz am roten Band
Sollst du aufs Herz mir legen;
Die Flinte gib mir in die Hand,
Und gürt'mir um den Degen.

So will ich liegen und horchen still,
Wie eine Schildwach, im Grabe,
Bis einst ich höre Kanonengebrüll
Und wiehernder Rosse Getrabe.

Dann reitet mein Kaiser wohl über mein Grab,
Viel Schwerter klirren und blitzen;
Dann steig'ich gewaffnet hervor aus dem Grab--
Den Kaiser, den Kaiser zu schützen!"

The external impetus for this poem—essentially a ballad—seems to have been the sight of wretchedly haggard French prisoners of war who had returned from Siberia. A group of them caught Heine's attention in Düsseldorf, while he was on a visit to his home town during a vacation. The war was long since over, but the soldiers had been kept in capitivity. Heine was always an enthusiastic supporter of Napoleon, who to him stood for progress, liberalism, tolerance of religious minorities (not, however, of the majority), and general enlightenment. Even toward the end of Napoleon's career, when he emerged as something less than a benefactor, Heine retained his attitude of hero worship. And that admiration for Napoleon made it impossible for Heine to fall into his customary irony in this poem.

The reading of a French account of the fate of prisoners of war in Russia is also regarded as one source for Heine's ideas, even for some of the actual lines. And a line or two may be based on the ballad *Edward* (e.g., *Lass sie betteln gehn, wenn sie hungrig sind*); Heine did make use of Herder's translation of that ballad in his play *William Ratcliff*.

Notes on the text:

1   *zogen:* implies that they had made the long journey from Russia, perhaps from Siberia, on foot.
3   *Quartier:* their quarters in Germany.
4   The rhyme with line 2 (*gefangen: hangen*) is repeated in 6, 8, 18, and 20.

5 *Mär:* archaic for "news, report, story" (*Märchen* "fairy tale" is a diminutive of this word).

6 *verloren gegangen (war):* with the omission of the auxiliary, common in nineteenth-century German.

7 Heine has *zerschlagen,* implying a more devastating rout than Schumann's *geschlagen.*
   Kaiser: "Emperor" (Napoleon). It is somewhat disconcerting to English-speaking people to encounter the word *Kaiser* in non-Prussian contexts. But it is, after all, the name Caesar to start with.

10 *ob:* "on account of."

13 *das Lied ist aus:* "it's all over; all is lost; the jig is up."

17 *Was schert mich:* "what do I care for."

25 *Das Ehrenkreuz:* the cross of the Legion of Honor.

29-36 Schumann and Richard Wagner both set these lines to a melody of part of the *Marseillaise,* although Wagner set the music to Heine's own French translation of the poem *Les deux Grenadiers,* which shows several differences from the original.

30 *Schildwach(e):* "sentry" is feminine. (Cf. French *la sentinelle,* Italian *la guardia,* both feminine. The words first applied to the post, then to the one occupying it.)

33-35 The verbs in these lines are present in form, future in sense.

On December 29, 1840, Richard Wagner wrote to Schumann:

. . . I hear that you have composed Heine's *Grenadiere* and at the end the *Marseillaise* appears in it. Last winter I, too, composed it and also brought in the *Marseillaise* at the end.

What a curious coincidence, and surely the only similarity between the two settings!

Besides favoring Heine's lyrical poetry, Schumann also composed music to several of Heine's ballads. Among the best known is the song the composer titled *Die beiden Grenadiere.* Here a refrain in the accompaniment reflects the sound of a bugle, a muffled drum, and the halting tread of a pair of tired soldiers (Ex. 25-a). A scalar melody alternates with monotone phrases for which Schumann has recourse to declamation and recitative (Ex. 25-b). A curious feature is the latent melody of the *Marseillaise* which can be

Ex. 25

SCHUMANN: *Die beiden Grenadiere*

Nach Frank reich zo gen zwei Gre - na - dier',

a.

Der an-dre sprach: "Das Lied ist aus,

b.

So will ich lie-gen und horchen still, wie ei - ne Schildwach', im Gra - be,

c.

found within the opening vocal melody (cf. Ex. 25-a and Ex. 25-c). Although the lied is *durchkomponiert,* the composer retains the outlines of the poetic stanzas in the following manner:

Stanza	Key	Section and style
1	B minor	*a a*
2		*b* monotone and sequence. Note also the rhythm of a funeral march.
		Piano interlude
3		*a c* and sequence
4		declamation
5		monotone with refrain (interlude and introduction) in accompaniment
6		monotone and new accompaniment
7		monotone and still another accompaniment (um-pah-pah)
8	B major	*Marseillaise* (Ex. 25-c)
9		*Marseillaise* and a four-bar postlude, bitter with dissonance and forming an ironic close

MENDELSSOHN (1809-47)

Mendelssohn, a fine musician, was equally gifted as a pianist, conductor, composer, critic, and musicologist. He wrote in all media with uniform competence, but rarely did he achieve true greatness. Of approximately seventy-five songs—most of which, for some unknown reason, appeared in groups of six—only a very few rank with those by Schumann or Schubert. Mendelssohn was trained by Zelter, one of Schubert's distinguished forerunners, who wrote a considerable number of pieces for the *Liedertafeln,* or singing societies, of his day. It is not surprising, therefore, that Mendelssohn, too, left some unusual secular songs for mixed chorus based on the poems of Goethe, Heine, and Eichendorff, among others.

Of his solo songs, unquestionably the best is his setting of Goethe's sonnet *Die Liebende schreibt.* His best-known lied, so popular that it is thought by many to be a folk song, is *Auf Flügeln des Gesanges.* Although Mendelssohn did not contribute to the development of the lied, an examination of his style in three songs should prove somewhat valuable, if only for the purpose of comparison with those by other composers.

HEINE

Auf Flügeln des Gesanges

Auf Flügeln des Gesanges,
Herzliebchen, trag ich dich fort,
Fort nach den Fluren des Ganges,
Dort weiss ich den schönsten Ort;

Dort liegt ein rotblühender Garten
Im stillen Mondenschein,
Die Lotosblumen erwarten
Ihr trautes Schwesterlein.

Die Veilchen kichern und kosen,
Und schaun nach den Sternen empor,
Heimlich erzählen die Rosen
Sich duftende Märchen ins Ohr.

Es hüpfen herbei und lauschen
Die frommen, klugen Gazelln,
Und in der Ferne rauschen
Des heilgen Stromes Well'n.

Dort wollen wir niedersinken
Unter dem Palmenbaum,
Und Liebe und Ruhe trinken,
Und träumen seligen Traum.

This is No. 9 in the *Lyrisches Intermezzo* and is apparently another by-product of Heine's Indic studies under Schlegel at Bonn and with Bopp at Berlin. The familiar words of the first line "On wings of song" follow numerous predecessors, but the most strikingly similar one is E. T. A. Hoffmann's *Kampf der Sänger: auf den Flügeln des Gesangs.* The delicacy of Indian poetry, with its characteristic personification of nature, is invoked again. Heine invites Amalie on an imaginary trip to India by the airy route of wings of song, which is the equivalent of the wings of imagination. Their destination would be the banks of the Ganges, a sacred stream, perhaps symbolizing love's fulfillment. Since, however, that is not to be, the entire proposal remains a dream. The poem is not a profound one, or even necessarily a very sincere one. The lotuses, violets, roses, gazelles, the palm tree, and the Ganges are all stock-in-trade devices of spurious Oriental poetry.

Notes on the text:

7 *Lotosblumen:* In several poems we find the lotus as the sweetheart of the moon. The lotuses await their "dear sister" (line 8), Amalie; Heine is, in one sense, the moon, as we have seen in earlier poems.

16 *Des heiligen Stromes Well'n:* The sacred stream is the Ganges. But it seems to represent Heine's love, too.

For *Auf Flügeln des Gesanges*, Mendelssohn returned to the *Bar* form, a pattern he had used for many songs. The last (third) stanza opens like the others, but soon takes off in another direction. The vocal melody is eminently singable; it was probably the single most important reason for the song's popularity. A flowing $\frac{6}{8}$ arpeggiated figure in the accompaniment continues unabated until the final vocal cadence, at which point the piano postlude concludes with a return to the same figure. Hardly an imaginative accompaniment, it does not double the vocal line, but supports it fully. The harmony is perfectly traditional; the A-flat tonality is somewhat less so. No Indian influence appears in the musical sonority, perhaps because Mendelssohn questioned the authenticity of the Orientalism.

GOETHE

Die Liebende schreibt

Ein Blick von deinen Augen in die meinen,
Ein Kuss von deinem Mund auf meinem Munde,
Wer davon hat, wie ich, gewisse Kunde,
Mag dem was anders wohl erfreulich scheinen?

Entfernt von dir, entfremdet von den Meinen,
Führ ich stets die Gedanken in die Runde,
Und immer treffen sie auf jene Stunde,
Die einzige; da fang ich an zu weinen.

Die Träne trocknet wieder unversehens:
Er liebt ja, denk ich, her in diese Stille,
Und sollst du nicht in die Ferne reichen?

Vernimm das Lispeln dieses Liebewehens;
Mein einzig Glück auf Erden ist dein Wille,
Dein freundlicher, zu mir; gib mir ein Zeichen!

The sonnet has not been a conspicuously successful or favored verse form in German. Goethe wrote some twenty-seven, seventeen of them in the period 1807-08, allegedly under the spell of two young women, Bettina Brentano and Wilhelmina Herzlieb.

Goethe's rhyme scheme is *a b b a, a b b a* for the two quatrains and *c d e, c d e* for the two tercets. Goethe uses feminine rhyme only. The line has eleven syllables and begins and ends with an unaccented beat. His interest in this verse form was aroused by reading the sonnets of Ariosto in August, 1807, and by the publication of an edition of Petrarch's poems, *Le rime di Francesco Petrarca*, by his friend Frommann, of Jena. Goethe was also visited by Zacharias Werner that same year, Werner being an accomplished sonneteer himself. He and Goethe read sonnets aloud to each other, and Goethe was seized with enthusiasm for the form. It is now a matter of debate how much effect the two young ladies mentioned really had upon Goethe's writing.

In this poem it is the girl who speaks. She is alone; her lover is far away. Memory awakens longing for a visible sign of his love. This brings tears. But consolation comes with the realization that just as his love reaches her, so too must hers be able to reach him. He will, she hopes, send her some assurance—possibly a sonnet in return?

Notes on the text:

1 *in die meinen:* accusative "into mine."
2 *auf meinem Mund:* dative (location—place where), a lasting kiss.
3 *gewisse Kunde:* "certain knowledge" (but really only in her feelings).
4 *mag:* the verb has the older sense "can" (cf. *vermag*, which still retains that meaning).
5 *entfremdet von den Meinen:* seems to indicate that she has either broken with her kith and kin or has fled from them. The mood is vaguely reminiscent of Mignon.

7-8 *auf jene Stunde, die einzige:* "that hour, the one and only" apparently means the time he declared his love for her. It can hardly refer to the moment of separation, because it is a time she prizes.

10 *liebt . . . her: her* indicates motion toward the speaker; the motion need not be tangible or visible. His love reaches her in this silent place.

11 *du:* the girl herself.

14 Much more than friendship is meant. A *Freund* is a very special person.

Die Liebende schreibt is an exceptional song for several reasons: it is through-composed, a form usually avoided by Mendelssohn until the end of his life; it shows Schumann's influence in texture, figuration, and general mood painting; and, according to Eric Werner *(Mendelssohn),* it was not published until after Mendelssohn's death. Rather than imitating the restrictive meter of the poem, Mendelssohn modeled his song on the rhyme scheme of the sonnet. He emphasizes the middle lines of the two quatrains (*b b* of *a b b a*) with a vocal cadence; and he does the same for each line in the next two tercets *(c d e).* Only the *a* is neglected. Although he follows the poet's meter for the first seven lines, he moves more freely (after *weinen*) in the last portion of the song. The composer used a predominantly stepwise melody and syllabic text setting. Unfortunately, his musical accents do not always coincide with the most significant words of the text (see *in,* bar 2). At the same time he displays a degree of sensitivity to the text with the vocal leap on *einzige* (bar 16) and the long-held note on *weinen* (bar 19).

In the accompaniment, the reiterated chords that support the first eight lines of the text change to an arpeggiated figure at *weinen,* in a kind of musical overlap before the beginning of the new line of text. The harmonies shift here also. Notice as well the interesting bass melody at *trocknet wieder,* unusual for Mendelssohn, who, despite his overwhelming interest in Bach's music, rarely infused his own songs with even a trace of counterpoint. The lover's final plea, *gib mir ein Zeichen,* is twice repeated, each time to slightly different music.

HEINE

Allnächtlich im Traume

This Heine text comes from the *Lyrisches Intermezzo,* where it is No. 56, and was used by Schumann as No. 14 of his *Dichterliebe* (see p. 126). How different from Schumann's is Mendelssohn's setting of *Allnächtlich im Traume*! Schumann, usually most precise in his performance instructions, must have believed that the meaning of the poem here would provide the solution to the tempo. He omits all mention of tempo for this lied. Mendelssohn, however, writes "Allegro," which tends to make singers take it too fast. Both composers use modified strophic forms. Schumann opens with the voice, but Mendelssohn writes four bars of a piano introduction which later serve to link the first two stanzas. The treble figure in bar 4 of the piano prelude is a Mendelssohn trademark; it appears in many of his instrumental compositions.

There is a breathlessness to this entire setting that is totally absent from Schumann's. A comparison of the opening bars of the two vocal parts brings up other differences: Schumann sets the text to tiny musical phrases, almost in little gasps. Mendelssohn, on the other hand, conceives of a longer-line melody, but he does not give it any well-defined shape. (Cf. Exx. 26-a and 26-b.)

Ex. 26

MENDELSSOHN: *Allnächtlich im Traume*

All - nächtlich im Traume   seh' ich dich und seh' dich freund - lich grü - ssen,
Du siehst mich an   weh - mü - thig - lich und schüttelst das blonde   Köpf - chen;

a.

SCHUMANN: *Allnächtlich im Traume*

All - nächtlich im Traume   seh' ich dich, und se - he dich freundlich, freundlich grüssen,

b.

V

The Romantic Ballad
and Rhapsody

THE BALLAD

A ballad ought, superficially at least, to afford the composer a facile text for composition, for it is a narrative song-poem with a rhythmic form adapted for singing. (We may merely mention its more ancient sense of "a song to dance to." Middle English *balade* was taken from Old French, which had itself borrowed the word from Provençal *balada,* from the verb *balar* "to dance." But the earlier meaning of the term has scant connection with our ballad, and the present-day popular use of "ballad" shows still another unrelated application of the same word to a different phenomenon.)

The composer's apparent advantage in form is offset, in the case of the folk ballad, by the knowledge that the text is already wedded to its own melody. His effort to provide a new setting might well be equated with abducting the text from its lawful mate and forcibly uniting it to a strange, more sophisticated partner. Nevertheless, such attempts have often been highly successful, and the new setting has sometimes supplanted the old to the extent that it alone is remembered.

It has been customary to distinguish between "literary" and "folk" (or "popular") ballads. But the major difference here is that the author of the literary ballad is relatively recent and known, while the folk ballad's author has been forgotten in the mists of time. Romantic enthusiasts in the eighteenth century (and later) claimed that folk ballads were created by the people as some mystical unity, rather than being the work of individuals. It is true that generations of people may have altered, modified, and reshaped a ballad in the course of its oral transmission. It is even likely that different stanzas could have been contributed by different people. But it is still difficult to envisage the first form of a ballad, or any other poem, as the product of a whole community acting in spontaneous creation.

LOEWE (1796-1869)

Loewe's ballads and Liszt's songs reveal another side of the lieder literature. Writing in the tradition of Zumsteeg, one of the earliest ballad composers whose works also influenced the young Schubert, Loewe favored narrative poems based on supernatural subject matter. Indeed, ghosts and goblins inspired his best works. We might speculate that his affinity for the underworld originated during his childhood, which he spent in the coal-mining town of Loebejuen, near Halle. Although Loewe wrote symphonies, concertos, numerous piano pieces, five operas, over a dozen oratorios, and approximately 360 songs, his most significant vocal compositions are his ballads, whose stylistic features are summarized below.

Loewe preferred syllabic text settings, with tremolando accompaniments that often resemble piano reductions of orchestral scores. Despite their pseudo-virtuoso appearance on the printed page, most figurations are simple to execute and unfortunately show little ingenuity. Occasionally the pianist begins the lied, but only rarely must he play a full-fledged prelude, postlude, or even interlude of extended length. Because Loewe was primarily a singer, we can understand his greater concern for the vocal line, which he invariably doubles in the treble or bass of the accompaniment. His melodies are eminently singable. Their simplicity and squareness make them easy to remember and therefore appealing to unsophisticated audiences. Loewe excludes fioriture in keeping with the folklike nature of the ballad, but often includes entire bars in monotone. The omission of melismata in the vocal line and the lack of unusual figurations in the accompaniment suggest that the composer tried to imitate the more natural, declamatory style of folk singers. Loewe rarely experiments harmonically. He reserves appoggiaturas and other dissonances for effective expression of the text. Occasionally he uses imitation between the voice and piano parts. Although he inserts lengthy sections of undifferentiated rhythmic figures, Loewe achieves variety with alternating and irregular meters as well as irregular phrase lengths, all of which help to underline the folksy nature of these ballads.

Of the five works we shall examine, *Edward* (No. 1), a setting of

Herder's translation of the Scots poem from his *Stimmen der Völker,* and Goethe's *Erlkönig* (No. 2) represent the work of the young Loewe. Besides *Erlkönig*—which was published the same year as Schubert's, although Schubert had written his setting three years earlier—Loewe set a number of Goethe's ballads, two of which (*Die wandelnde Glocke,* No. 3, and *Der getreue Eckart,* No. 4) we have included. *Prinz Eugen* (No. 5) by Ferdinand Freiligrath, a poet less well known to American readers, inspired one of Loewe's best ballads. This song, too, has an element of the supernatural about it.

HERDER (1744-1803)

Edward

Dein Schwert, wie ist's von Blut so rot?
Edward, Edward!
Dein Schwert, wie ist's von Blut so rot?
Und gehst so traurig da? O!

Ich hab geschlagen meinen Geier tot,
Mutter, Mutter!
Ich hab geschlagen meinen Geier tot,
Und das, das geht mir nah. O!

Deines Geiers Blut ist nicht so rot,
Edward, Edward!
Deines Geiers Blut ist nicht so rot,
Mein Sohn, bekenn mir frei. O!

Ich hab geschlagen mein Rotross tot,
Mutter, Mutter!
Ich hab geschlagen mein Rotross tot,
Und's war so stolz und treu. O!

Dein Ross war alt und hast's nicht not,
Edward, Edward!
Dein Ross war alt und hast's nicht not,
Dich drückt ein andrer Schmerz. O!

The German form of the ballad *Edward* is obviously one step removed from the Scottish original, for it is a translation by Johann Gottfried von Herder, a friend and, for a time, mentor of Goethe's. He was a passionate collector and skilled translator of folk poetry of many nations, his enthusiasm being linked to a belief that man sang before he spoke, or that poetry preceded prose, and that folk literature was somehow the expression of a "folk soul." These romantic and discredited notions did not impair his art as a translator, however, and his rendition of the Scottish ballad captures much of the spirit and sense of the original. What it does not impart is the characteristic flavor of the Scots dialect. It would, in fact, be incongruous to attempt to duplicate this in German. The antiquarian air is lightly indicated by the occasional use of more archaic word order, rather than by resorting to archaic vocabulary. Herder retains the meter and general verse form of the original, including the recurrent interjection "O" at the end of every fourth line. It is customary to call such a syllable a "meter-

> "Why dois your brand sae drap wi bluid,
> Edward, Edward,
> Why dois your brand sae drap wi bluid,
> And why sae sad gang yee O?"
>
> "O I hae killed my hauke sae guid,
> Mither, mither,
> O I hae killed my hauke sae guid,
> And I had nae mair bot hee O."
>
> "Your haukis bluid was nevir sae reid,
> Edward, Edward,
> Your haukis bluid was nevir sae reid,
> My deir son I tell thee O."
>
> "O I hae killed my reid-roan steid,
> Mither, mither,
> O I hae killed my reid-roan steid,
> That erst was sae fair and frie O."
>
> "Your steid was auld, and ye hae got mair,
> Edward, Edward,
> Your steid was auld, and ye hae got mair,
> Sum other dule ye drie O."

Ich hab geschlagen meinen Vater tot!
Mutter, Mutter!
Ich hab geschlagen meinen Vater tot!
Und das, das quält mein Herz! O!

Und was wirst du nun an dir tun,
Edward, Edward?
Und was wirst du nun an dir tun,
Mein Sohn, das sage mir! O!

Auf Erden soll mein Fuss nicht ruhn!
Mutter, Mutter!
Auf Erden soll mein Fuss nicht ruhn!
Will wandern übers Meer! O!

Und was soll werden dein Hof und Hall,
Edward, Edward?
Und was soll werden dein Hof und Hall,
So herrlich sonst, so schön? O!

Ach immer steh's und sink und fall
Mutter, Mutter!
Ach immer steh's und sink und fall,
Ich werd es nimmer sehn! O!

Und was soll werden aus Weib und Kind,
Edward, Edward?
Und was soll werden aus Weib und Kind,
Wann du gehst über's Meer? O!

Die Welt ist gross, lass sie betteln drin,
Mutter, Mutter!
Die Welt ist gross, lass sie betteln drin,
Ich seh sie nimmermehr! O!

Und was soll deine Mutter tun,
Edward, Edward?
Und was soll deine Mutter tun,
Mein Sohn, das sage mir? O!

Der Fluch der Hölle soll auf euch ruhn!
Mutter, Mutter!
Der Fluch der Hölle soll auf euch ruhn!
Denn ihr, ihr rietet's mir! O!

"O I hae killed my fadir deir,
Mither, mither,
O I hae killed my fadir deir,
Alas, and wae is mee O!"

"And whatten penance wul ye drie for that,
Edward, Edward,
And whatten penance wul ye drie for that?
My deir son, now tell me O."

"Ile set my feit in yonder boat,
Mither, mither,
Ile set my feit in yonder boat,
And Ile fare ovir the sea O."

"And what wul ye doe wi your towirs and your ha,
Edward, Edward,
And what wul ye doe wi your towirs and your ha,
That were sae fair to see O?"

"Ile let thame stand tul they doun fa,
Mither, mither,
Ile let thame stand tul they doun fa,
For here nevir mair maun I bee O."

"And what wul ye leive to your bairns and your wife,
Edward, Edward?
And what wul ye leive to your bairns and your wife,
Whan ye gang ovir the sea O?"

"The warld is room, late them beg thrae life,
Mither, mither,
The warld is room, late them beg thrae life,
For thame nevir mair wul I see O."

"And what wul ye leive to your ain mither deir,
Edward, Edward?
And what wul ye leive to your ain mither deir,
My deir son, now tell me O."

"The curse of hell frae me sall ye beir,
Mither, mither,
The curse of hell frae me sall ye beir,
Sic counseils ye gave to me O."

filler," but its employment in the ballad is almost an expected feature, an idiomatic mark of the genre. It is clearly more at home in the original work, where it is practically felt as part of the preceding word. In the German translation this is not so, and the "O!" is separated by an uneasy pause, after which it is duly inserted as an addendum. This separation, slight as it is, calls attention to the ugly duckling and imparts to the syllable an emphasis which it was never meant to have. Part of the essence of the balladic idiom consists of the matter-of-fact utterance of such syllables. They must not be turned into great amens. Herder provides each "O" with an exclamation point, whereas the Scots ballad employs only one, in the sixth stanza, and even that has reference to other words ("wae is mee").

Herder chooses to vary the austere rhyme scheme of the original and to replace the unvarying rhyme of the final line in each stanza (yee, thee, mee, etc.) with greater diversity. The final lines of Herder's stanzas 1 and 2 rhyme (*da: nah*), as do those of 3 and 4 (*frei: treu*, which counts as a rhyme in German verse), 5 and 6 (*Schmerz: Herz*), 9 and 10 (*schön: sehn* = a rhyme); in 7 and 8, assonance is employed (*mir: Meer*), while 11 and 12 have "perfect" rhyme in standard German (*Meer: mehr*), although this may well have been assonance in Herder's East Prussian pronunciation. The last two stanzas show identity (*mir: mir*).

To offset this gratuitously introduced variety, Herder uses rather less diversity of rhyme than the Scots ballad in the first two lines of each stanza. It is debatable whether the alteration is an improvement or not. It is not easy to transform a Scots scone into German gingerbread. The division into stanzas, by the way, is an arbitrary procedure. Herder's fourteen stanzas correspond to seven in the Scots original, as usually printed. To a composer there is, of course, a difference, unless he uses through composition. A natural division is given by the dialogue form and the alternation between mother and son, a feature which can be exploited in music.

The opening line of the original "Why dois your brand sae drap wi bluid [Why does your sword so drip with blood]?" is deprived of its ghastly actuality by Herder's more passive rendition, *Dein Schwert, wie ist's von Blut so rot?* ("Your sword, why is it so red with blood?"), and this difference between graphic process and static result is seen more than once in the German. Once or twice the rendition is infelicitous in the extreme: *Und was soll deine Mutter tun?* ("And what is your mother to do?") hardly reproduces the force of "And what wul ye leive to your ain mither deir?" which leads inexorably to the "curse of hell."

The choice of *Geier* ("vulture") to translate "hauke" is somewhat baffling. German has *Habicht* "hawk" and *Falke* "falcon," each of which would suit metrically and would be more appropriate in the present context than their carrion-consuming cousin, the vulture.

The mood and subject matter of a ballad are out of the ordinary. There is frequently an uncanny atmosphere of tragedy, of supernatural occurrences, of phantoms, of bloody crimes. Sometimes there is a clash between man and the forces of evil. But there is usually no specific preaching or underscored moral.

This ballad increases in intensity as the actual source of the dripping blood on Edward's sword is revealed, after two patently evasive explanations. It is the mother, despite her complicity, who elicits the truth with the cold-bloodedness of Lady Macbeth. We know that neither hawk nor steed can be the source; and while anticipating a human foe, we are shattered, upon our first reading, at learning who has been slain: "My father." Then, in another sequence, the mother asks what will become of Edward's possessions and family, and, finally, what he will leave her. "The curse of hell" is the devastating answer, "sic [such] counseils ye gave to me." Herder's translation of this line partly destroys the indirectness of the Scots version by saying too bluntly that the mother counseled the patricidal deed, whereas the original lets us surmise this while allowing us to think there is more to those counsels, perhaps a lifetime of twisted upbringing. The last line is shattering enough, and it is to the artistic credit of the unknown author that there is no reply on the mother's part. At any rate, both the Scots and the German succinctly sketch a stark drama with overtones of a "Greek" tragedy. Consummate economy is employed in delineating the characters, and the motives behind the deed are only dimly suggested. A successful musical setting should achieve no more and no less.

Notes on the Scots text:

1   *dois:* "does"; *brand:* "sword."
4   *gang:* "go."
5   *guid:* "good."
8   *nae:* "no"; *mair:* "more."
9   *reid:* "red."
13 *reid-roan steid:* "red-roan steed."
16 *erst:* "once"; *frie:* "good, fine."
20 *dule:* "pain"; *drie:* "suffer, bear."
29 *feit:* "feet."

33 *ha:* "hall."
37 *fa:* "fall."
41 *bairns:* "children."
45 *thrae:* "through."
49 *ain:* "own."
53 *frae:* "from"; *sall:* "shall."
56 *Sic:* "such."

Notes on the German text:

13 *Rotross: Ross* "steed" has the same poetic flavor as English "steed." The compound is not a usual one.
25 The German is ambiguous; cf. the original "whatten penance."
37 *steh's:* 's "it," or the whole complex of towers and hall; hence "them."
40 *nimmer:* poetic and archaic for "never" (otherwise *nie, niemals*).
45 *lass sie betteln drin:* reminiscent of Heine's *Lass sie betteln gehn* in *Die beiden Grenadiere,* with an obvious difference of motivation. The anticipated fate of the innocent family is here connected with the father's treachery; in Heine's ballad, loyalty to the Emperor is the cause.

Op. 1 (1818)

Pianist and vocalist begin together with the singer's stepwise melody doubled in the treble of the accompaniment. The recurrent rhythmic figure in the singer's part is also duplicated by the pianist in a homo-rhythmic pattern for the first stanza, the last five bars of which appear opposite (Ex. 27-a).

In order to stress the agitation of the mother and her son, Loewe has cleverly given each of them a different meter: $\frac{6}{8}$ for the boldly questioning mother (see Ex. 27-a) and $\frac{2}{4}$ (considerably varied within the basic beat) for her nervous, excitable son. Having established two basic musical designs for the first two stanzas, Loewe repeats them almost literally for the next two stanzas, giving the listener the sense of a strophic setting that follows the stanzaic divisions of the poem. From this point (Ex. 27-b) to the end of the ballad, Loewe varies the accompanimental figures and ends finally with arpeggios in contrary motion.

Ex. 27

LOEWE: *Edward* †

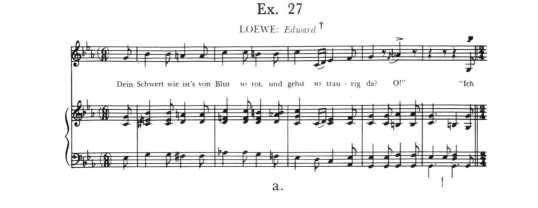

Dein Schwert wie ist's von Blut so rot, und gehst so trau - rig da? O!" "Ich

a.

Ich hab ge - schlagen meinen Va - ter tot!

Mut - ter! Mut - ter! Ich hab ge - schlagen meinen

b.

The vocal melody, following the syllables of the text, suggests the breathlessness of the narrators, which the composer controls with a slow harmonic rhythm (infrequent chord changes) or a pedal point.

Edward is through-composed, the music changing with the text. Nevertheless, because Loewe has coordinated his changes of accompaniment, rhythm, meter, melody, and harmony to parallel the stanzas of the poem,

† Original key: E minor.

the listener hears the separate strophes as he would see them in the printed poem. The composer uses irregular nine-bar phrases through Edward's second statement, at which point (see * in Ex. 27-b) he starts extending his musical sections first to eighteen bars and later to twenty-four bars, before returning to his original nine-bar phrase. In sum, *Edward* is a remarkable achievement for a very young man. Among several other settings of this poem, the reader might compare Schubert's *Eine altschottische Ballade,* which exists in two versions (D. 932 a and b), both published posthumously, and also Brahms's setting for alto and tenor, Op. 75, No. 1, of his *Balladen und Romanzen* of 1878. Brahms also wrote a *Ballade* for solo piano, Op. 10, No. 1 (1856), based on this grisly tale.

GOETHE

Erlkönig, Op. 1, No. 3

Loewe's *Erlkönig* was written in 1818, a mere three years after Schubert wrote his setting of the same text (see p. 37). Loewe immediately captures the eerie atmosphere of the poem in his use of a tremolando over the tonic pedal with which the pianist begins the song (see Ex. 28-a). After two introductory bars, the singer starts his narrative fully supported by bass octaves in the accompaniment which double his vocal line. The pianist's scalewise figure spans two octaves (see * Ex. 28-a), stretching far beyond the ninth (F sharp to G) required of the singer and unfortunately losing its effectiveness through its extension. The composer's choice of compound-triple meter ($\frac{9}{8}$), in combination with a syllabic text setting, forces the vocalist to crowd six to nine syllables into one bar. Although clear-cut enunciation of the text is consequently difficult, it is nevertheless mandatory for an effective rendition.

Three different persons as well as the narrator are heard in the course of the ballad: the narrator has the outer stanzas, the father the second, the Erlking the third, fifth, and seventh, and the boy the fourth and sixth. The accompaniment changes for each stanza, the new material usually beginning in the short piano interlude before the singer starts the next stanza. Sometimes the composer changes the key or the mode (from minor to major) as well. Unfortunately, in Loewe's *Erlkönig* none of these changes is sufficiently sharp to catch the listener's attention the first time he hears

Ex. 28
LOEWE: *Erlkönig*[†]

Wer rei - tet so spät durch Nacht und Wind?

a.

them. Then too, we notice changes occurring in the middle of a phrase (see bar 8 at *Knaben wohl*), without any rational justification for the alteration at this point in the poem. Whereas Loewe achieves a degree of contrast by means of these slight diversifications of key and figuration, he attains effective unification of the entire ballad through the inclusion of a persistent sixteenth-note tremolando that appears in all but about ten of the ninety-five bars of the piece. By and large, the vocal part consists of a stepwise melody with leaps within the chord. Occasional bars in monotone may reflect his desire to retain the ballad singer's style.

In five of the eight stanzas, Loewe repeats the last line of the text, presumably to round off the musical phrase. (Goethe does not seem to have resented these alterations. We know he preferred this setting to Schubert's.) At bar 47 the tritone (F sharp/C) pierces the accompaniment; inasmuch as the pianist is alone at this point, we cannot say that the sound reflects the meaning of the text. Instead, it might be considered a warning. Toward the close of the ballad, on *grauset's*, Loewe begins a descent by thirds through the supermediant, the mediant (in major mode), the tonic major, and finally the tonic minor home key. The last four words are in recitative, with the pianist's final bars providing the musical resolution for both singer and pianist. (See Ex. 28-b.)

† Original key: G minor.

b.

After listening to Loewe's *Erlkönig*, it is difficult not to compare it with Schubert's well-known treatment of the poem. Schubert represents each of the four characters with a particular key, figuration, range, melodic profile, and color. He does not repeat any section of the text and often uses the accompaniment to reflect the meaning of the words. Compare, for example, both composers' settings of the fourth stanza; notice particularly Schubert's use of minor seconds (D–E flat) as the child shrieks *Mein Vater!* (Cf. Ex. 6-c, on p. 38.) Compare also the musical caresses that Schubert bestows on the Erlking's vocal line at *spiel' ich mit dir* and at *wiegen und tanzen . . . ein.* Perhaps as a result of his having seen the Schubert piece before he composed his own setting of the poem, Loewe has taken considerably more pains with the pianist's material here than with the vocalist's part. According to his daughter, however, he was not influenced by Schubert's version other than to say that he felt he could do better. Both composers use recitative to close, but Loewe's last few bars seem more appropriate than Schubert's two chords.

Die wandelnde Glocke

Es war ein Kind, das wollte nie
Zur Kirche sich bequemen,
Und Sonntags fand es stets ein Wie,
Den Weg ins Feld zu nehmen.

Die Mutter sprach: Die Glocke tönt,
Und so ist dir's befohlen,
Und hast du dich nicht hingewöhnt,
Sie kommt und wird dich holen.

Das Kind, es denkt: die Glocke hängt
Da droben auf dem Stuhle.
Schon hat's den Weg ins Feld gelenkt,
Als lief' es aus der Schule.

Die Glocke Glocke tönt nicht mehr,
Die Mutter hat gefackelt.
Doch, welch ein Schrecken! hinterher
Die Glocke kommt gewackelt.

Sie wackelt schnell, man glaubt es kaum!
Das arme Kind im Schrecken,
Es lauft, es kommt, als wie im Traum:
Die Glocke wird es decken.

Doch nimmt es richtig seinen Husch,
Und mit gewandter Schnelle
Eilt es durch Anger, Feld und Busch
Zur Kirche, zur Kapelle.

Und jeden Sonn- und Feiertag
Gedenkt es an den Schaden,
Lässt durch den ersten Glockenschlag,
Nicht in Person sich laden.

A rather sadistic joke on a small boy is behind this ballad. Goethe's son August and the latter's tutor, Riemer, convinced the boy that the bell might come down from the belfry, come waddling across the marketplace, and let itself down over him. August demonstrated with an open umbrella the waddling motion of the bell. This was allegedly reinforced by the sight of bell-shaped hills in Bohemia, which gave Goethe the impression, as he rode by, that they were moving toward him, chasing him.

The child in this ballad has reason to be just as terrified as the boy in *Erlkönig*, yet Goethe takes it far less seriously. In fact, a cheap moral is drawn which is almost unworthy of the poet.

Notes on the text:

2   *sich bequemen:* "reconcile himself to the idea of going."
3   *stets:* "always."
    ein Wie: "a how, a way." This nominalization (turning into a noun) of practically any part of speech is called "hypostasis." Cf. English "no ifs, ands, or buts."

6   The first indication of personification of the bell is in the word
     befohlen ("you've been ordered").

7   *und hast du dich nicht hingewöhnt:* "if you haven't got used to
     the idea of going there," from *dich gewöhnen* ("accustom your-
     self") and *hin* ("hither, to that place").

8   *sie:* "it" (the bell; perhaps the bell is conceived of as a sort of
     female monster, being feminine).

9   *Das Kind, es denkt:* "folksy" style.

10   *Stuhl:* "belfry."

11   *Schon hat's:* 's=es (the child).

13   *Glocke, Glocke:* the repetition is possibly intended as imitation
     of child's speech.

14   *gefackelt: fackeln* formerly meant "to hem and haw, hesitate"
     (from the uncertain flickering of a torch [*Fackel*]), then "to fib."

16   *kommt gewackelt:* "comes waddling." Where English has a present
     participle, German has, in these constructions, a perfect participle
     (cf. *kommt ein Vogel geflogen*).

20   *decken:* "cover, enclose, smother."

21   *Husch:* "whisk, whir, rapid flight."

27-28:   These last two lines mean "accepts the invitation at the first
     stroke of the bell and doesn't wait to be asked in person." Despite
     the rather mocking tone used by Goethe, this ballad has appealed
     to several composers.

Op. 20 (1832)

Die wandelnde Glocke sounds like a good example of an anonymous
folk song of the nursery variety. The carefree, casual air of this lied, however, belies the efforts the composer has expended on its construction. It is
a genuine tone poem in miniature. The simple, unpretentious accompaniment does all that is required of a musical background without drawing
attention to itself. It is in the accompaniment that we hear the sound of
the pealing bell. Through the pendulum-like movement of the bell we
sense the pulse as well as the pace of the story.

On first hearing, the lied sounds strophic, as if the composer had used
the same melody for each group of two stanzas; Loewe, however, has
written a through-composed setting. He captures the strophic divisions of
the poem through the recurrence of one catchy tune. Singer and pianist

state this playful melody at the outset and remain together with precise regularity. The undifferentiated eighth notes of the tune are doubled in the treble of the accompaniment. The two groups of four bars that shape each stanza fit together in the manner of antecedent and consequent phrases. They form a single unit which Loewe states twice before concluding with a four-bar transition for the piano. The diagram below illustrates the subtlety of what appears to be a straightforward design:

4 + 4 bars	=	first stanza
4 + 4 bars	=	second stanza
4 bars	=	transition
4 + 4 bars	=	third stanza
4 bars	=	half of fourth stanza
2 bars	=	interlude
4 bars	=	last half of fourth stanza
4 + 4 + 2 bars	=	fifth stanza
4 + 4 bars	=	sixth stanza
4 + 4 + 1 bars	=	seventh stanza
2 bars	=	postlude

Despite the limitations of a simple setting, Loewe is able to accentuate the highlights of the poem. Notice that at *Die Mutter sprach* (see Ex. 29) the bell strikes three times in the inner voice of the accompaniment (at *).

Ex. 29

LOEWE: *Die wandelnde Glocke*

The mother's concern, heightened by the clanging bell, the carefree mood of the children, and their subsequent flight when they feel threatened by the moving bell are all reflected in the accompaniment. Notice, for example, how the figuration that represents the repeated bell sound accelerates from the eight notes per bar (bars 33 ff.) to twelve notes in each bar (see triplets in bars 53 ff.), increasing the children's terror and causing them to run away even faster.

On a trip to Karlsbad, Goethe was told a ghost story by his secretary, Mr. John. Goethe put it into verse form the same day. The story was

Der getreue Eckart

"O wären wir weiter, o wär' ich zu Haus!
Sie kommen. Da kommt schon der nächtliche Graus;
Sie sind's die unholdigen Schwestern.
Sie streifen heran und sie finden uns hier,
Sie trinken das mühsam geholte das Bier,
Und lassen nur leer uns die Krüge."

So sprechen die Kinder und drücken sich schnell;
Da zeigt sich vor ihnen ein alter Gesell:
"Nur stille, Kind! Kinderlein, stille!
Die Hulden sie kommen von durstiger Jagd,
Und lasst ihr sie trinken wie's jeder behagt,
Dann sind sie euch hold die Unholden."

Gesagt so geschehn! und da naht sich der Graus
Und siehet so grau und so schattenhaft aus,
Doch schlürft es und schlampft es aufs beste.
Das Bier ist verschwunden, die Krüge sind leer;
Nun saust es und braust es, das wütige Heer,
Ins weite Getal und Gebirge.

Die Kinderlein ängstlich gen Hause so schnell,
Gesellt sich zu ihnen der fromme Gesell:
"Ihr Püppchen, nur seid mir nicht traurig."--
"Wir kriegen nun Schelten und Streich' bis aufs Blut."--
"Nein keineswegs, alles geht herrlich und gut,
Nur schweiget und horchet wie Mäuslein.

Und der es euch anrät und der es befiehlt,
Er ist es, der gern mit den Kindelein spielt,
Der alte Getreue, der Eckart.
Vom Wundermann hat man euch immer erzählt,
Nur hat die Bestätigung jedem gefehlt,
Die habt ihr nun köstlich in Händen."

Sie kommen nach Hause, sie setzen den Krug
Ein jedes den Eltern bescheiden genug
Und harren der Schläg' und der Schelten.
Doch siehe man kostet: ein herrliches Bier!
Man trinkt in die Runde schon dreimal und vier
Und noch nimmt der Krug nicht ein Ende.

Das Wunder es dauert zum morgenden Tag.
Doch fraget wer immer zu fragen vermag:
Wie ist's mit den Krügen ergangen?
Die Mäuslein sie lächeln, im stillen ergetzt:
Sie stammeln und stottern und schwatzen zuletzt
Und gleich sind vertrocknet die Krüge.

Und wenn euch, ihr Kinder, mit treuem Gesicht
Ein Vater, ein Lehrer, ein Aldermann spricht,
So horchet und folget ihm pünktlich!
Und liegt auch das Zünglein in peinlicher Hut,
Verplaudern ist schädlich, verschweigen ist gut;
Dann füllt sich das Bier in den Krügen.

one of local tradition. It is found, in one version, in the *Thuringian Chronicle*. Once, in the Thuringian village of Schwarze, Frau Holla (or Hulda) and her raging host of female furies passed through, after Faithful Eckart had gone ahead to warn the people to keep out of the way. Two boys on the way home from a neighboring village, where they had bought beer for their parents, saw the approaching shadows and hid in some nook or cranny. But some of the furies rushed at them, emptied the beer jugs, and moved on with a great rush and roar. When the commotion had ceased, the boys resumed their homeward way, wondering how they could convincingly explain the incident to their parents. While they were deliberating, Eckart came to them and said that they had done right to let the furies have the beer, for, had they resisted, the pleasant supernatural ladies would have wrung their necks. The boys found this to be only cold comfort, for they expected their fathers to emulate the furies in punishing them for the loss of the precious beer. But old Eckart urged them to proceed unafraid: "When you get home, the jugs will be full, and they will remain so as long as you keep quiet about this little happening. But as soon as you break your silence, the jugs will be empty."

That is probably the gist of the story as told to Goethe. There are other versions, and Eckart and the furies are known in other stories. Goethe omits any reference to the nature symbolism of Eckart and the wild nocturnal host. He seems, however, to emphasize the didactic side of the tale: "Children, obey your elders, especially when they tell you to keep quiet!"

The mysterious female spirits in Goethe's ballad are not excessively malevolent. Grimm thought that Christianity had turned the old *Hulden* ("gracious spirits") into *Unholden* ("demons"). But the designation of such

spirits as "gracious" is an example of euphemism—calling something unpleasant by a pleasant name. The Greek Eumenides ("well-meaning ones")
were the Furies.

In Goethe's poem, Eckart refers to the furies by both names, *die
Hulden* ("the gracious ones") and also *die Unholden* ("the demonic ones").
The children refer to them as *unholdige Schwestern* ("monstrous sisters").
Goethe leaves the figure of Eckart himself slightly obscure, apparently on
purpose. In German legend he is an old man with a white wand who pre-
cedes the raging horde of furies and warns people to go home or keep out
of the way. He is also the kindly admonisher who sits at the entrance to
the Venusberg and warns mortals (like Tannhäuser) not to enter. In any
case he is a sort of protective go-between, or buffer character, between man
and the supernatural. Goethe calls him, among other things, the *Wundermann*, of whom all children have heard.

In the first strophe the terror of the children is shown. At first, all
speak ("If only we were nearer home!"); then each thinks to himself ("I
wish I were home!"). The repeated awed reference to the spirits as "they"
is a sign of the horror the children feel. "They're coming!" The children
also stumble over words. Eckart appears; at first he is only "an old fellow"
(*ein alter Gesell*). He informs the children that the "gracious ones" are
coming from a hunt that has made them thirsty and says that it would be
advisable to let them drink. In the third strophe the rapidity of action is
indicated, as well as the vagueness of the shadowy forms. They come and
guzzle noisily—they are real enough for that—and then roar away like
the wind. In this strophe there are some twenty-five instances of sibilant
sounds (*s* or *sch*), no doubt to represent the eerie rushing of the ghostly
horde. The children pick themselves up and hurry home, terrified by
their experience and unhappy at the prospect of the beating they all
expect. Then the assurance of Eckart is inserted, plus the admonition
"All will be well if you keep quiet." In the fifth strophe, Eckart identifies
himself by name and by the title *Wundermann*, which he is sure they have
often heard. Now they are to have vivid proof of his effectiveness. In
strophes six and seven the narration continues in childlike tones, as Goethe
takes many "folksy" liberties with the language. Despite Eckart's assurances,
they are still frightened. But the miracle does occur, and it lasts as long
as the children do not reveal the source of the beer. When they finally can
no longer restrain themselves, the beer dries up. The final strophe contains the moral, a not entirely consistent one, for Eckart is equated with

their elders, whereas he is certainly something more than a human being of advanced age!

Notes on the text:

5   *das mühsam geholte das Bier:* the children stumble over the words; but this kind of structure is part of folk language anyway.

7   *drücken sich:* "duck down" in the hope that the uncanny spirits will fly over them.

9   *Kind! Kinderlein:* Eckart speaks first to one, then to all. This is an inverted parallelism to line 1: first they all speak, then one.

13 *Gesagt so geschehn:* refers to Eckart's admonition and prophecy of what was about to happen. (Pedantically we might expect *so gesagt, so geschehn,* or *gesagt, geschehn*).

15 *schlampft:* not a common verb (*schlampt* is more usual, but not much more). It means to drink up noisily and to lick one's chops while so doing—to guzzle.

19 *Kinderlein:* one of those striking formations in which the diminutive ending -*lein* follows the plural ending. In line 26 Goethe uses still another form, *Kindelein,* which is, however, differently derived.

31 *sie setzen* instead of *vorsetzen* is colloquial, or folk language.

35 *dreimal und vier* instead of *drei oder viermal,* or the like.

40 *Mäuslein:* a word of endearment for children; it also harks back to line 24 and to Eckart's warning to them to be still as mice.

44 *Aldermann:* as the "d" indicates (for expected "t"), this cannot be an inherited word of ancient Germanic vintage; it seems to be from English or Low German dialect.

The rhyme scheme should be noted: *a a B c c D*

The third and sixth lines are not rhymed with anything. Such a jagged, jarring device is often used to indicate the uncanny, the imperfect, the unfinished, the uncertain. The rhymes are all masculine: *Haus: Graus, hier: Bier.* The unrhymed lines end in an accented beat followed by an unaccented one. (These would, if rhyming, constitute feminine rhymes.)

Op. 44 (1835)

Here we turn again to a folk tale with elements of the supernatural. Loewe divides the eight stanzas of the poem into two musical parts, *a* and *b*. Part *a*, characterized by a densely textured accompaniment with persistent movement in sixteenth notes, appropriately underlines the first three stanzas. Part *b*, set in another key, features a different melody, rhythm, meter, and texture; it provides the musical background for the last five stanzas.

Stormy, chromatic, and in the minor mode, the first part consists of rapidly alternating figurations in the accompaniment that support a stepwise melody in the voice. Loewe uses a succession of arpeggiated diminished seventh chords, recognizing their suspenseful quality. Although he maintains a predominantly syllabic text setting, he also includes occasional instances of neumatic setting (a few notes to one syllable) as in *Schwestern* (bar 10) and *Gebirge* (bar 46). The excellent rhythmic drive in this ballad is closely related to the composer's artful juxtaposition of different phrase lengths. In the first stanza, notice how he progresses from groups of four bars (in the piano introduction and also in the opening vocal phrase) to eight bars which are extended to ten by the addition of two transitional bars for the pianist. Except for slight modifications in their melodic profile, the next two stanzas repeat the music and pattern of the first. Notice also that the first two stanzas end on the dominant and press to resolve to the tonic at the conclusion of the third stanza. Loewe employs this harmonic design also in *Die wandelnde Glocke* (see p. 197), holding back from the tonic

Ex. 30

LOEWE: *Der getreue Eckart*

in order to establish a stronger point of articulation on arrival there. The pianist closes this first section of the ballad with furiously rushing arpeggios in contrary motion.

The lovely second section in the relative major, $\frac{6}{8}$ meter, and Mahlerian type of *Ländler* melody (see Ex. 30) describes the events that lead to the moral of the story. Loewe uses his customary syllabic text setting stated in relatively undifferentiated rhythmic patterns, but he achieves variety and contrast again through phrase lengths, three groups of four bars with piano interludes occurring at unexpected places. For example, there is no musical pause between the fourth and fifth stanzas. Instead, a piano interlude in the middle of the fifth stanza supplies a change of texture, incorporating Eckart's motive in imitation between the treble and bass of the accompaniment. The sixth and seventh stanzas duplicate this procedure. The last stanza contains the melody of the opening of the fourth and the closing of the fifth stanzas, thereby integrating the material. The pianist concludes with echoes of Eckart's motive in a short postlude.

FERDINAND FREILIGRATH (1810-76)

Ferdinand Freiligrath combined, in strange medley, the feelings and activities of a revolutionary with lively interest in exotic verse. Evidently an honest man, he voluntarily renounced the king's proffered patronage and went into exile because of his political convictions. He collaborated with Karl Marx in editing the *Neue Rheinische Zeitung*.

Prinz Eugen, der edle Ritter

Zelte, Posten, Werderufer!
Lust'ge Nacht am Donauufer!
Pferde stehn im Kreis umher
Angebunden an den Pflöcken;
An den engen Sattelböcken
Hangen Karabiner schwer.

Um das Feuer auf der Erde,
Vor den Hufen seiner Pferde
Liegt das östreichsche Piket.
Auf dem Mantel liegt ein jeder;
Von den Tschackos weht die Feder,
Leutnant würfelt und Kornet.

Neben seinem müden Schecken
Ruht auf einer wollnen Decken
Der Trompeter ganz allein:
"Lasst die Knöchel, lasst die Karten!
Kaiserliche Feldstandarten
Wird ein Reiterlied erfreun!

Vor acht Tagen die Affaire
Hab ich, zu Nutz dem ganzen Heere,
In gehör'gen Reim gebracht;
Selber auch gesetzt die Noten;
Drum, ihr Weissen und ihr Roten!
Merket auf und gebet Acht!"

Und er singt die neue Weise
Einmal, zweimal, dreimal leise
Denen Reitersleuten vor;
Und wie er zum letzten Male
Endet, bricht mit einem Male
Los der volle, kräft'ge Chor:

"Prinz Eugen, der edle Ritter!"
Hei, das klang wie Ungewitter
Weit in's Türkenlager hin.
Der Trompeter tät den Schnurrbart streichen
Und sich auf die Seite schleichen
Zu der Marketenderin.

The ballad *Prinz Eugen, der edle Ritter* ("Prince Eugene, Noble Knight") has as its theme "a song is born"; it tells of the imaginary origin of a folk song, *Prinz Eugen vor Belgrad,* which had as its first line *Prinz Eugenius, der edle Ritter.* It is noteworthy that Freiligrath does not regard the birth of that song in the traditionally believed way, with the whole folk participating as joint authors. Rather, he ascribes words and music to a specific individual, the trumpeter. But it quickly becomes common property, for it catches on after it is sung two or three times by the composer, being taken up by the whole chorus of soldiers and lustily sung as if already an old favorite. Having created a hit, the trumpeter roguishly steals away to join the canteen woman.

But the origin of that song, while apparently the theme of the ballad, is really the excuse for Freiligrath's verses, which are more concerned with the atmosphere of army life and the goings-on in the Austrian camp between battles. The sentries, horses, officers and men, the campfire, uniforms, the dice games—all are fully as important as the newly composed song celebrating a victory over the Turks one week before. The strains of that song, fittingly enough, carry across to the Turkish camp.

Missing from the ballad are the elements of uncanniness, the supernatural, violent passions, clashes of will; the only feature approaching any of them is the spectacular way in which the new song spreads, but this is far from magical. A poem of mood, atmosphere, and word pictures, this ballad must be regarded as atypical. Yet it has, for all that, much of the flavor we associate with the ballad, and it affords the composer an opportunity to apply his art.

Notes on the text:

1   *Werdarufer: Wer da* = "Who goes there?" "Who-goes-there-callers" = sentries, guards.

11   *Tschacko, Tschako:* a military cap, cylindrical or in the form of a truncated cone, with a visor and plume (a Hungarian word originally; cf. *csákó* "hussar's helmet"). The English name is "shako."

12   *würfelt:* "shoots dice, plays dice." (*Würfel* "die" is from *werfen* "throw.")
     Kornet: "cornet," an officer in a troop of cavalry who carried the colors.

13   *Scheck(en):* "checked"; a dappled horse.

16   *Knöchel:* literally "knuckles, bones," then "dice" (cf. slang "bones").

36   *Marketenderin:* a "canteen woman," a female follower of the troops who sold all sorts of wares to the soldiers.

Op. 92 (1844)

Prinz Eugen represents one of Loewe's most felicitous efforts to blend text and tone. Not one unessential note or superfluous ornament mars this fine setting, in which pianist and singer together relate the origin of the ballad *Prinz Eugen* with one basic accompanying figuration. Again a syllabic text setting receives its support in the accompaniment, in this instance the low bass. Observe how this opening triadic melody—unusual for

Loewe, who seems to prefer scalar melodies—resembles the beginning of Kurt Weill's "Mac the Knife." The melody that serves for the third and fourth stanzas reverts to the conjunct style; the last two stanzas are also predominantly stepwise, except for significant octave and fourth leaps meant to be brought out by singer and pianist.

Loewe ingeniously employs a $\frac{5}{4}$ meter and frequently stresses the last eighth or quarter note in the bar, avoiding the customary accent of the first beat. Extremely significant is the complete absence of a long note as the first in any bar of the song. This intentional diminution of the note immediately following the barline attracts the listener and draws him further and further into the story. The divisions in these $\frac{5}{4}$ bars appear to be basically three and two, with the fermata falling on the last quarter of a group of two (see Ex. 31). The pattern of the fermatas within each seven-measure stanza is in itself interesting:

The musical accentuation created by the fermatas is, curiously, totally independent of the accentuation of the text.

Ex. 31

LOEWE: *Prinz Eugen* †

Zel - te, Po - sten,   Wer da rufer! Lust'ge Nacht am Donau ufer! Pferde stehn im Kreis umher

Loewe divides the six stanzas into three basic musical units: the first two stanzas are set to melody *a;* the next two are set to *b;* the last two differ slightly from one another (we might indicate them as *c* and *c¹*) in that the second time the tune is presented in its entirety. Except for the last two, which follow one another without any intervening bar, each stanza is separated from the next by one bar for the piano alone. This bar features a recurrent rhythmic motive (♪♪♪♩ ♩ ♪♪♩), conceivably an attempt to imitate the trumpet's fanfare. It is also the last measure in

† Original key: G major.

a seven-bar phrase, a most unusual phrase length, for which Loewe has a marked propensity (cf. *Edward*).

Each of the first two stanzas begins in the tonic minor and moves to the key of the dominant minor at the close, switching rapidly to the true dominant in the piano's solo bar. Subtle chromatic alterations in the inner voices of the accompaniment (see bar 5 and bars 16-17, which anticipate Brahm's style) add a colorful touch. The combination of $\frac{5}{4}$ meter, off-beat accents, seven-bar phrase lengths, and harmonic novelties provides ample evidence that this composer understood the folk idiom. Notice, finally, that this is a difficult song; the singer must be able to negotiate two complete octaves.

LISZT (1811-86)

Liszt, greatly underestimated as a composer of instrumental music, was also never properly acknowledged for his innovations in lieder composition. Although known primarily as a composer of symphonic poems—a genre he was among the first to use—and virtuoso piano pieces, Liszt had already shown an interest in the art song with his early transcriptions of lieder by Beethoven and Robert Franz. In addition, most of his fifty-seven transcriptions of Schubert's songs stem from the period before 1860. Of nearly seventy-five original songs written between 1843 and 1883, the vast majority—indeed some of the best—are in German. For example, his six Goethe songs—among them *Mignons Lied, Es war ein König in Thule, Freudvoll und Leidvoll,* and *Über allen Gipfeln ist Ruh*—reveal interesting departures from their traditional settings by Schubert and Schumann. Liszt's Heine songs (see p. 213, *Vergiftet sind meine Lieder*) are among the finest devoted to this poet's work. After Goethe and Heine, the poet whose works occupied him most often is Victor Hugo. Surprisingly, despite the Italian inspiration of many of his piano pieces, Liszt set very few Italian texts.

Occasionally, Liszt utilized a melody both as a song and as a piano piece. For example, his early settings of three Petrarch sonnets (Nos. 47, 104, and 123) and his *Liebestraum No. 3* are better known in their piano arrangements than in their original settings as lieder. Then too, many of the songs exist in various versions: perhaps two slightly different settings of the same basic melody for voice and piano (see Heine's *Morgens steh' ich auf und frage,* Liszt No. 290); or one setting for voice and piano (with an alternate version of the piano accompaniment) and another for piano solo, followed by yet another for voice and piano (see Heine's *Am Rhein*, Liszt No. 272); or four different versions of the same melody for the same medium (see Goethe's *Der du von dem Himmel bist*, Liszt No. 279).* Liszt has also set the same poem to two completely different melodies (see Goethe's *Wer me sein Brot mit Tränen ass*, Liszt No. 297). Indeed, even a casual glance at the list of songs (Nos. 269 to 340 in Grove) will show that all but about twenty can be found in multiple versions, demonstrating that Liszt's tendency to rework material or to transfer it from one medium to another affected his song composition as well as his instrumental music. His habit of creating these different versions at approximately the same time makes it exceedingly difficult to date these songs.

Liszt allows the vocalist considerable independence, while at the same time providing a thickly cushioned piano accompaniment. Despite some violations of textual accentuation—German was not his native tongue—his technique in text underlay is generally good. He prefers through-composed settings, in some instances not even retaining the stanzaic divisions of the poem.

Liszt appeals to the listener by incorporating sharp rhythmic motives and richly ornamented melodies into the accompaniments. Although he employs folk elements and dance rhythms in several lieder, we can find only one song with distinct gypsy flavor, *Die drei Zigeuner* (p. 221), a setting of Lenau's poem in the original German. Even in his other songs, Liszt does not strive for the concentrated intimacy of the earlier lieder composers. (*Es muss ein Wunderbares sein*, p. 218, is an exception.) Instead, his conception of the lied is more dramatic, broad, rhapsodic. Many of his episodic, sectional lieder might even be described as vocal rhapsodies.

Just as his harmonic experimentation and individual orchestration predate Wagner and his piano figurations prepare the way for the piano pieces of Debussy and Ravel, so, too, do his lieder, with their frequent use of recitation and declamation (see *Alpenjäger*, p. 216), anticipate the later songs of Hugo Wolf and Alban Berg. Often Liszt's dramatic handling of the material resembles the approach of an operatic composer rather than that of a lied specialist, a treatment most surprising in view of the complete absence of opera from his *oeuvre*.

Of the six songs we shall discuss, each shows the composer treating

---

* The numbering corresponds to that used in Humphrey Searle's catalogue of Liszt's works in Grove's *Dictionary of Music and Musicians* (5th ed., 1954).

the problems of text and tone in a different fashion. Liszt's virtuoso style appears most often in the songs of his middle period, 1840-60, but the pianist is never more important than the singer, nor are the sections for solo piano at any time more extensive than those similar portions of Schumann's lieder.

JOHANN LUDWIG UHLAND (1787-1862)

Uhland emerged as a poet when only seventeen years of age. He was equipped by inclination and talent to become a master writer of ballads, having a special affinity for Germanic antiquity and medieval poetry, plus a facile skill in the melodious use of the language. He combined in appropriate proportion the narrative, the lyrical, and the dramatic. Yet he was not immediately hailed as a new literary star. For one thing, Goethe criticized him harshly. Yet the feature to which Goethe objected, the "melancholy tone" of his poems, is an almost indispensable element of the ballad, which is frequently a tragedy in miniature. Uhland was able to survive Goethe's ill-founded attack and to become the leading figure in the development of the German ballad. He has suffered reverses from period to period, and successive evaluations of his work have been alternatively laudatory and disparaging.

Perhaps the most significant vindication of his poetry is the fact that several of his poems are thought of as *Volkslieder*. They are sung even now, and few are aware of who the author was. (*Es zogen drei Burschen wohl über den Rhein* and *Ich hatt' einen Kameraden* are two such songs.)

Die Vätergruft

Es ging wohl über die Haide
Zur alten Kapell' empor
Ein Greis im Waffengeschmeide
Und trat in den dunkeln Chor.

Die Särge seiner Ahnen
Standen die Hall' entlang,
Aus der Tiefe tät ihn mahnen
Ein wunderbarer Gesang.

"Wohl hab' ich euer Grüssen,
Ihr Heldengeister, gehört;
Eure Reihe soll ich schliessen:
Heil mir! ich bin es wert."

Es stand an kühler Stätte
Ein Sarg noch ungefüllt,
Den nahm er zum Ruhebette,
Zum Pfühle nahm er den Schild.

Die Hände tät er falten
Aufs Schwert, und schlummert' ein.
Die Geisterlaute verhallten;
Da mocht' es gar stille sein.

Notes on the text:

Title. *Vätergruft: Gruft* is a blend of "crypt" and "grave"; *Väter* "fathers" = "ancestors; forefathers."

1 *es:* this introductory word would ordinarily be regarded as a meter-filler, but it is more than that, for it occurs frequently in prose narration, too (like English "there"). *Wohl* is a favorite meter-filler in folk songs and ballads.

4 *Chor:* the choir of a church, the portion between the nave and the altar.

5 *Ahnen:* "ancestors." They, though long dead, apparently are the source of the wondrous singing (line 8).

7 *tät ihn mahnen:* "did admonish him" (*tät* is an old-style indicative, not subjunctive).

8 *wunderbarer:* this adjective embraces a wider range of meaning than English "wonderful." It means that, but also "wondrous, amazing, awesome."

11 *Reihe . . . schliessen:* can mean "to close ranks" but also "to fill the last remaining gap in the ranks," as here.

12 *Heil mir, ich bin es wert:* this line does not imply overweening pride or conceit; it is, rather, a factual statement that the old knight has won his right to take a place beside ancestral heroes. The threefold utterance of this statement in Liszt's song may be open to question. The *es (ich bin es wert)* is an old genitive, "worthy of it," although speakers of modern German do not realize this.

13 *Es stand:* the *es* is introductory, as in line 1; "there stood."
15 *zum Ruhebette:* despite *-m* (definite article), this corresponds to English "as a resting place."
16 *zum Pfühle:* "as a pillow." Cf. *zum Ruhebette* above.
17 *tät:* as in line 7.

Liszt No. 281 (1842)

Typical of Liszt's lieder, *Die Vätergruft* opens with a few bars for solo piano. A minor scale with a clearly defined rhythmic profile rises slowly in the bass. The singer follows in almost identical imitation, with his melody doubled in the accompaniment. Heroic piano figurations emerge in the middle section only to be interrupted by a sharp rhythmic snap that serves as a bridge to the song of the spirits, which reappears twice before the conclusion of the piece. The mysterious sonority of the low register of the keyboard seems particularly appropriate because this song is a genuine ballad. Later in the piece, Liszt builds up tension by moving

Ex. 32

LISZT: *Die Vätergruft*

the melody in long notes over undifferentiated quarters in the accompaniment. Constantly changing the music with the text, Liszt combines melody, rhythm, and harmony to articulate the separate sections of the poem. Observe, for example, where the composer changes meter and texture, particularly in the parlando section (Ex. 32). Notice the effective *sotto voce* codetta wherein the spirits' song recurs and is then followed by staccato octaves before the final chords.

Like Berlioz, and later Strauss and Ravel, Liszt successfully orchestrated several of his songs; the orchestration of *Die Vätergruft* represents the last work completed before his death in 1886.

HEINE

Vergiftet sind meine Lieder

Vergiftet sind meine Lieder,
Wie könnt' es anders sein?
Du hast mir ja Gift gegossen
Ins blühende Leben hinein.

Vergiftet sind meine Lieder,
Wie könnt' es anders sein?
Ich trag' im Herzen viel Schlangen,
Und dich, Geliebte mein.

This poem is No. 51 in Heine's *Lyrisches Intermezzo*. He claims that his songs are poisoned, and that they could not be otherwise. His beloved has, by her refusal of his love, poured venom into his young life (and his poems spring from this life). But there are serpents in his heart (reminiscent of *Ich grolle nicht,* in which Heine saw the snake of remorse and frustration which ate at *her* heart). Serpents are sources of poison, too. Whether they remain from earlier painful experiences is left for us to guess. Right beside them is his beloved, the prime source. The "punch line," as frequently, incorporates all the might of his bitter irony, as the very juxtaposition of *viel Schlangen* and *dich* achieves this typical Heine effect.

There is extreme paucity of rhyme in the poem—*sein: hinein; sein: mein*—and the first two lines are repeated in the second strophe. Yet there is no resulting monotony, and the lyric quality of the verses is not destroyed even by our suspicion that the experience was less devastating than the poet would have us believe.

Notes on the text:

1   *Vergiftet:* "poisoned," from *Gift* "poison." In Medieval German a *gift* was a "dose" of medicine (from *geben* "to give"); later German confines it to the sense of "poison." English "gift," of the same origin, preserves an earlier sense.

3   *ja:* "after all," providing a connection between the question in line 2 and the answer in lines 3 and 4.

7   *viel:* an old singular meaning "a multiplicity of, a lot of"—not merely an apocopated (lopped-off) form of the plural *viele.*

8   *Geliebte mein:* the order may well be for the rhyme's sake, but it is a well-established construction in Germanic poetry (and even prose).

Liszt No. 289 (1842)

It is customary for the singer today to open this song with the upbeat at bar 4, eliminating the piano introduction. Abbreviated accompanimental figures, none lasting very long, give way to a vigorous rhythmic motive that separates the first two stanzas. The vocal part is declamatory; the wide leaps reflect the meaning of the text. Liszt differentiates the various sections of the poem by changing his accompanimental figures. He builds in tempo changes by decreasing the note values (cf. bars 22 and 23). A recurrent chromatic motive (beginning at bar 19) beneath an inverted pedal serves to unify the piece. Compare, for example, the bass in the piano postlude with the bass at bar 23. Much of the intensity of the piece results from its limited vocal range, a major seventh.

SCHILLER

Der Alpenjäger

Willst du nicht das Lämmlein hüten?
Lämmlein ist so fromm und sanft,
Nährt sich von des Grases Blüten
Spielend an des Baches Ranft.
"Mutter, Mutter, lass mich gehen,
Jagen nach des Berges Höhen!"

Willst du nicht die Herde locken
Mit des Hornes munterm Klang?
Lieblich tönt der Schall der Glocken
In des Waldes Lustgesang.
"Mutter, Mutter, lass mich gehen,
Schweifen auf den wilden Höhen!"

Willst du nicht der Blümlein warten,
Die im Beete freundlich stehn?
Draussen ladet dich kein Garten,
Wild ist's auf den wilden Höhn!
"Lass die Blümlein, lass sie blühen!
Mutter, Mutter, lass mich ziehen!"

Und der Knabe ging zu jagen,
Und es treibt und reisst ihn fort,
Rastlos fort mit blindem Wagen
An des Berges finstern Ort,
Vor ihm her mit Windesschnelle
Flieht die zitternde Gazelle.

Auf der Felsen nackte Rippen
Klettert sie mit leichtem Schwung,
Durch den Riss geborstner Klippen
Trägt sie der gewagte Sprung,
Aber hinter ihr verwogen
Folgt er mit dem Todesbogen.

Jetzo auf den schroffen Zinken
Hängt sie, auf dem höchsten Grat,
Wo die Felsen jäh versinken
Und verschwunden ist der Pfad.
Unter sich die steile Höhe,
Hinter sich des Feindes Nähe.

```
Mit des Jammers stummen Blicken
Fleht sie zu dem harten Mann,
Fleht umsonst, denn loszudrücken
Legt er schon den Bogen an.
Plötzlich aus der Felsenspalte
Tritt der Geist, der Bergesalte.

Und mit seinen Götterhänden
Schützt er das gequälte Tier.
"Musst du Tod und Jammer senden,"
Ruft er, "bis herauf zu mir?
Raum für alle hat die Erde,
Was verfolgst du meine Herde?"
```

Schiller based this pastoral ballad upon a legend of elderly parents whose son is unwilling to tend the cattle but insists on hunting chamois in the mountains. He loses his way in the snow and doubts that he will ever get back alive. Then the spirit of the mountain appears and says the chamois are his flock: "Why do you pursue them?" He nevertheless shows the hunter the way back. Returning home, the boy now tends the cattle of his parents.

In the first strophe the boy's mother tries to persuade him to take care of their lamb, but he finds her words feeble and wants to head for the heights to hunt. Then she begs him to tend the flocks, to blow the horn and round them up; there is equally little allure for him in that occupation; he longs for the mountain heights. With increasing despair, she asks him to tend the flower garden. Finally he tears himself away and rushes impulsively into the mountains. We are told that he is hunting the gazelle, which seems unlikely. The hunted prey tries its utmost to escape with bold leaps, but it is unable to elude the persistent hunter, who takes aim with bow and arrow. In the nick of time the spirit of the mountain appears and saves the animal. There is no indication here, as in the legend Schiller had read, that the boy is lost. Nor are we told that he lives to return home again, although we surmise as much from the words of the old *Geist*.

Notes on the text:

4   *Ranft:* ordinarily means "crust of bread," but here it means "edge"; cf. *Rand,* to which it is probably related.

16 *Wild ist's auf den wilden Höhn:* in her desperate attempt to restrain her son, the mother falls into the hyperlogical argument that it is "wild on those wild heights."

20 *es:* in this impersonal construction the *es* refers to all the irresistible urges moving him.

24 *Gazelle:* it is surprising to find this name for a European animal; the gazelle is related to the chamois, apparently, but Schiller's use of the word may be for reasons of rhyme. It is, nevertheless, somewhat incongruous in an Alpine setting.

28 *Trägt sie der gewagte Sprung:* the object of the verb is *sie*.

31 *Jetzo:* archaic for *jetzt*.

32 *Grat:* "mountain ridge."

38 *Mann:* the son is called a boy (line 19, *Knabe*); in his capacity of hunter he presumably assumes the character and vices of a man.

42 *der Bergesalte:* "the old man of the mountain; the mountain spirit."

43 *mit seinen Götterhänden:* the spirit is thus regarded as a mountain deity.

Liszt No. 292 (1845)

Three of Schiller's poems from *Wilhelm Tell* represent the only works by this poet to have been set by Liszt. *Der Alpenjäger,* one of the three, has an orchestral opening in true Lisztian transcription style (Ex. 33). Alternating diminished sevenths and tonic chords over a pedal point (F sharp) provide sonorous excitement. Again a pronounced rhythmic motive, which begins in the bass and extends upward through two octaves, serves to unify the piece. Liszt does not allow the repetitions of this motive to become

Ex. 33

LISZT: *Der Alpenjäger*

monotonous, a feat that Loewe, unfortunately, could not duplicate. Modulations occur at textually significant points, and expressive devices further illustrate the poem. For example, notice the pictorialism at *tief unter* and the expressive melodic leaps at *grünende Feld.* Producing a faithful musical characterization of the hunter, Liszt concludes this dramatic-action lied forte. Observe also the unusual Phrygian cadence at the close (A flat to G).

OSKAR VON REDWITZ (1823-91)

Von Redwitz now belongs to the host of the great unknown. No one reads his sentimental lyrical-epic poem *Amaranth,* and his historical plays, few in number, have not excited attention for almost a century. Histories of literature seldom mention him.

Es muss ein Wunderbares sein

Es muss ein Wunderbares sein
Ums Lieben zweier Seelen,
Sich schliessen ganz einander ein,
Sich nie ein Wort verhehlen,
Und Freud und Leid
Und Glück und Not
So miteinander tragen,
Vom ersten Kuss bis in den Tod
Sich nur von Liebe sagen.

Notes on the text:

Title. *ein Wunderbares:* the adjective is nominalized or substantivized (turned into a noun); it is here the equivalent of "a wonderful thing" (neuter) or "something wonderful." The poet says, "It *must be* a wonderful thing," as if it had not been part of his experience to know such love. One may well ask whether such love exists at all, or if it would be desirable "from the first kiss until death to talk of naught but love."

3 *sich:* accusative.
4 *sich:* dative.

The repeated lines are Liszt's own contribution. They are not demanded by the verse, but almost everyone will agree that Liszt enhances the poem and imparts to it perhaps even more of the element of the wondrous/wonderful than the author himself perceived.

Liszt No. 314 (1857)

With its simple, unobtrusive accompanimental figure, *Es muss ein Wunderbares sein* represents the closest example of an intimate lied in the manner of Schumann or Brahms. There is relatively little doubling of the melody, which nevertheless derives from the harmonic accompaniment. Again the composer ignores the stanzaic divisions of the poem, preferring instead to produce a through-composed setting. The text is expressively illustrated, with *Leid* at bar 14 underlined by the dissonant sound of the tritone, and *Tod* at bars 25-26 emphasized through the use of a descending fifth. Where he repeats the text *so miteinander tragen,* bars 17-22, Liszt employs a musical parallel, repeating the vocal part a half-step higher while intensifying the harmonic support.

NIKOLAUS LENAU (1802-50)

Nikolaus Lenau's real name was Nikolaus Franz Niembsch, Edler von Strehlenau, obviously in need of shortening. From the last part of his name the final two syllables, not exactly divided philologically, give the pen name (Streh-lenau). Born in the old Austria-Hungary, Lenau was of German, Hungarian, and Slavic descent, and some literary historians have attempted to discern a conflict among those three elements, attributing to genes and chromosomes the same shortcomings found in individuals and nations.

After desultory attempts to study at the University of Vienna (law, medicine, agriculture), he was encouraged by some of the so-called Swabian poets—Kerner, Mörike, and others—to publish some of his poems (*Gedichte,* 1832). These verses met with an enthusiastic reception, for they echoed the *Weltschmerz* of the times. One reviewer said that they "brought fresh breath from the *pusztas* [plains] of Hungary." But there was also in them the note of melancholy and pessimistic discontent that ran through all his later work. A restless man, he was nowhere at home. In 1832 he traveled to America with high hopes of finding a better way of life:

Du neue Welt, du freie Welt,
An deren blütenreichem Strand
Die Flut der Tyrannei zerschellt,
Ich grüsse dich, mein Vaterland.

(O thou new world, o thou free world,
on whose fair flower-bordered strand
the sea of tyranny, tide-hurled,
is shattered; hail, my fatherland.)

A few optimistic poems resulted—*Der Indianerzug, Drei Indianer, Niagara*—but his old melancholy soon returned, and the land of freedom proved to be a disappointment. He returned to Europe, remaining ten years in Vienna. From there he went to Württemberg, Germany. His complex personality, always unstable, deteriorated, and Lenau finally became quite insane, spending the last five years of his life in an asylum.

Although he attempted an epic drama, *Faust,* he is best known for his lyrical poetry. Influence from many quarters is clearly detected: Goethe, Eichendorff, Byron. He had little in common with Mörike, who was far too placid and well adjusted for him. To Lenau, life was one long autumn of continued, unrelieved despair. *Die ganze Welt ist zum Verzweifeln traurig* ("The whole world is sad to the point of despair") was his theme song.

His lament was that of many sensitive creative natures of the time. Such figures were by no means confined to Central Europe. There were Leopardi and Manzoni in Italy; Pushkin, Goncharov, and Lermontov in Russia; Byron in England; and so on. Lenau's special sense of kinship with the gypsies was based on his admiration for their nomadic way of life, their apparent predilection for wild, lonely campsites on the heath, and for the glorious wildness of their music. There is certainly something akin to this in the verbal melody of his poems. There is also a subtlety and even delicacy that is not easily reproduced in song.

Three free men—free in Lenau's sense—express their disdain for the world and its bourgeois cares and duties. The first, the most active, plays his violin, and there is traditionally powerful magic when that happens. The second, more passive, smokes his pipe. The third, most passive of all, sleeps. His cimbalom * hangs from a branch of a tree; if it gives forth any sound at all, that sound will be caused by the wind.

* The English translation of *Zymbal* as "cymbal" is incorrect. *Zymbal* should be translated as "cimbalom," a contemporary Hungarian dulcimer.

Die drei Zigeuner

Drei Zigeuner fand ich einmal
Liegen an einer Weide,
Als mein Fuhrwerk mit müder Qual
Schlich durch sandige Heide.

Hielt der eine für sich allein
In den Händen die Fiedel,
Spielt', umglüht vom Abendschein,
Sich ein lustiges Liedel.

Hielt der zweite die Pfeif' im Mund,
Blickte nach seinem Rauche,
Froh, als ob er vom Erdenrund
Nichts zum Glücke mehr brauche.

Und der dritte behaglich schlief,
Und sein Zymbal am Baum hing;
Über die Saiten der Windhauch lief,
Über sein Herz ein Traum ging.

An den Kleidern trugen die drei
Löcher und bunte Flicken;
Aber sie boten trotzig frei
Spott den Erdengeschicken.

Dreifach haben sie mir gezeigt,
Wenn das Leben uns nachtet,
Wie man's verschläft, verraucht, vergeigt,
Und es dreifach verachtet.

Nach den Zigeunern lange noch
Musst ich schaun im Weiterfahren,
Nach den Gesichtern dunkelbraun,
Nach den schwarzlockigen Haaren.

Notes on the text:

17   The use of the verb *trugen* is effective, for it implies that the holes are a part of the gypsies' raiment: "they wore holes and colorful patches."

22   The verb *nachtet* is an interesting instance of a "denominative" verb, that is, a noun turned into a verb (cf. in English, to *foot* the bill, to *book* passage, etc.).

23 The order of fiddling, smoking, sleeping (strophes 2, 3, and 4) is now reversed in Lenau's recapitulation: *verschläft, verraucht, vergeigt* "sleeps away, smokes away, fiddles away."

24 *dreifach:* conveys not only the notion that they have defied mundane existence in three different ways but also that they have scorned it threefold, three times over.

The final strophe is sung as the gypsies grow smaller and smaller when the poet moves further away from them. The opportunity for a composer is obvious. But Liszt seems to offer us the chance to omit this strophe, if we choose. Does he consider it too contrived?

Liszt No. 320 (1860)

Ex. 34

LISZT: *Die drei Zigeuner*

a.

The solo piano opening of *Die drei Zigeuner* (see Ex. 34-a) resembles the start of many of Liszt's Hungarian Rhapsodies. A long narrative poem which Liszt has set in its entirety, *Die drei Zigeuner* continues with a vocal introduction in parlando style, followed by three sections in which Liszt gives three different musical characterizations of the gypsies. The composer uses a syllabic text setting, except for the ornaments in gypsy style (see bars 2 and 4 of Ex. 34-b). In addition to the Czardas and gypsy ornaments, an-

Hielt der Zwei - te die Pfeif im Mund blick - te nach sei - nem

Rau - che,

b.

other folk element—the Hungarian minor scale with its augmented-second interval, here with a short dotted rhythm—opens the song. Curiously, the German word for gypsy, *Zigeuner,* contains this dotted rhythm (♪♪. ♪) in its pronunciation.

Liszt suggested that the brusque, truncated conclusion at bar 94 would be a more effective ending in concert than continuing to the actual end of the piece. Concluding the song at bar 94, however, necessitates omitting the last stanza of the poem.

EMIL KUH (1828-76)

Emil Kuh has not made a name for himself in literature and he is remembered chiefly as a friend of Friedrich Hebbel, the distinguished nineteenth-century dramatist, whose plays he edited with some scholarly acumen. After unsuccessful efforts in business, Kuh, a journalist, subsequently became a professor of German literature. Such people are not destined to drink very deeply of the spring of poetic inspiration.

Yet this poem, *Ihr Glocken von Marling*, is a felicitous exception, a song that virtually sings itself. It obviously struck a responsive chord in Liszt, who endowed it with a haunting beauty, such as bells often have.

Ihr Glocken von Marling

Ihr Glocken von Marling, wie braust ihr so hell!
Ein wohliges Lauten, als sänge der Quell.
Ihr Glocken von Marling, ein heil'ger Gesang
Umwallet wie schützend den weltlichen Klang.
Nehmt mich in die Mitte der tönenden Flut--
Ihr Glocken von Marling, behütet mich gut!

Marling is southwest of Merano, where Kuh spent the last years of his life; once part of Austria, it is now in that disputed area of Italy, South Tyrol. The significance of the bells must be a part of Emil Kuh's own experience. Evidently the church bells of that town had a special magic of their own.

The selection of consonants seems to be an attempt at onomatopoeia: *Glocken, Marling, sänge, Gesang, Klang* suggest the resonance of certain bell tones; *hell* and *Quell* are brighter and lighter tones; in *der tönenden Flut* we hear something of the continued vibrations and wavelike persistence of the lower tones. One is tempted to think of a carillon playing sacred tunes. Despite the comfort which the author finds in the reassuring sounds of the bells, there is a hint of dissonance which inevitably accompanies their ringing.

Liszt No. 328 (1874)

As Liszt grew older, he began to favor a simpler style of lieder composition. While his harmony became increasingly complex, his textures and figurations became less dense. (A comparison of the earlier and later settings of the Petrarch sonnets mentioned above offers tangible evidence of these stylistic changes.) *Ihr Glocken von Marling*, a late work, is a short song in which Liszt presents a persistent accompaniment of undifferentiated eighth notes that slow down—the steady eighth-note motion replaced by quarter notes—only in the last ten bars of the piece. Text setting is almost completely syllabic, with several unaccompanied bars for the singer. The general mood of the poem is one of relative tranquillity, transmitted through the rhythmic regularity of the accompaniment. Tension is created by the use of unresolved seventh and ninth chords (in the manner of Debussy and Ravel), but no virtuoso figurations mar the essential peacefulness. The delicate, ethereal sound of the bells (the persistent eighths) reveals a completely different facet of Liszt's style.

The composer repeats the last line of the poem and its accompaniment almost literally. It is in this phrase that the first unaccompanied bars occur, with the piano reentering on the last note of the vocal phrase (*gut*). At the second reentrance of the piano the anticipated final cadence does not occur. Rather, the eighth-note motion continues. The voice sings the final line of text once more in the same rhythm as previously, but the vocal line is compressed in range (the original octave leap is replaced by a fourth), quieter in dynamics (piano throughout, rather than forte and then piano), extended (the second syllable of *behütet*, originally a dotted quarter note, now lasts for four beats), and slower (poco a poco ritardando). It ends inconclusively on the fifth of the dominant. Quarter-note motion begins the final ritardando. The phrase *behütet mich gut* is repeated (sempre ritardando and pianissimo), the vocal line ending finally but uncertainly on the third of the tonic scale. The piano continues, ever slower, for several measures, dying out at last on a first-inversion chord. Liszt uses twenty-five measures, out of a total of sixty-six, to conclude the song in a mood of delicate meditation.

VI

Minor Poems and Major Lieder

BRAHMS (1833-97)

Whereas Schuman was more discriminating than Schubert in his choice of texts to set to music, Brahms differed from both in his approach to the poetry he selected for his lieder. Except for the baker's dozen devoted to the works of Goethe and Heine and the fifteen Romances of Ludwig Tieck, his songs are based on texts of lesser-known poets, among them G. F. Daumer (19), Klaus Groth (12), Lemcke (7), Wenzig (10), Uhland (4), and Hölty (6). Brahms may have felt, as Goethe so plainly stated, that the best poems are complete without music. Or he may simply have been inspired most by those poets who were his friends and contemporaries, responding more profoundly to their poetic utterances.

Brahms's songs are predominantly minor, gloomy, dark, and in a low register that best suits the alto voice. He evinces no particular fondness for *Tonmalerei*. Outside of Tieck's Romances, the so-called *Magelone Lieder*, he wrote no cycles. Death, unrequited love, frustration, nostalgia for lost youth are the topics we encounter most frequently. Exceptions are the folklike settings culled either from anonymous collections of poetry or song, or from those assembled by Zuccalmaglio. This dichotomy is not unusual for Brahms. In the instrumental works as well, we notice the introspective, meditative Intermezzi and slow pieces side by side with the exuberant, enthusiastic Capriccios, Hungarian Dances, and Rhapsodies. Brahms's music presents a study in sharp contrasts. In vocal and instrumental music, both of which he wrote intermittently during his lifetime, he maintains this duality.

His melodies are generally triadic; that is, each can usually be reduced to some form of arpeggio. Brahms also has a habit of relating two different melodies in the same song, either through inversion (changing the direction of the pitches) or by incorporating other modifications—as, for example, filling in a melodic interval that had previously been a leap. These relationships, more often than not, are less noticeable to listeners than another technique he employs: unification through recurrence of specific rhythmic profiles. Two or more melodies will have the same rhythmic shape, and the listener then has a sense of familiarity on hearing them successively. Finally, there are more instances of bass melodies or of structurally significant bass lines in Brahms's songs than in those of other composers.

Brahms's piano accompaniments are not unusual. They, too, focus on the arpeggio. He prefers a thick, muddied sound in the low bass. Notice, for this reason, the frequent octave doublings. Sometimes the bass line doubles the singer's melody several registers away. Linear writing appears even more frequently in Brahms's songs than in Schumann's. His accompaniments may be incredibly contrapuntal. Whereas these figures never sound terribly difficult, they do not lie easily under the fingers. This criticism applies equally to the piano pieces, most of which sound much less difficult than they really are. Because Brahms wrote piano and vocal works throughout his entire lifetime, the styles of piano writing in both lied and solo piece are distinctly similar.

Rhythm is a controlling element in all of Brahms's music. He reintroduces the techniques of baroque fugal writing: augmentation, diminution, hemiola, cross rhythms, and alternating meters. Often the singer and the pianist have completely independent rhythmic lines.

Prevalent harmonic relationships outline major or minor keys a third apart (F sharp to A or C to E) or keys related through a common pivot note, perhaps enharmonically spelled, such as E and A flat (= G sharp). Modality, too, makes frequent appearances in his scores. Altered chords, particularly the lowered sixth note implanted in a major scale, as well as pedal points and ostinatos to blur the tonality all provide considerable harmonic interest.

Brahms preferred strophic form, although only rarely does he set all stanzas to exactly the same music. Instead, each strophe contains slight modifications. Sometimes he just changes the mode for one stanza, setting it in the parallel minor key.

Among Brahms's approximately two hundred and fifty lieder we find some extraordinary works that even today have not achieved the recognition they merit.

L. C. H. HÖLTY (1748-76)

Hölty belonged to a group of poets called the *Göttinger Hain* ("Grove") or *Göttinger Bund*, founded by a number of talented but eccentric students, who inaugurated their circle with strange rites and hocus-pocus· (invoking the moon and stars, swearing eternal friendship). The Germanic *Hain* was supposed to be the opposite of the lofty temple on the hill that symbolized classical poetry. Starting as imitators of predecessors, these poets gradually achieved some independence of creation and, while never soaring to the heights of true genius, threw off the shackles of artificiality and were not too remote from life and nature. Hölty has been called the most gifted of the group. His life was a short one, and he did not live to see his poems published; that came posthumously. He was ill for the greater part of his life, yet many of his poems show an optimistic affirmation, even though he is aware that he has not long to live. But some, like the present one, are pervaded by a dreamy melancholy.

Die Mainacht

Wann der silberne Mond durch die Gesträuche blinkt,
Und sein schlummerndes Licht über den Rasen streut,
Und die Nachtigall flötet,
Wandl' ich traurig von Busch zu Busch.

Überhüllet von Laub girret ein Taubenpaar
Sein Entzücken mir vor; aber ich wende mich,
Suche dunklere Schatten,
Und die einsame Träne rinnt.

Wann, o lächelndes Bild, welches wie Morgenrot
Durch die Seele mir strahlt, find ich auf Erden dich?
Und die einsame Träne
Bebt mir heisser die Wang herab!

The sights and sounds of a night in May should not be sad: the gentle moonbeams, the singing of the nightingale, the cooing of a pair of lovebirds. But none of the tranquillity of the night or the joy of nature is imparted to the melancholy man who wanders sadly from bush to bush, purposely seeking out the darker shadows. He weeps for the love which is not his, and which he almost despairs of knowing.

Rhyme is a characteristic of most of Hölty's poems, but there is none in *Die Mainacht.*

Notes on the text:

1   Brahms alters *Wenn* to *Wann. Gestreuche* is changed to *Gesträuche,* which merely brings the word up to date orthographically. For *blickt* Brahms has *blinkt.*
2   Brahms replaces *geusst* (archaic for *giesst* "pours") with *streut* "strews."

A second strophe, which partly accounts for the man's sorrow, is omitted by Brahms. (The nightingale, unlike the man, has a mate.)

Op. 43, No. 2

Typical of many of Brahms's songs, the subject here is night. The setting is low, the vocal melody rising. Compare both rhythm and melody of the opening vocal lines of stanzas 1 and 2 in Exx. 35-a and 35-b. Notice

Ex. 35

BRAHMS: *Mainacht*

Wann der sil - ber - ne Mond durch die Ge - sträu - che blinkt,

a.

Ü - ber hül - let vom Laub

b.

the similarities as well as the slight differences in the directions of the last two eighth notes. The arpeggio, in one of its many formations, appears in the accompaniment. The top line of the bass chords anticipates the vocal melody while the low B flat sounds as a sustained tone anchoring the entire passage and setting the fundamental mood of the lied. Brahms emphasizes formal outlines here by key changes in the figurations of the accompaniment. The modulation from E-flat major, one of Brahms's favorite keys, to B major is not so remote as it seems. Consider E flat as D sharp, its enharmonic equivalent, and the gap between the two keys appears narrower.

An impassioned, richly textured transition leads into the return of the opening material, this time supported by a different accompaniment. Brahms, as we shall see, rarely repeats himself in exactly the same way. The four bars that underline *und die einsame Träne* in the transition include many Brahmsian elements: texture, figuration, melody, and harmonic progression (see Ex. 35-c).

und   die   ein - sa - me   Thrä - ne bebt.

c.

MAX VON SCHENKENDORF (1783-1817)

Like most of his contemporary poets, Schenkendorf was inspired by the struggle against Napoleon. Despite a paralyzed right hand (the result of a duel), he rushed off, sword in his left hand, to fight against Napoleon. He participated in the battle of Leipzig and other engagements. He cherished the hope and belief that the German Empire of old would one day be restored. Much of his material would be found boring today, but at least a third of his poetry is truly lyrical and of a quality superior to that of most of his fellow poets. It is reminiscent of Eichendorff. One song, *Freiheit, die ich meine, die mein Herz erfüllt,* is as well known as any in the language.

Todessehnen

Ach, wer nimmt von meiner Seele
Die geheime, schwere Last,
Die, je mehr ich sie verhehle,
Immer mächtiger mich fasst?

Möchtest du nur endlich brechen,
Mein gequältes, banges Herz!
Findest hier mit deinen Schwächen,
Deiner Liebe, nichts als Schmerz.

Dort nur wirst du ganz genesen,
Wo der Sehnsucht nichts mehr fehlt,
Wo das schwesterliche Wesen
Deinem Wesen sich vermählt.

Hör es, Vater in der Höhe,
Aus der Fremde fleht dein Kind:
Gib, dass er mich bald umwehe,
Deines Todes Lebenswind.

Dass er zu dem Stern mich hebe,
Wo man keine Trennung kennt,
Wo die Geistersprache Leben
Mit der Liebe Namen nennt.

Notes on the text:

2 *Die geheime, schwere Last:* the burden of living.
7 *hier:* in this life.
9 *Dort:* in the hereafter.
  genesen: "to be healed" (of the sickness of living).
11 The mysterious reference to a "sisterly being" (*schwesterliches Wesen*) occurs in more than one poem of Schenkendorf's. Whether he alludes to an actual person or is speaking figuratively of some such phenomenon as Death is difficult to determine.
14 *Aus der Fremde: Fremde* is exile; here it means life.
16 *Deines Todes Lebenswind* is a paradox; death is represented as the breath of life. Yet there is a religious strain here (Schenkendorf was the author of some hymns): in heaven at least there is presumably a life worth living. But life in the present world

is, for him, suffering, sickness, and exile. Not all of his poems are as pessimistic as this.

Op. 86, No. 6

The six songs of Op. 86 are all for low voice, and each is to a poem by a different poet. In this lied a walking bass line in octaves characterizes the brooding opening section. On its repeat for the second stanza, the direction of the octaves is reversed (cf. Ex. 36-a and Ex. 36-b), while the melody undergoes slight changes. Syncopated material in the transition leads into

Ex. 36

BRAHMS: *Todessehnen*

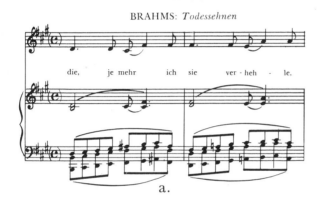

a.

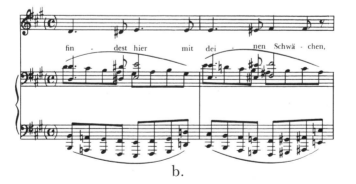

b.

the second section, *Hör es Vater*, bars 31 ff., the melody of which appears again in the Andante of Brahms's B-flat Piano Concerto (1881). He draws attention to the unusual concept of *Deines Todes Lebenswind* (bar 49) by making it the vocal highpoint of the song.

The original key and the opening melody never return. Instead, Brahms follows this formal scheme: $a\ a^1\ b\ c\ c^1$. He articulates the sections here through the use of metric as well as textural changes.

THEODOR STORM (1817-88)

Like Groth and Hebbel, Storm was a northerner, born in Schleswig. His native language, therefore, was Plattdeutsch (usually called, with woeful misunderstanding, Low German), but he wrote in standard German. After embarking on a legal career, he soon left Husum because of objections to Danish policy in Schleswig-Holstein. (It is difficult to think of Danes as persecuting Germans, but it happened then.) He went to Heiligenstadt in Prussia, where life was freer and the government more liberal. Later he returned to his native province.

Storm is known to generations of American students of German because of his extremely sentimental (but beautiful) short story *Immensee*. His stories are his best works; his lyrical creativity was rather limited.

Über die Heide

Über die Heide hallet mein Schritt;
Dumpf aus der Erde wandert es mit.
Herbst ist gekommen, Frühling ist weit,
Gab es denn einmal selige Zeit?

Brauende Nebel geisten umher;
Schwarz ist das Kraut und der Himmel so leer.
Wär'ich nur hier nicht gegangen im Mai!
Leben und Liebe, wie flog es vorbei!

Notes on the text:

   Title. *Heide:* like the English moors, the heath usually sets the mood as mysterious, wild, uncanny, or supernatural.
   1 *hallet:* conveys the impression of empty surroundings; his tread echoes in the void.

2 *Dumpf aus der Erde wandert es mit:* the sense is that the echo of his footsteps accompanies him as he walks, as if the echo arose from the ground.

3 Unlike Lenau, Storm does not welcome *Herbst* (autumn); to him it is the melancholy time in which we long for spring, as is seen in line 4. "Was there ever a blissful time?"

5 *geisten:* a denominative verb from the noun *Geist* ("roaring mists ghost all around").

6 *Kraut:* "vegetation" (with none of the comic overtones the word has for us in English).

7 "If only I had not walked here in May!" (I would not now be suffering because of the appalling contrast.)

8 *Leben und Liebe, wie flog es vorbei!* We now realize that he once loved here in spring. We also realize, however, that he is probably speaking not of last spring but more likely the spring of his life.
Mai: "May" = youth.

Op. 86, No. 4

Über die Heide is the only poem by Storm that Brahms set. Observe several typical features: a low register and a rising melodic line, perpetual syncopation throughout, sequences in the middle section, and two related melodies. (Compare the opening with the vocal melody at *Brauende* and again notice similarities and differences.) Instead of using a triadic skeleton for his melody, Brahms fashions his tune from a scale. Somehow the $\frac{6}{8}$ meter does not prove monotonous in this song.

GEORG FRIEDRICH DAUMER (1800-75)

After studying theology and classical philology at the universities of Erlangen and Leipzig, and showing such passionate interest in Eastern religions that people regarded him as mad (a fitting comment on their own state of bliss), Daumer assumed a teaching position in the secondary school (*Gymnasium*) at Nuremberg. His feeble state of health made it necessary for him to retire early. He pursued scholarly and poetic studies, and in a few years he passed from violent rationalism to ultra-Romanism, becoming converted to Catholicism.

Daumer translated some of the Persian works of Hafiz, stimulated by Goethe's *West-östlicher Divan,* and also works of classical literature. Brahms was an admirer of Daumer's poetry and set nineteen of his poems to music.

Nicht mehr zu dir zu gehen

Nicht mehr zu dir zu gehen,
Beschloss ich und beschwor ich,
Und gehe jeden Abend,
Denn jede Kraft und jeden Halt verlor ich.

Ich möchte nicht mehr leben,
Möcht' augenblicks verderben,
Und möchte doch auch leben
Für dich, mit dir, und nimmer, nimmer sterben.

Ach rede, sprich ein Wort nur,
Ein einziges, ein klares!
Gib Leben oder Tod mir,
Nur dein Gefühl enthülle mir, dein wahres!

Notes on the text:

2 *Beschloss ich und beschwor ich:* "I resolved and swore" (to go to you no more).
3 *und:* "and yet" (all resolutions are broken, because I have lost my power of resistance).
6 *augenblicks:* "in the twinkling of an eye" = "at once."
7 The line contradicts the preceding; he is in a paradoxical state in which he cannot live with her or without her, in which he wants to die, and yet to live. Startling contrasts like this may have been learned from Hafiz, whom Daumer copied to some extent.
8 *nimmer:* poetic and obsolescent word for "never" (from *nie mehr* "nevermore").
9-12 These verses explain what will determine whether he lives or dies.

Op. 32, No. 2

This lied is the first of the settings of Daumer poems written by Brahms. Again, a listener hearing only a few beats of the opening bars will recognize his personal imprint. A brooding, melancholy song in D minor, Brahms's tragic key, its texture and rhythmic treatment are typical of the composer's style. For example, notice the bass octaves that double the melody. For the first stanza, they rise in a scale pattern; for the second, they descend, reversing the direction of the opening melody. At *Ich möchte nicht mehr* the underpinning has changed, and the triplet accompaniment, pitting two notes against three, adds to the general feeling of uneasiness. Curiously, the rhythmic homogeneity (persistent quarter notes) in the first stanza is unusual for Brahms. He compensates by using several levels of rhythmic activity in the middle section of the lied, bars 11 ff. Brahms delineates the formal sections of the song through modulations to and from the relative major key.

The melody is declamatory, rather than lyrical, in a style often associated with Brahms's instrumental music. Another feature of his instrumental music borrowed for this song is the significant three-note motive that appears first in bar 2 in the treble of the accompaniment. It is based on the interval of a minor second. In an undulating motion, it persists throughout the *a* section, reappearing at the return of *a* for the last stanza. Usually Brahms does not concern himself much with *Tonmalerei*. Here, however, we get the feeling that the ambivalence of the lover is reflected in the movement, first away from and then toward his beloved.

KLAUS GROTH (1819-99)

Groth wrote mostly in his native Plattdeutsch dialect. He was from the same locality (Dithmarschen) as Friedrich Hebbel and the same province (Schleswig-Holstein) as Theodor Storm, but Hebbel ridiculed him for his use of the local idiom; Storm and Hebbel both wrote standard German only. Plattdeutsch, or Low German (the language of the "Lowlands," i.e., the northern part of the country), embraces a number of dialects that have not undergone certain consonantal changes which have affected the dialects of the South. English resembles Plattdeutsch in the same respect (English *water,* Plattdeutsch *water,* German *Wasser;* English *tongue,* Plattdeutsch *tunge,* German *Zunge;* English *book,* Plattdeutsch *bok,* German *Buch*). There are also differences in vocabulary and grammar.

A collection of Groth's poems in his native dialect (*Quickborn,* "Fountain of Youth," 1852) showed that Low German could serve as an artistic means of poetic expression no whit inferior to that in the standard language. Before Groth it had been customary to regard Low German poetry as something coarse, funny, and awkward, the product of illiterate yokels or oafs smelling of fish. And speakers of Low German had allowed themselves to be persuaded that "low" meant "inferior." Groth's lyrics were the means of establishing a new self-respect. They are melodious, sincere, polished, at times even sophisticated, while not losing touch with the nature of the folk song.

Groth also wrote in standard German, a language which he, like all of his fellow northerners, learned in school. Any author aspiring to a wide audience is practically forced to adopt the standard language, but it is not on his writings in that idiom that Groth's literary fame rests. The present poem is, obviously, in standard German.

O wüsst' ich doch den Weg zurück

O wüsst' ich doch den Weg zurück,
Den lieben Weg zum Kinderland!
O warum sucht' ich nach dem Glück
Und liess der Mutter Hand?

O wie mich sehnet auszuruhn,
Von keinem Streben aufgeweckt,
Die müden Augen zuzutun,
Von Liebe sanft bedeckt!

Und nichts zu forschen, nichts zu spähn,
Und nur zu träumen leicht und lind;
Der Zeiten Wandel nicht zu sehn,
Zum zweiten Mal ein Kind!

O zeig'mir doch den Weg zurück,
Den lieben Weg zum Kinderland!
Vergebens such' ich nach dem Glück,
Ringsum ist öder Strand!

The *ich* is certainly the poet. He unashamedly wishes he were back in his childhood, whatever psychoanalytical critics may make of that. He implies that there might be a way back: *O wüsst' ich doch* ("If I only knew"). He regrets now, later in life, that he left his mother's tender care to seek his fortune and to be involved in the killing pace of such a life. He longs to escape the world of reality and to return to childhood—not the real childhood, with fright and dirt and illness, but a paradisical time that he recalls. (Groth's Low German account of the years of his youth is significantly entitled *Min Jungsparadies,* "The Paradise of My Youth").

After the first three strophes have expressed his wish to become a child again, he then asks someone to show him the way: *O zeigt mir doch den Weg zurück,* with partial repetition of the words of the first strophe. In place of the question "Why did I seek?" we have the admission that the search has been in vain. The final line sums up a fearful, terrifying prospect: all around is a desolate shore. Groth's introduction of the word *Strand* is itself somewhat abrupt, for there has been no intimation of any sea. Yet such a figure is natural to one of Groth's early environment, which involved the sea, the shore, the battle of dikes against encroaching waves— all, of course, the concern of the grownups, not of the child Klaus Groth.

Nostalgia is the keynote. The desire is hopeless, because the way back can be achieved only through the tragedy of second childhood, unless the simpler substitute of memory and imagination is invoked, as here.

Notes on the text:

2 *Kinderland:* childhood is almost a *place* to the poet.
5 *mich sehnet:* an impersonal, poetic expression (*sehnet* itself being archaic for *sehnt*) for what is now *ich sehne* "I long."
6 *Streben:* a two-edged word meaning, on the one hand, "striving, aspiration," on the other, "frantic ambition, mad striving [rat-race]." It will amuse some to learn that the hectic career to which Groth refers was that of a professor at the University of Kiel.
8 *Von Liebe sanft bedeckt:* reminiscent of a *Wiegenlied* and suggestive of a child being tucked into bed.
13 Groth has *zeigt* (plural imperative), which Brahms altered to *zeig'* (singular). In either case, he is begging someone, anyone, to show him the way—an impossible task.

15 *such' ich:* The present tense implies that he has been searching right up to now for fortune and happiness, both of which are included in the ambiguous word *Glück.*

Op. 63, No. 8

A meandering arpeggiated figure, its intervals sometimes filled in with a chromatically altered note, immediately establishes the nostalgic mood of the poem. The rising melody of the first stanza (Ex. 37-a) undergoes slight changes for its use in the second stanza, but the accompaniment is considerably altered (Ex. 37-b). Notice the avoidance of rests in the widespread, long-line legato melodies. Brahms follows a triadic pattern in his choice of keys for the first two stanzas: E major, G major, B major. The

Ex. 37

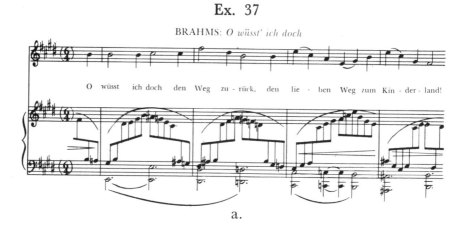

a.

b.

third stanza is almost identical with the second; the final stanza follows the pattern of the first except for the following changes at the close: inclusion of a syncopated accompaniment (more like that used in stanza 2) that underlines *Vergebens such'*; and a tritone built on the lowered sixth degree of the scale that highlights the text at *öder Strand*.

JOSEF WENZIG (1807-76)

Wenzig was born in Prague, which has been the birthplace of several authors in the German language, e.g., Rilke, Kafka, Werfel. Unlike these three, he has not achieved fame. Wenzig was bilingual (in German and Czech) and translated Czech folk songs and tales into German. Despite his German writings, he fought, as an educator, to have Czech made the language of instruction in the schools of Bohemia, where it had long been banned by Austrian decree. He was among the most active workers in the cause of the Czech national revival.

Von ewiger Liebe

Dunkel, wie dunkel in Wald und in Feld!
Abend schon ist es, nun schweiget die Welt.
Nirgend noch Licht und nirgend noch Rauch,
Ja, und die Lerche sie schweiget nun auch.

Kommt aus dem Dorfe der Bursche heraus,
Gibt das Geleit der Geliebten nach Haus,
Führt sie am Weidengebüsche vorbei,
Redet so viel und so mancherlei:

"Leidest du Schmach und betrübest du dich,
Leidest du Schmach von andern um mich,
Werde die Liebe getrennt so geschwind,
Schnell wie wir früher vereiniget sind.
Scheide mit Regen und scheide mit Wind,
Schnell wie wir früher vereiniget sind."

Spricht das Mägdelein, Mägdelein spricht:
"Unsere Liebe sie trennet sich nicht!
Fest ist der Stahl und das Eisen gar sehr,
Unsere Liebe ist fester noch mehr.

> Eisen und Stahl, man schmiedet sie um,
> Unsere Liebe, wer wandelt sie um?
> Eisen und Stahl, sie können zergehn,
> Unsere Liebe muss ewig bestehn!"

The setting of the poem *Von ewiger Liebe* is evening, darkness, woods, and field. The boy escorts his beloved home. Implying that her relationship with him has brought her shame and mistreatment, he offers to sever that relationship at once, as quickly as it had been formed (love at first sight?). Perhaps he is of "inferior" social status; perhaps he has a bad reputation. But the girl will not hear of any such thing. She sees their love as something eternal, more lasting than iron or steel. Her figures of speech are extreme but clear—also traditional.

The meter is predominantly dactylic:

$$\text{Dúnkel, wíe dúnkel ín Wáld únd ín Féld,}$$

but each line ends on a stressed syllable.

Notes on the text:

4   *die Lerche:* traditional songbird of the daytime (as opposed to the nightingale).

5   *Kommt aus dem Dorfe:* the word order of folk speech and poetry, verb first in a statement (not standard syntax). The same applies to lines 6-8.

7   *Weidengebüsch:* the willow is sacred to the moon goddess; hence it is an appropriate ingredient in night poetry.

9   *Leidest . . . betrübest:* unlike lines 5-8, this is not folk word order but shows initial position of verb in a condition.

11   *werde:* optative subjunctive, "Let love be broken . . ."

15   *Spricht das Mägdelein, Mägdelein spricht:* two expressions of the same utterance, both *volkstümlich*, as is the word *Mägdelein* itself.

16   *Unsere Liebe, sie:* this usage of the pronoun, recapitulating the subject, is also folk language, although the girl's speech in general is a watered-down version of proverbial style.

Op. 43, No. 1

This lied and *Die Mainacht* belong to the same group of songs. Both are among the most frequently performed of Brahms's solo songs. Another passionate love song, *Von ewiger Liebe* reveals the Slavic origin of the poet Wenzig. A triadic melody begins in the low bass (Ex. 38-a) and anticipates the singer's presentation of the same notes in a slightly altered

Ex. 38

BRAHMS: *Von ewiger Liebe*

a.

"Lei - dest du Schmach und be - trü - best du dich.

lei - dest du Schmach von An - dern um mich,

b.

rhythm. Observe that the accompaniment, too, is arpeggiated. Compare the melodic line at *Nirgend noch* (bar 14) with the opening melody of the song. Also notice their similarity to the melody of the third stanza (Ex. 38-b). As so often happens with Brahms's music, we sense or hear relationships that defy explanations. Observe also that the two parts of the first stanza are set to keys a minor third apart. The formal scheme of the entire song might be represented in the following manner:

Stanza 1	*a*	(B minor/D minor/B minor)
Stanza 2	*a*^{1}	(B minor/D minor/B minor)
		Slight rhythmic changes are made to suit the text.
Stanza 3	*a*^{2}	(B minor/F-sharp minor/B minor)
		The melodic profile shows a relationship to *a;* the key is the same initially, but the triplet movement in the accompaniment and the persistent accents on the second beat make for considerable variety.
Stanza 4	*b*	(B major)
		The most extensive section; a fuller texture, an insistent inner motive in $\frac{6}{8}$ meter, and an inverted pedal in the treble of the accompaniment characterize this concluding portion, all of which is in the tonic major key. Observe the built-in ritard as the meter changes in the accompaniment on the final statement of *Unsere Liebe* (bar 113).

The musical form *a a*^{1} *a*^{2} *b* is a variant of the traditional *a a b, Bar* form. Except for the *Magelone Lieder,* this song is one of Brahms's longest.

HEINE

Der Tod, das ist die kühle Nacht

Der Tod, das ist die kühle Nacht,
Das Leben ist der schwüle Tag.
Es dunkelt schon, mich schläfert,
Der Tag hat mich müd' gemacht.

Über mein Bett erhebt sich ein Baum,
Drin singt die junge Nachtigall;
Sie singt von lauter Liebe,
Ich hör' es sogar im Traum.

This poem is No. 87 in the series called *Die Heimkehr* ("Homecoming"), written during the years 1823-24. Day is life; night, death. Day is sultry and exhausting; it has made the poet tired. He is sleepy and approaches, apparently, his eternal sleep. Yet this poem was written when Heine was still a young man!

Notes on the text:

3 *Es dunkelt:* cf. *Die Lorelei.*
   mich schläfert: an archaic impersonal construction ("it makes me sleepy"—with no specification of what the "it" is), used elsewhere by Heine (cf. *ihn schläfert* in the poem *Ein Fichtenbaum steht einsam*).
6 *Nachtigall:* typical songbird of the night. Why "young"? Is his night young?
7 *lauter:* an indeclinable adjective; "nothing but, sheer."
8 *es:* does not mean the bird (which would require a feminine pronoun) but the act of singing. *Im Traum* is perplexing; the first strophe leads us to believe that sleep will be the sleep of death. What sort of dream will Heine have in death? Or is death a sleep in which one dreams of life? Heine is indulging in his customary extravagance of utterance. There is a contrast between the two strophes that is not easily resolved—except, perhaps, in music.

Op. 96, No. 1

Opus 96 was supposed to include only a group of Heine songs. Before its publication, however, Daumer's *Wir wandelten* was added as the second of the four lieder. *Der Tod, das ist die kühle Nacht,* the first Heine song in the group, opens with a slowly rising melody moving from the mediant upward to the tonic in this splendid example of Brahms's lyrical gifts. A syncopated accompaniment accents beats 2 and 5 in the $\frac{6}{8}$ meter. Before and after *Es dunkelt schon* (bar 7), the piano part contains several different altered chords, most of them belonging to the key of D, the supertonic, as if the *dunkelt* were reflected in the groping within the harmonic pattern before settling unexpectedly into the dominant major at *müde gemacht,* bar 12. A new texture and accompanimental figure support the second stanza, where the voice moves upward and outward in lush Brahmsian sonorities. The dominant pedal point in the accompaniment emerges as the single sustaining element. The pianist elaborates on the notes of *Liebe* (bars 19 and 21), filling in the gaps in the melodic line from A to C and then F to G. The music does not return to the opening strains. Both Brahms and the poet apparently welcome death with little sense of anxiety. The tonic pedal point in the bass adds a touch of finality to the last seven bars.

UHLAND

Der Schmied

Ich hör meinen Schatz,
Den Hammer er schwinget,
Das rauschet, das klinget,
Das dringt in die Weite,
Wie Glockengeläute,
Durch Gassen und Platz.

Am schwarzen Kamin,
Da sitzet mein Lieber,
Doch geh ich vorüber,
Die Bälge dann sausen,
Die Flammen aufbrausen
Und lodern um ihn.

The song is sung by the blacksmith's sweetheart. Uhland's rhythm reproduces—or gives the reader or composer the opportunity to reproduce—the beats of the hammer on the anvil. When his sweetheart goes by, the smith puts on a special show, the bellows whir, the flames shoot up, and sparks fly. And all this light and heat no doubt have something to do with symbolizing his love.

Note that the first and last lines of each strophe rhyme. This necessitates an "attention span" that may not endure, for it is not easy to recollect, for example, *Schatz* in line 1 upon reaching *Platz* in line 6. Yet there seems to be no impression that the sixth line is left hanging. Somehow the sense of rhyme comes through.

Op. 19, No. 4

One of the few absolutely strophic settings we shall discuss, *Der Schmied* appeared in manuscript (differently from the way it is printed today) with the two verses placed one under the other between the voice part and the accompaniment. (Ex. 48-a, p. 283.) Notice again how Brahms employs the basic triad in the melody of this folksy song. The piano part makes an instant impression: one rhythmic motive recurs to unify the song, whose tunefulness, also, is exceptional for Brahms.

Several composers were inspired to use blacksmiths and their profession as the subject matter of songs: cf. the Anvil Chorus from Verdi's *Il Trovatore* and the smithy motives of the Nibelungen in Wagner's *Ring*. Traditionally, people who wielded steel and made swords were exceptional. Uhland's poem appealed to numerous musicians, and other settings include Schumann's arrangement for mixed choir, Op. 145, No. 1, and Konradin Kreutzer's setting for male choir and soloist.

FRANZ KUGLER (1808-58)

Kugler is not a well-known figure in German literature. He is better known as the author of a history of art, and he was professor of that subject at the University of Berlin. A few plays by him are now completely forgotten, but he is remembered because of this serenade and its setting by Brahms. Another poem, *An der Saale hellem Strande,* is still known, perhaps on its own merits. One could compile a list of otherwise obscure writers who once or twice achieved in a lied lasting merit, whereas the vast mass of their literature is assigned to oblivion.

Ständchen

Der Mond steht über dem Berge,
So recht für verliebte Leut';
Im Garten rieselt ein Brunnen,
Sonst Stille weit und breit.

Neben der Mauer im Schatten,
Da stehn der Studenten drei,
Mit Flöt' und Geig' und Zither,
Und singen und spielen dabei.

Die Klänge schleichen der Schönsten
Sacht in den Traum hinein,
Sie schaut den blonden Geliebten
Und lispelt "Vergiss nicht mein!"

A serenade does not need to be a solo. Here three students serenade the lady with flute, fiddle, and zither. The mood is set with moonlight. A fountain ripples in Eichendorffian fashion in the garden; all else is still. And even the music-making of the serenaders does not cause the girl to awake. The notes softly insinuate themselves into her dream, and she sees her blond lover there. Is he one of the three? Or are they singing on his behalf? We do not know. She murmurs in sleep, *Vergiss nicht mein!*

Notes on the text:

2 *So recht für verliebte Leut':* "made to order" for people in love.
4 *Stille:* a noun derived from the adjective; cf. English "quiet."
6 *der Studenten drei: Studenten* is genitive ("three [of] students, a trio of students").
9 *der Schönsten:* dative.
12 *lispelt:* "whispers" (rather than "lisps").
   mein: an old genitive of the pronoun; *vergessen* formerly took that case. An archaic touch is imparted to the whole poem by one or two such strokes.

Op. 106, No. 1

Kugler's *Skizzenbuch* included not only poems but also drawings and some musical compositions by this versatile artist and musician, who had set Chamisso's *Frauenliebe und -leben* earlier than either Loewe or Schumann. In contrast to the preceding songs, Kugler's poem brings out another side of Brahms. A picaresque, light, carefree mood permeates the song. The vocal melody rises to a twelfth above its starting point, and the accompaniment sounds like the plucked strings of a guitar.

The three stanzas are set in an *a b a* pattern. We can see how Brahms links the two phrases of the initial melody by comparing, for example, the direction of the pitches under *Im Garten rieselt* with those of *Der Mond steht über*. Notice also that the rhythmic profile of the two phrases is identical. Subtle associations like these are common in Brahms's music. Broadly spaced arpeggiated triplets, a feature of the transition, reflect the words *singen und spielen* (bars 21 ff.) before a resumption of the opening *a* section.

TRADITIONAL

Wiegenlied

Guten Abend, gut Nacht,
Mit Rosen bedacht,
Mit Näglein besteckt,
Schlupf unter die Deck:
Morgen früh, wenn Gott will,
Wirst du wieder geweckt.

Guten Abend, gut Nacht,
Von Englein bewacht,
Die zeigen im Traum
Dir Christkindleins Baum:
Schlaf nun selig und süss,
Schau im Traum's Paradies.

There are no poetical complications in this traditional lullaby, but a few archaisms of language could be troublesome to those who have learned standard German. Like many traditional poems of popular origin, this has apparently been modified by more sophisticated hands, but not excessively so. The somewhat gruesome note struck in lines 5 and 6 is found in other lullabies. The same theme is found in "If I should die before I wake," and the insertion of such sentiments was doubtless a superstitious safeguard of the child's soul.

Notes on the text:

2 *bedacht:* an older form of the past participle of *bedecken* "cover"; standard German has *bedeckt*.

3 *Näglein:* "carnations, pinks." Standard German has *Nelken* (plural of *Nelke*). The word can also mean "cloves," which makes
slightly clearer the etymological connection with "little nails."

4 *Schlupf':* the form *schlüpf'* (with umlaut) is more usual.

10 *Christkindleins Baum* ("Christ Child's tree"): Christmas tree.

12 *Traum's:* the *'s* is a contraction of the neuter definite article *das*
and belongs with *Paradies.*

Op. 49, No. 4

A version of this poem known as a love letter dates from the fifteenth
century. In 1868, Brahms, however, used the text that had appeared in
Arnim and Brentano's *Des Knaben Wunderhorn,* where it was titled *Gute
Nacht, mein Kind.* For the accompaniment, he borrowed a typical Viennese waltz song, which he had heard sung by his friend Fräulein Porubsky
in Hamburg in 1859. By means of syncopation and insertions, Brahms
disguised the piano part and added to it a delightful lullaby containing
one exceptional feature: a rising vocal line. Most lullabies descend, lulling
the child to sleep. Perhaps because of this unique feature, but more probably as the result of the combination of Viennese flavor and the delightfully singable melody, the song became an immediate success. Brahms
dedicated it to Frau Bertha Faber (formerly Porubsky) in celebration of
the birth of her second son.

Fritz Simrock, Brahms's publisher, added the second stanza, which
was written by Georg Scherer and printed in his *Illustriertes deutsches
Kinderbuch* in 1849, but the composer was never pleased with the text.
Notice how even in this simple setting Brahms employs contrary motion
in an inner voice of the accompaniment at the very end of the song.

Some doubt persists whether this is a traditional poem of unknown
authorship or whether it was written by Anton Wilhelm Florentin von
Zuccalmaglio (a sufficiently unbelievable name itself), who collected folk

Vergebliches Ständchen

"Guten Abend, mein Schatz, guten Abend, mein Kind!
Ich komm aus Lieb zu dir,
Ach, mach mir auf die Tür,
Mach mir auf die Tür!"

Mein' Tür ist verschlossen, ich lass dich nicht ein;
Mutter die rät mir klug,
Wärst du herein mit Fug,
Wär's mit mir vorbei.

"So kalt ist die Nacht, so eisig der Wind;
Dass mir das Herz erfriert,
Mein Lieb erlöschen wird.
Öffne mir, mein Kind!"

Löschet dein Lieb, lass sie löschen nur!
Löschet sie immerzu,
Geh heim zu Bett, zur Ruh;
Gute Nacht, mein Knab!

songs and published them under one or two pseudonyms. He may have collected this; the matter is hardly of world-shattering importance.

This "Vain Serenade," or "Serenade in Vain," differs from others in having a conversation between the would-be lover and the unwilling maiden. Thus it is, strictly speaking, not a serenade at all but a poem *about* a serenade. There is considerable humor here in the girl's rejection of the proffered affections, and no real heartbreak is perceived. When the man pleads "Let me in or my love will grow cold and die!" her answer is "Let it! Then you can go home and go to bed!" And perhaps that is for the best.

Notes on the text:

3   *mach' mir auf die Tür:* for more standard *mach' mir die Tür auf.*
6   *Mutter die:* "folksy" word order.
8   *Wär's mit mir vorbei:* "it would be 'all up' with me."
13   *Löschet:* verb first, in a condition (= "If your love goes out"). Any attempt to treat this case of unrequited love as something tragic would be ludicrous.

Op. 84, No. 4

Brahms, when he took this poem from Zuccalmaglio's collection *Deutsche Volkslieder,* was deceived by the poet's title *Niederrheinisches Volkslied,* not realizing that he had set to music an old folk-song theme, not a folk song. The composer employed a modified strophic pattern, writing a slightly different accompaniment for each of the four stanzas, changing to minor for the third stanza. The arpeggiated vocal melody is typical of Brahms; the tunefulness is not. This lied obviously belongs to the lighter side of his works. The composer himself added the words *Er* and *Sie* to the appropriate stanzas. Each stanza is divided into two parts; the first has the piano following the vocal line (Ex. 39-a), and the second (Ex. 39-b) has staccato chords in the piano. The two sections are unified, however, by the triadic nature of the vocal melodies.

Ex. 39

BRAHMS: *Vergebliches Ständchen*

VII

Folk Influence

MAHLER (1860-1911)

Although primarily concerned with large-scale orchestral works, Mahler also wrote about forty songs, many of which form the kernel of particular movements of his symphonies. For example, the fourth movements of his Second, Third, and Fourth Symphonies are song movements requiring a soloist to sing with the orchestra; and the fifth movements of the Second and Third are choral movements. In addition, the first three symphonies have movements based on material culled from the songs. Finally, two additional symphonies—the Fifth and the unfinished Tenth—incorporate melodies that closely resemble thematic material found in the songs.

It is easy to isolate the principal sources and subject matter of Mahler's lieder: folk music and folk poetry appear in about twenty songs from *Des Knaben Wunderhorn*. Accompanimental figures in these songs include many imitations of nature, such as bird calls, besides military fanfares and the *Ländler* type of dance tune. Fate, death, and the elemental forces of nature prove irresistible, particularly in the Rückert songs. Mahler set ten of this poet's texts, all with orchestral as well as piano versions. Five of these make up the *Kindertotenlieder* cycle. Mahler provided his own words for his other orchestral song cycle, *Lieder eines fahrenden Gesellen*.

Although Berlioz was one of the first composers to write a song cycle for voice and orchestra, this genre usually calls to mind the works of the Germans Mahler and Strauss. Whereas Mahler did write two such cycles, most of his songs appeared originally for voice and piano and were orchestrated only later. Occasionally he tries for orchestral effects at the keyboard. Sometimes he achieves them, and at other times the results resemble those emanating from under the fingers of young, aspiring conductors as they "read" an orchestral score at the piano. Mahler was not a pianist; at no time do his figurations show any correspondence to those employed by composers like Schumann or Brahms, or even his closer contemporary, Hugo Wolf.

Both of the songs we have included were published in Mahler's early *Lieder und Gesänge aus der Jugendzeit* (1880-83). Leander's *Erinnerung* reveals the dark, anxious side of Mahler's personality, the Viennese *Angst* and *Weltschmerz* he so thoroughly enjoyed. *Ich ging mit Lust,* the text of which derives from *Des Knaben Wunderhorn,* portrays the other side of his nature. A carefree folksiness pervades the entire composition, a splendid foil to *Erinnerung.*

Des Knaben Wunderhorn

This most popular of all collections of German folk songs was published in 1806-08 by Achim von Arnim and Clemens Brentano. It was the first such collection of any importance, for Herder's work (1778-79) was largely devoted to collecting and translating the folk songs of other nations. Yet Arnim and Brentano evinced more enthusiasm than scholarship and tried to improve many a song by rewriting it. There have been several such collections after them, although none has achieved the same esteem. The title, "The Boy's Magic Horn," which is also one of the songs in the collection, refers to a horn sent as a gift from a mermaid to the Empress. The boy is the bearer of the gift. It is a wondrously wrought horn of ivory, gold, and silver, with countless precious stones and a hundred gólden bells. The boy tells the Empress that if she merely presses the horn with her finger, the bells will emit such beauteous music as has never been heard on earth or elsewhere. She does so, and the promised result is realized.

In the *Wunderhorn* this poem is called *Waldvöglein* ("Little Woodbirds"). Mahler's "sleepyhead" version contrasts with the original by the omission of two stanzas and the addition of another, for which he may have authority, however. The original has the lover appear and explain his delay in coming. Boastfully, and somewhat cruelly, he says he has been detained by three great attractions, beer, red wine, and a brown-haired maiden. "I almost forgot all about you!" But he does come to see his girl, however late.

Ich ging mit Lust

Ich ging mit Lust durch einen grünen Wald,
ich hört' die Vöglein singen;
sie sangen so jung, sie sangen so alt,
die kleinen Waldvöglein im grünen Wald!
Wie gern hört' ich sie singen!

Nun sing, nun sing, Frau Nachtigall!
Sing du's bei meinem Feinsliebchen:
Komm schier, wenn's finster ist,
wenn niemand auf der Gasse ist,
dann komm zu mir!
Herein will ich dich lassen!

Der Tag verging, die Nacht brach an,
er kam zu Feinsliebchen, Feinsliebchen gegangen.
Er klopft so leis' wohl an den Ring:
"Ei schläfst du oder wachst,mein Kind?
Ich hab so lang gestanden!"

Es schaut der Mond durchs Fensterlein
zum holden, süssen Lieben,
die Nachtigall sang die ganze Nacht.
Du schlafselig Mägdelein, nimm dich in Acht!
Wo ist dein Herzliebster geblieben?

Notes on the text:

1 This line has a swinging, promising lilt.
3 *so jung . . . so alt:* some tunes were youthful and sprightly, others sounded graver and philosophical.
8 *schier:* an older meaning is "soon" (later "almost").
9 *Gassen:* an older dative singular (now *Gasse*).
13 *kam . . . gegangen:* "came walking."
14 *Ring:* the knocker or doorknob.
20 *schlafselig:* "blissfully sleeping, sleepy."

The verses show assonance in addition to rhyme (sometimes "perfect" or identical rhyme: e.g., *singen: singen*).

The drone bass heard first in the opening bars, the sound of the horns in the treble, and the triadic melody in the vocal part (see Ex. 40-a) all

point to a folksy setting of a simple tune. Mahler, however, has here combined several folk-music features with other sophisticated techniques of
lieder composition. Prone to employing imitations of nature, he inserted
the sound of birds singing at bars 6 ff., directly over the drone bass (Ex.
40-b). His text setting is basically syllabic, with only an occasional neumatic
passage. Throughout most of this lied the treble of the accompaniment
doubles the vocal line. Always, however, on each restatement of a, the
accompaniment changes somewhat, as if Mahler the orchestrator were
thinking in terms of different instrumentation for each appearance of the
theme.

Ex. 40

MAHLER: *Ich ging mit Lust*

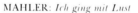

Ich   ging   mit   Lust   durch ei - nen grünen Wald

a.

b.

The formal pattern is clearly discernible. The composer separated
the four stanzas in the following manner:

Text	Stanza	Formal unit	Key
Ich ging . . .	1	a	D major
Nun sing . . .	2	a^1	D major
Der Tag . . .	3	b	G major
Es schaut . . .	4	a^2	D major

Mahler varied the *a* material with modifications in the accompaniment. These changes are less figural than harmonic or modal alterations. Compare, for example, bars 5 and 34, bars 13 and 42, or bars 21 and 50. The IV^9 chord at bar 18 and a few appogiaturas are only slight departures from the commonplace I-IV-V progressions.

Curiously, the opening of the *b* section (Ex. 40-c) reveals a distinct melodic relationship to the material in bar 21, similar to the correspondence we often find between the two parts of a Brahms song. In the *b* section, Mahler has also used a tonic pedal, but in a figuration different from the drone bass of the opening. Compare the bass of Ex. 40-a and Ex. 40-c.

c.

Finally, observe that what begins as a balanced symmetrical phrase structure turns into irregular groupings so characteristic of Bohemian folk songs. Mahler extends his musical line through text repetition.

RICHARD LEANDER (1830-89)

Leander was the pseudonym of Richard von Volkmann (Leander—"Man of the people"—being a Greek translation, in Latin guise, of Volkmann), who was a physician as well as author. He wrote lyrical poetry and stories, some of which were best-sellers. His medical writings were important in their day. As Surgeon General of the Prussian Army, he was a pioneer in the introduction of antiseptic procedure. In 1885 he was elevated to the nobility (hence the *von*), surely for his contributions to medicine rather than to literature. Nevertheless, although he is almost

completely forgotten as a literary figure, some of his verse is not inferior
to that of remembered authors.

Erinnerung

Es wecket meine Liebe die Lieder immer wieder!
Es wecken meine Lieder die Liebe immer wieder!
Die Lippen, die da träumen von deinen heissen Küssen,
In Sang und Liedesweisen von dir sie tönen müssen!
Und wollen die Gedanken der Liebe sich entschlagen,
So kommen meine Lieder zu mir mit Liebesklagen!
So halten mich in Banden die Beiden immer wieder!
Es weckt das Lied die Liebe!
Die Liebe weckt die Lieder!

The theme is the mutual inextricability and reciprocal reaction of
love and song (poetry). His love reawakens his songs, and his songs reawaken love, even if his conscious thought might want to dismiss it. The
poet and lover is held captive by love and song. His lips, appropriately
enough, participate in both activities; that they dream of past kisses and
are thus compelled to sing is a conceit worthy of Heine at his most
extravagant.

The first seven lines consist of fourteen syllables each—six accented—
whereas lines 8 and 9 are each half that length. The division is somewhat
arbitrary, for the last two lines could just as well constitute one line; or
every line could be divided into two, for there is a slight metrical pause
in each, as is partly taken into account in Mahler's setting.

Notes on the text:

Title. As emerges from the poem itself, *Erinnerung* embraces several
connotations, including "remembrance" and "memory" but also
"reminding, admonition."

1, 2 *Es:* particle anticipating the subject (as in line 8 also). In line
1, the verb is singular (the subject is *Liebe*); in line 2, it is
plural (for *Lieder*).

4 *Liedesweisen:* "melodies of song, melodies."
tönen: "sound" = "sing."

The word order, as well as the gratuitous insertion of *sie,* is irregular for reasons of metrics and rhyme.

5   *und wollen:* "even if my thoughts would . . ."
    sich entschlagen (with dative): "get rid of, give up, dismiss."

7   *die Beiden:* "these two" (love and song).

8   *das Lied:* generic; not one particular song but all songs, represented by the singular.

That Mahler is predominantly a song composer or that his symphonies are in essence overblown lieder may be argued by some critics. Others, however, find this criticism indefensible. True, like Schubert, he was essentially a lyrical composer. But unlike the earlier Viennese musician, he could not contain his lyricism within the confines of the miniature song form. Intimacy was unknown to Mahler. When he was happy, he wanted the world to know, and when he was sad, he wanted everyone to share his grief. Even a typical lied, *Erinnerung,* one of the early *Lieder und Gesänge aus der Jugendzeit,* cries out for orchestration, a treatment it received at the hands of one of Mahler's younger disciples. Voice and piano are inadequate for the sonority Mahler required.

In *Erinnerung,* the voice is doubled in the accompaniment throughout all but the latter half of the middle section (*So kommen . . . . ,* bars 28 ff.,), at which point the register also changes sharply. Persistent triplets in the bass reflect the ambivalence so characteristic of Mahler's personality. As a pedal point or ostinato, they provide a stable element; at the same time, rhythmically they produce the uneasiness that always accompanies the sound of three notes set against two. (Compare the bass and the treble of the accompaniment.) Indeed, the recurrence of triplet eighths in all but the final four bars of the song colors the entire lied.

Ex. 41

MAHLER: *Erinnerung*

a.

The rhythmic profile of the melody, too, is constantly repeated. (See ⌐ in Ex. 41-a.) Except at the initial climax of the piece, bars 16-17, this phrase is always preceded by a rest. By means of this pause (see * in Ex. 41-a), Mahler accounts for the implied division within each line of the text. Thus a seven-syllable textual phrase occupies two and a half bars, and the complete fourteen-syllable line covers five bars, which become the basic larger musical unit.

At the conclusion of the first statement of section *a*, bars 1-10, the accompaniment concludes the chromatic descent of the vocal line. Following the repeat of *a*, after *müssen,* the pianist has a longer chromatic descent. At the final appearance of *a* (see Tempo I, bars 40 ff.), Mahler writes an extended descending chromatic scale in the Aeolian mode. Trace it in the treble of the accompaniment from bar 48 to the close of the piece.

The melody is basically stepwise, the fourth being favored for leaps. The highest pitch in the entire song is at bar 32, where the voice begins and the piano ends an eleven-note chromatic descent with a tritone drop to underline the meaning of *Klagen* (Ex. 41-b). In addition to the ostinato,

b.

the recurrent rhythmic profile of the melody, and the repeated fragments of a descending scale, a fourth feature, the melodic interval of a minor second, serves to unify this lied. It appears five times in the first five bars of the piece. (See it in the first two and a half bars in Ex. 41-a.) Although the song is in ternary form, the opening tonality does not reappear at the close. Compare bars 12 and 40, which present the same material, and notice that the concluding section affords a good example of Mahler's technique of progressive tonality. Beginning in G minor, *Erinnerung* ends in A minor.

VIII

Poems for Voice and Piano

HUGO WOLF (1860-1903)

Hugo Wolf's career in music is unique in two respects. First, his reputation rests almost exclusively on the 242 songs for voice and piano that he completed during his short lifetime; second, the actual time spent in the composition of the vast majority of these songs is approximately six months! He often wrote two or three lieder in one day. When Wolf worked, it was in a creative frenzy. We can believe him when he writes, "I am working incessantly with a thousand horsepower from dawn till late at night." Forty-three of the Mörike songs were written in three months. From the age of seventeen, he had begun to write music, but not until he came across the poems of Mörike did he feel that he had found a kindred soul, a man whose thoughts corresponded so well with his own that the poet's words and his music would sound made for one another. Truly grateful to Mörike for a renewal of his self-confidence, the composer called his work *Gedichte von Eduard Mörike für eine Sing-stimme und Klavier*. He titled the first song *Der Genesene an die Hoffnung* ("A Convalescent's Ode to Hope").

Wolf had studied the lieder of his predecessors, particularly Schubert, Schumann, and Loewe; he also understood Wagner's new kind of *Sprech-gesang*. This latter technique appealed to him, and we find numerous lieder in this new style. His musical gifts, his original approach to melody, rhythm, and harmony enabled him to set each song in a unique fashion. We cannot, as we could with Schubert's works, for example, point to particular pianistic figurations reused in numbers of songs. Wolf had an uncanny knack for selecting just the right combination and figuration for each song. Furthermore, he rarely made more than one setting of a poem. He would not set poems that he felt had already been well treated by others. When he set the *Harfenspieler* songs from *Wilhelm Meister,* for which both Schubert and Schumann had already composed music, it was simply because he believed he could do better.

Wolf was an intellectual composer, and his reputation, as Ernest Newman says, outstripped his popularity. Wolf's songs are the caviar of lieder literature, showing a highly refined sense of style. As a result, songs from the Mörike cycle would seem as out of place among the Goethe songs as Wagner's writing for *Tristan und Isolde* would sound conspicuously wrong in *Die Meistersinger.* Wolf's Eichendorff songs are the fewest in number. Although the composer reveals humor as a hitherto untouched dimension of Eichendorff's personality, as a group these songs are less remarkable than those of Goethe or Mörike. Besides the fifty-three Mörike songs, twenty Eichendorff lieder (and an additional eight early songs), and fifty-one Goethe settings (ten more are among his early works), the balance of Wolf's works are settings of poetry translated by Heyse and Geibel. First, he set the *Spanisches Liederbuch,* whose forty-four songs are divided into ten sacred and thirty-four secular songs. These were completed in 1890. Then the *Italienisches Liederbuch* appeared, the first part in 1890-92, the second in 1896. The two parts provide a total of forty-six songs. Actually, almost half of Wolf's songs are settings of foreign works in translation.

Lovers, rogues, poets, sailors, hunters, kings, humorists, and philosophers are portrayed in Wolf's music. Flowers, mountains, clouds, sunset, dawn, and the middle of the night are subjects for reflection. Elves and birds, fairy-tale objects as well as real people, are the topics that appeal to him. Curiously, no two characters are alike; Wolf is not a generalist. Indeed, in his lieder we encounter again the kind of attention to detail, to specific words, that we noticed in many of Schubert's songs.

EDUARD MÖRIKE (1804-75)

The outstanding lyric poet of Swabia (whether there was a "Swabian school" or not is a question left undebated here), Mörike was one of the best German poets of the nineteenth century. He did not have literature as his profession, being first a pastor (many Swabian poets studied theology) but leaving that calling for reasons of health. He was subsequently a teacher of German literature at a girls' secondary school in Stuttgart.

Many of his poems have become the "common property" of the people and virtually rank as folk songs. Hugo Wolf's settings have no doubt helped to preserve his immortality, but he had sufficient merit of his own to enjoy lasting fame. The heir of Goethe, of romanticism, and of the tradition of classical antiquity, he is unpretentious in his lyrical utterances, not given to hyperbole and extravagance or to literary posing. A good sense of proportion prevents conceit. Many of his poems reflect a lost happiness, nostalgia, or an unsatisfied yearning, but his poetry is never maudlin. He was a promising novelist, and his short story *Mozart auf der Reise nach Prag* maintains its place as a treasure of German literature.

Verborgenheit

Lass, o Welt, o lass mich sein!
Locket nicht mit Liebesgaben,
Lasst dies Herz alleine haben
Seine Wonne, seine Pein!

Was ich traure, weiss ich nicht,
Es ist unbekanntes Wehe;
Immerdar durch Tränen sehe
Ich der Sonne liebes Licht.

Oft bin ich mir kaum bewusst,
Und die helle Freude zücket
Durch die Schwere, so mich drücket,
Wonniglich in meiner Brust.

Lass, o Welt, o lass mich sein!
Locket nicht mit Liebesgaben,
Lasst dies Herz alleine haben
Seine Wonne, seine Pein!

The notions are not simple. Can the heart alone be the source of its joy and sorrow independently of others, of the world? He admits that his sorrow and grief are of unknown origin (thus not necessarily the creation of the heart itself), and here he resembles those romantic authors who, like him, spoke of a "wild, unknown woe." Often he is hardly aware of what is happening (but aware enough to write a poem) as radiant joy flashes through the "heaviness" that otherwise oppresses him. Despite his pain, he rejects the "gifts of love" with which the world allegedly tempts him. He repeats the first strophe at the end, as if to underscore the desire to be let alone as he shies away from love. Mörike, we are told, was a shy man; *Verborgenheit* can mean "secrecy, seclusion, privacy"—even "withdrawal," as Philip Miller has it (with possibly anachronistic application of psychoanalytical terminology).

Notes on the text:

2 *Locket:* Mörike shifts the imperative from the singular in line 1 (where, however, he addresses the world) to the plural, where he seems to think of several individuals.
9 "I scarcely realize; I am scarcely aware."
12 *Wonniglich* implies that the troubles he endures are somehow accompanied by blissful pleasure; this recalls the bitter-sweet experience of many *Sturm und Drang* poets.

The composer has so carefully followed the formal plan of the poet that we should do well to examine his procedure. Wolf shapes the four stanzas into a ternary lied in the following way:

Stanzas	Musical form	Length	Accompaniment
1	*a*	2 bars intro., 8 with text	drone bass
2		8 bars with text	thick-textured chords
	b	1 bar interlude	
3		8 bars with text	thick-textured chords
4	*a¹*	8 bars with text, 1 bar extension	drone bass

Observe that where Mörike employed the same text, Wolf reused the same music. The piano figurations in the two middle stanzas (*b*) sound practically identical; the only modification is the appearance of a fragmentary bass melody at the opening of the third stanza. The melodies in these two stanzas, seemingly different, on close inspection reveal a subtle relationship to one another. Compare, for example, G–F sharp–C in the voice part in bars 11 and 12 with F–C–B in bar 21. Furthermore, *Verborgenheit,* like *Anakreons Grab* (see p. 277), contains a distinct three-note motive, which, appearing as it does in each of the separate sections of the song, links them together. (See Exx. 42-a, 42-b, and 42-c.) The voice enters with this motive above the open-fifth drone, which already in the two-bar piano introduction emphasizes the essentially lonely mood of the poem. In the second stanza, see the motive in bar 13 in the bass (Ex. 42-b); in the third, in bar 21 as well as bars 24 ff. (Ex. 42-c).

Ex. 42

WOLF: *Verborgenheit*

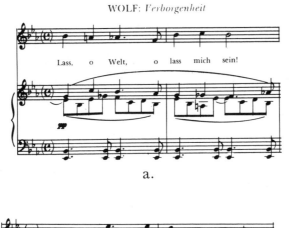

Lass, o Welt, o lass mich sein!

a.

es ist un - be - kann - tes We - he;

b.

durch die Schwere, so mich drü - cket, won -

c.

Verborgenheit is one of the most popular of Wolf's songs, although many critics do not rank it among his best. Structurally, however, it gives evidence of extremely careful workmanship. Wolf does well to borrow Schumann's favorite performance instruction, *sehr innig*. At the opening, and later when the music swells to a climax (Ex. 42-c), *Innigkeit* is the order of the day. The composer has taken the title of the poem literally; the tonal/modal opening defies classification. The surprisingly lyrical melody proceeds to a welcome cadence at bar 10. Once again, the composer's excellent rhythmic control allows him to offer several different rhythmic schemes perfectly compatible with one another (Ex. 42-a). Underlining the fundamental meaning of the second stanza, the music moves upward and outward harmonically and melodically, the texture becoming ever more dense. (See Ex. 42-b.) In the third stanza, the passionate vocal line, straightforward, powerful, but without ornamentation, moves to a climax. Because of Wolf's concern for strict economy of means, he rarely indulges in fioriture. (One of the only examples of vocal acrobatics of any kind can be found in Ex. 45-c, from *Die Zigeunerin*.) He illuminates such words as *Wonne* (bar 9), *Licht* (bar 18), and *wonniglich* (bar 26), but always with taste.

Er ist's

Frühling lässt sein blaues Band
Wieder flattern durch die Lüfte;
Süsse, wohlbekannte Düfte
Streifen ahnungsvoll das Land.
Veilchen träumen schon,
Wollen balde kommen.
Horch, von fern ein leiser Harfenton!
Frühling, ja du bist's!
Dich hab ich vernommen!

The imminent arrival of Spring is excitedly sensed by the poet with successive perception through sight, smell, and sound (blue sky, the nascent scent of flowers, the sounds of the harp). Spring is not quite here, but it (he) is ready to break forth at any moment, and all nature is poised to receive him. The last two lines are addressed to Spring himself, as *Er ist's* of the title yields to the direct (but apostrophic) *du bist's,* "It's you!"

Notes on the text:

Title. *Er* is obviously masculine because of *der Frühling*, but the gender facilitates personification. English has "It is I, you, he," but German says, "I am it, you are it, he is it."

1 *blaues Band:* evidently the blue ribbon is a strip of blue vernal sky.

2 *wieder:* "once again," because the welcome arrival of spring is a recurrent phenomenon, as is further indicated by *wohlbekannte* in line 3.

4 *streifen:* "brush, stroke"; a verb of tactile connotation is neatly applied to scents (synesthesia).
ahnungsvoll: "full of presentiment, premonition" = anticipating the imminent arrival.

5 The violets dream, as it were, that they are soon to be born.

7 The significance of the sound of the harp is ambiguous. Perhaps the instrument is associated with spring, or the playing of the harp is resumed after a long winter, or the harp is now played outdoors in the mild air. (The spring season in Central Europe is different from that of America.)

9 *vernommen:* past participle of *vernehmen* "to perceive" (through any of the senses, but most frequently through hearing).

The rhyme scheme is *a b b a, c d c (e) d*. Line 8, the climax of the poem, is conspicuous by being the only unrhymed line in it. The *a*'s and *c*'s are masculine, the *b*'s and *d*'s feminine rhymes. The meter is trochaic in the main, but the syllabic count is uneven, especially in the last five lines. Lines 1 and 4 have seven syllables; lines 2 and 3, eight; lines 5, 8, 9 have only five syllables; 6 has six; and the overlong line 7 has nine.

Three famous lieder composers—Schumann, Robert Franz, and Wolf —all set Mörike's poem *Er ist's*. The Franz song need not concern us here. Sufficiently startling are the differences between Schumann's version of the poem and Wolf's setting. Apparently, spring meant different things to each composer. Their responses reflect the differences in their personalities. For example, Schumann marked his lied with his favorite expression, *Innig*.

Wolf wrote *sehr lebhaft, jubelnd*. And a more jubilant setting would be hard to find: *Er ist's* surely ranks among Wolf's liveliest songs. One can almost sense the feeling of rebirth brought by the new spring season: the leaves rustling in the breeze, the earth pulsating with renewed youth.

The piano is most important here. One figuration (Ex. 43) prevails in forty-five of the total fifty-five bars of the lied. Short piano interludes and a twenty-bar postlude are significant structural features. Fleet fingers are essential for the accompanist, also a leggiero quality that rarely finds its way into lieder accompaniments. The delightfully lyrical melody is exceptional for the composer. The rhythmic figure, too, duplicates the breathlessness inherent in the setting. Notice the rest (see * in Ex. 43) within each alternate grouping of triplet sixteenths.

Ex. 43

WOLF: *Er ist's*

Früh - ling lässt sein

The poet did not subdivide the lines into stanzas. The composer, on the other hand, has separated the song into sections, each—owing to the variations in the number of syllables in each line—of different length. (Curiously, all three of the composers mentioned above made the same musical divisions. Furthermore, each repeats *Frühling, ja du bist's*, the only unrhymed line, several times in the course of the song.) Here is Wolf's scheme:

2   bars introduction
8   bars with text, 2 bars extension
2   bars interlude

4   bars with text
1   bar interlude
4   bars with text—2 bars extension

6 bars with text—1 bar extension
2 bars with text—2 bars extension

20 bars postlude

The accompanimental figure and the recurrence of several short motives (cf. bar 5 and the opening of the postlude, for example) join the sections tightly together.

In an unexpected harmonic progression in bars 9-12, where we anticipate a modulation to A major, Wolf resolves instead to C-sharp major, a refreshing change. He also compresses a series of unresolved dominant seventh chords (bars 15-25), successfully building tension which resolves only at the conclusion of the vocal part (bars 33 ff.). Following this section, the listener is catapulted into the fiery conclusion of what is unquestionably one of Wolf's most accessible songs.

An eine Äolsharfe

Angelehnt an die Efeuwand
Dieser alten Terrasse,
Du, einer luftgebornen Muse
Geheimnisvolles Saitenspiel,
Fang' an,
Fange wieder an
Deine melodische Klage!

Ihr kommet, Winde, fernherüber,
Ach! von des Knaben,
Der mir so lieb war,
Frisch grünendem Hügel.
Und Frühlingsblüten unterwegs streifend,
Übersättigt mit Wohlgerüchen,
Wie süss bedrängt ihr das Herz!
Und säuselt her in die Saiten,
Angezogen von wohllautender Wehmut,
Wachsend im Zug meiner Sehnsucht,
Und hinsterbend wieder.

Aber auf einmal,
Wie der Wind heftiger herstösst,
Ein holder Schrei der Harfe
Wiederholt, mir zu süssem Erschrecken,
Meiner Seele plötzlich Regung;
Und hier--die volle Rose streut, geschüttelt,
All'ihre Blätter vor meine Füsse!

There is an autobiographical connection of an *ex post facto* sort on the part of the composer. After Wolf had set the poem to music, he was hiking with a friend in Southeast Austria. As they came to the old castle of Hoch-Osterwitz, Wolf stopped and listened. It sounded as if a piano were being played somewhere, which did not seem likely. In the most remote room of the castle they discovered the source of the music: an Aeolian harp was set in the window. Wolf was highly delighted, for he claimed that he had never heard one before but had caught it just right in his song.

This may be debatable. It is hardly likely that Mörike intended the harp to be the only motif of the poem, despite the title. For it may be secondary to the lyric themes of spring versus death, of sound and feeling, of interaction of heart and harp, of flowers and scent; these are all present in a somewhat elusive measure.

After addressing the harp and begging it to resume its plaintive music once more, the poet speaks to the winds which come from the distant grave of a boy once dear to him (possibly his brother in reality, although this is not evident from the poem). Coming from the grave, the winds could conceivably bring a message. The theme of death contrasts with the motif of spring, and this is even seen at the grave, where the vernal green is fresh on the house of death. The same winds which come from the grave and set the harp to playing are saturated en route by the scent of spring flowers; they also set the strings of the poet's heart vibrating, as they sigh in the more tangible Aeolian harp, and they reawaken in him the note of melancholy and longing. Then they die down, and the music stops.

In the next, shorter strophe, after the winds have stopped for a while, there is a sudden new gust, and a *holder Schrei* of the harp, as if taken unawares; this is matched by similar agitation in the poet himself. All of this new burst of inspiration is really a reversal of the music that was stirred by the winds of grief. The harp utters a glad cry, and the rose petals at the author's feet are, while borne by the same winds, symbols of spring and beauty and life.

This poem, whatever its autobiographical origin may be, is a reflection of Mörike's classical background. He prefaces it with a quotation from an ode of Horace, in which the great Roman poet addresses a literary friend, beseeching him to dry his tears for the loss of a favorite slave boy, Mystes, and to turn his literary powers to more positive pursuits. Is Mörike exhorting himself to do the same?

Notes on the text:

There is no rhyme in the poem, and there is considerable metrical irregularity. Whether Mörike is aiming to imitate classical meters is not clear. The poem has the effect of a classical ode or the like.

1 *Angelehnt:* "leaning."
3 *Du:* the Aeolian harp.
   einer luftgebornen Muse is genitive ("air-born," *not* "airborne," because of the source of the stirring of the strings). Aeolus was god of the winds.
4 *Saitenspiel: Saiten* = "strings," here "lyre."
11 *frisch grünendem Hügel:* goes with *des Knaben.*
12 *streifend:* "brushing, stroking, touching."
25 *Blätter:* here "petals."

Wolf must have taken the poet's reference to the harp literally, because an arpeggiated figure persists throughout the entire lied, continuing even into an extensive piano postlude, rare for the composer. Widely spaced bass arpeggios combine with full-textured chords in the high treble to provide a lush, luxuriant sound, difficult to obtain within the prescribed *immer pp* or *ppp*. The singer has a high tessitura, although frequently the voice part lies considerably lower than the lowest note of the treble chord.

Wolf separates the song into an introduction and two stanzas. These divisions do not exist in the original poem. The vocal line begins in a declamatory style. (Brahms, who set this poem only thirty years earlier in 1858, actually wrote *recit* for the opening.) Only at *melodische Klage,*

the close of the introduction, do we have a hint of the lyricism to follow.
A piano interlude separates *wieder* from *Aber auf einmal,* which starts
the second stanza. The song is completely *durchkomponiert,* the melody
unwinding endlessly. Notice the irregular phrase lengths and unexpected
melodic turns, perhaps in imitation of the poet's omission of rhyme. Except
for the constant accompanimental pattern and several recurrent intervals
—minor and major seconds and a gapped scale figure—one gets a strong
feeling of amorphism. Wolf adds to this sense of formlessness with a tension-
building device straight out of Wagner's music dramas. He refuses to
allow the voice part a resolution to the tonic. Notice that at *Klage* the
voice is left with the supertonic and the piano gets the E two octaves
down. At *wieder* the voice remains on the leading tone and the tension
is unresolved, the tonality completely blurred at this point. The singer
even ends on the mediant instead of the tonic. *An eine Äolscharfe* opens
in C-sharp minor and closes in E major, reflecting the changing mood
of the poem.

Das verlassene Mägdlein

Früh, wann die Hähne krähn,
Eh' die Sternlein schwinden,
Muss ich am Herde stehn,
Muss Feuer zünden.

Schön ist der Flammen Schein,
Es springen die Funken.
Ich schaue so darein,
In Leid versunken.

Plötzlich, da kommt es mir,
Treuloser Knabe,
Dass ich die Nacht von dir
Geträumet habe.

Träne auf Träne dann
Stürzet hernieder;
So kommt der Tag heran--
O ging' er wieder!

This is a theme of folk poetry, but the poem is not quite a *Volkslied*. The syntactic and idiomatic coloration of *Volkspoesie* are absent. If there is such a thing, it may be called *Kunstvolkspoesie* (like, for example, Goethe's *Heidenröslein*).

The servant girl has been deserted. Was the boy an apprentice staying a while, or is he one who has forsaken her for another local beauty? Was there a tale of conquest, betrayal, desertion? Before the day dawns, when the rooster crows, her duties start, deserted or no. In the course of the mundane act of lighting the fire, the girl sees the magic behind this commonplace phenomenon. The gleam of the flames, the flying sparks capture her attention and she is fascinated, while simultaneously plunged in grief. She is especially sad because she dreamed of *him* last night. As day dawns she wishes it would go away.

This is a song of quiet suffering, not of passionate condemnation. *Treuloser Knabe* is a soft, though biting reproach. The rhyme scheme is simple: *a b a b, c d c d, e f e f.*

Here we have a rare instance of Wolf's approaching a poem that had already been exceptionally well handled by a composer whom he respected. Schumann's setting (entitled *Das verlassne Mägdelein*) is simplicity itself. He used no introduction and no postlude for this monothematic lied written almost exclusively in three-part harmony. The piano accompaniment is delicately transparent. Usually the treble doubles the voice part; occasionally the pianist strikes the note a shade sooner than the singer. They start together, however, with two bars that contain the only motive of the song (Ex. 44-a). As the song continues, this material is altered or extended, transposed to the dominant in its repetition at *Ich schaue,* and returned to the tonic at *Träne auf Träne:* a simple ternary form. The

Ex. 44

SCHUMANN: *Das verlassne Mägdelein*

Früh wann die Häh - ne krähn,

a.

bass line descends (see beginning at * in Ex. 44-a) in a scalewise pattern sinking two and a half octaves without letting up until reaching *Funken.* Schumann inserts two bars for piano solo, and the bass resumes its downward movement. *Funken* would appear to be the end of the stanza, but it is not. Schumann did not respect the poet's stanzaic divisions.

Wolf knew that this deceptively simple poem had already been set to "heavenly music by Schumann," as he reports in a letter to a friend. Indeed, in 1885, three years before Wolf wrote his own version, Challier's *Liederlexikon* listed fifty different settings of the poem. However, the young composer, seduced by the beauty of *Das verlassene Mägdlein,* for once could not restrain himself.

Wolf's approach differs considerably from Schumann's. A four-bar introduction sets the mood (Ex. 44-b); the seconds (see * in Ex. 44-b)

WOLF: *Das verlassene Mägdlein*

b.

reflect the distress of the jilted lass; the drop of a fifth in the singer's opening melody is further indication of her feelings. Wolf closely follows the poet's plan. At the end of the first stanza, after *zünden,* he inserts two bars of piano interlude; after *versunken,* the end of the second stanza, the pianist plays four bars alone; and three bars for solo piano separate the last two stanzas. For the last stanza, Wolf returns to the opening music, varying it slightly and in conclusion adding a bitterly morose piano postlude. From this description, it would seem that Wolf divided the lied into symmetrical phrases, but he did not. Notice his organization below:

Stanza 1	4 bars piano introduction
	8 bars with text
	2 bars for piano

| Stanza 2 | 8 bars with text |
| | 4 bars for piano |

| Stanza 3 | 8 bars with text |
| | 3 bars for piano |

Stanza 4	6 bars with text
	1 bar of rest *
	2 bars with text
	6 bars for piano

At * Wolf showed his depth of understanding. Much as Schubert has Gretchen speechless at the thought of *sein Kuss,* Wolf's *Mägdlein* is, for just a moment, unable to contemplate another day. Before the last two bars of text *(o ging' er wieder!)* is a bar of silence. The material is artfully arranged, and never contrived.

Curiously, Wolf duplicates Schumann's melodic line at the start of the second stanza, *Schön ist* (Exx. 44-c and 44-d).

SCHUMANN: *Das verlassne Mägdelein*

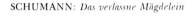

Schön ist der Flam ; me Schein.

c.

WOLF: *Das verlassene Mägdlein*

Schön ist der Flam - men Schein,

d.

EICHENDORFF

Eichendorff here captures some of the fascination that Lenau so enthusiastically displayed for the life of the gypsies, although Eichendorff's poem is more subdued in tone. That life is reflected in the motifs of the crossroad, the fires, the forest, the delights of wandering, as well as in the lusty exuberance of the gypsy girl, *die Zigeunerin,* who, despite the free-

Die Zigeunerin

Am Kreuzweg, da lausche ich, wenn die Stern'
Und die Feuer im Walde verglommen,
Und wo der erste Hund bellt von fern,
Da wird mein Bräut'gam herkommen.

"Und als der Tag graut', durch das Gehölz
Sah ich eine Katze sich schlingen,
Ich schoss ihr auf den nussbraunen Pelz,
Wie tat die weit überspringen!"--

's ist schad' nur ums Pelzlein, du kriegst mich nit!
Mein Schatz muss sein wie die andern!
Braun und ein Stutzbart auf ung'rischen Schnitt
Und ein fröhliches Herze zum Wandern.

dom of her nomadic existence, must conform to the customs of the gypsies and take a sweetheart with dark-brown hair and Hungarian-style whiskers, like all the others.

The incident of the cat and the cryptic remarks of the girl, "Too bad about the fur; but you won't get me," leave the reader perplexed, for there is no context to which to relate them. It is conceivable that she has toyed briefly with the idea of accepting the attentions of a gorgio (non-gypsy) lover, an almost impossible step that would violate a principal article in the code of the *Zigeuner*. There is a remote similarity to a poem of Goethe's, *Zigeuner* ("Gypsies"), in which a gypsy shoots a cat belonging to a witch, whereupon seven witches transform themselves into werewolves to avenge the cat, but it is difficult to find in this poem (incorporated into the gypsy scene of the fifth act of the play *Götz von Berlichingen*) an explanation of the Eichendorff motif.

To a composer, the setting and mood are more important than the details of a story that must be surmised.

Notes on the text:

1 *Kreuzweg:* The crossroads play an important role in gypsy lore, for it is there that the gypsies leave their secret markings to

impart messages and directions to later arrivals. Witches also meet at the crossroads, and Hecate received sacrifices there.

2   *verglommen:* from *verglimmen* "cease to glow, fade away, die out"; belongs with *Stern(e)* and *Feuer.*

4   *Bräut(i)gam:* "fiancé" (not usually "bridegroom").

5   *graut':* shift of tense from present to imperfect; "was dawning." (The verb is derived from the adjective *grau* "gray.")
    Gehölz: the *Ge-* has collective significance; "wood, copse."

6   *sich schlingen:* "to wind its way, sneak, creep."

8   *die:* demonstrative "she."
    tat . . . überspringen shows colloquial use of *tat* as an auxiliary (like English "did," which, however, is standard); "how high did she leap up!"

10 *die andern:* the other young gypsy ladies.

11 *braun:* brown-haired; does not usually refer to complexion, although that may be included in the brunet effect.
    Stutzbart: "trimmed beard, close-cropped beard."
    Schnitt: "cut, style."
    ung'rischen for *ungarischen.*

12 *Herze:* archaic for *Herz.*

Wolf had hoped to write a supplement to Schumann's *Liederkreis,* Op. 39, in which the older composer had captured those elements of the poet's style relating to night and nature, twilight, fairies, medieval castles, and woodlands. Wolf honestly believed that there were aspects of Eichendorff's writing that Schumann had missed entirely. Several of Wolf's Eichendorff songs are inconsequential early works. In a later group, however, Wolf concentrated on humorous and realistic figures. Some of his best settings are musical portraits: soldiers, minstrels, a gypsy.

Die Zigeunerin offered Wolf a rare instance for bravura writing, but he hesitated to indulge himself. Within his self-imposed restrictions, we might recognize limited devil-may-care attitudes. Wolf was just incapable of more. Compare Liszt's conception of the gypsy in *Die drei Zigeuner* (p. 221) for another approach to gypsy music. Liszt opened with an extensive cadenza for the piano soloist, anticipating the excitement to come. Wolf's opening is measured (*Mässig*), deliberate but calm. (See Ex. 45-a.) His gypsy is named Azucena, not Carmen.

Ex. 45

WOLF: *Die Zigeunerin*

a.

The formal outlines are distinctly ternary. Nonsense syllables and melodic fioriture (see * Ex. 45-b)—exceptional for Wolf—together delineate the close of each stanza. A sharply different accompanimental figure supports the speechlike vocal part in the second stanza (Ex. 45-b).

b.

The third stanza resembles the first, but concludes with considerable variation. Superficially, the song seems disconnected. Upon examination, however, we notice recurrent elements. One of these is the repeated *La, la* inserted by the composer, and another, the rising and falling scale figures

c.

that appear in each stanza (bars 9, 20, 24 ff., etc.). Wolf emphasizes the structural significance of the scale by closing the lied with a chromatic scale, one of the only ad lib passages in any of his works (see Ex. 45-c). Much depends on the performers for the success of this song.

GOETHE

Anakreons Grab

Wo die Rose hier blüht, wo Reben um Lorbeer sich schlingen,
Wo das Turtelchen lockt, wo sich das Grillchen ergötzt,
Welch ein Grab ist hier, das alle Götter mit Leben
Schön bepflanzt und geziert? Es ist Anakreons Ruh.
Frühling, Sommer, und Herbst genoss der glückliche Dichter;
Vor dem Winter hat ihn endlich der Hügel geschützt.

This poem, highly lauded by those for whom Goethe could do no wrong, owes its origin in part to Herder's translations from the *Greek Anthology*. It teems with conventional devices: the rose, the vine, the laurel, turtledoves. It also imitates classical meters. It is hardly the product of real experience or non-literary inspiration. Wolf has perhaps enhanced the words even beyond their deserts.

The real Anakreon was born in Asia Minor about 550 B.C. Later he went to Athens and died there at the age of eighty-five. Of his poems only a few genuine ones have been preserved. What is traditionally referred to as Anacreontic poetry was the product of those taking his name in vain with frothy verses on the themes of wine, women, and song. In their hands the term "Anacreontic" became a condemnation.

Notes on the text:

1　*Reben:* "vines" = wine.
　　Lorbeer: "laurel," the symbol of athletic victory or poetic excellence (cf. poet laureate).
6　Implies that Anakreon died before reaching the "winter" of his life. This hardly accords with the facts, if the poet lived to be eighty-five.

The unusual opening cadence of the two-bar piano introduction provides immediate tranquillity. Despite the absence of a clearly defined piano figuration, the descending thirds in the upper register of the treble sustain a very real sense of repose. Wolf writes a momentary *mf* but twice. For the balance of the song, the performers alternate between varying degrees of piano. *Anakreon* offers two examples of *Tonmalerei:* the considerable ornamentation in the accompaniment that underlines *geziert,* bars 9-10, and Wolf's placement of the lowest note in the song on *Ruh,* bar 12. The melody, more conjunct than usual, again allows the singer complete independence. The range of the vocal part is often sandwiched between treble and bass of the accompaniment.

Rhythm emerges as a controlling element. Observe the diversification of rhythmic patterns comprising each of the bars in the $\frac{12}{8}$ meter; notice also the triple-layered rhythmic activity (see bar 4 of our Ex. 46). The

Ex. 46

WOLF: *Anakreons Grab*

Wo die Rose hier blüht, wo Reben um Lorbeer sich schlingen,

lied is *durchkomponiert,* but the composer reuses the pianist's opening material before the concluding vocal statement. Wolf writes it here in the key of G major, the subdominant, not in the tonic D. His use of D major for this serene song parallels Brahms's employment of this key to provide a feeling of restfulness.

Each note is important as Wolf eliminates everything that is not absolutely vital to the whole. Above his richly luxuriant harmonies, it is Wolf's basic three-note motive that gives this song formal unity. Not easily perceived, but certainly sensed with repeated listening, are the related melodic progressions that hover about three notes: 7-8-2 (leading tone, tonic, and supertonic) or 3-5-4 (see * and ** in Ex. 46), always retaining the same rhythmic profile. This subtle use of a melodic or rhythmic cell is a feature common to many of Wolf's songs.

Goethe's *Mignon Lieder* *

Nur wer die Sehnsucht kennt

Mignon's plaintive melody in Schubert's setting (p. 44), the last of all his Goethe songs, haunts all who hear it. Wolf's Mignon does not have a singable tune. However, the *Stimmung* he created for this entire poem has made it one of great beauty. Like Schubert, he used ternary form, seizing upon the poet's repetition of the first two lines of the text as a reason to return to the opening music. Schubert, generally less mindful of the preservation of the poet's text, immediately repeats the two lines *Nur . . . leide*

Ex. 47

a.

b.

* The following table shows the different sequence accorded the *Mignon Lieder* by Schubert and Wolf:

Schubert	Wolf
Lied der Mignon No. 1 (Op. 62, No. 2)	Mignon I
(Heiss mich nicht reden)	*(Heiss mich nicht reden)*
Lied der Mignon No. 2 (Op. 62, No. 3)	Mignon II
(So lasst mich scheinen)	*(Nur wer die Sehnsucht kennt)*
Lied der Mignon (Op. 62, No. 4)	Mignon III
(Nur wer die Sehnsucht kennt)	*(So lasst mich scheinen)*
Mignons Gesang	Mignon
(Kennst du das Land)	*(Kennst du das Land)*

at the onset of his lied. Wolf does not. Then to conclude his song, Schubert offers the same pattern, two statements of the text. Schubert's quadruple statement of these words is not as effective as Wolf's retention of the original. Although Schubert modifies his fourth statement of the words, it is Wolf's treatment that proves more penetrating to the listener. He alters the melody and accompaniment of the second phrase *weiss . . . leide,* allowing the music to sink gradually through melodic and rhythmic sequences to its close. The tension on *leide* is almost unbearable, and it finds no release until the tonic octave rumbles ambiguously in the bass. Unexpectedly it resolves in D major in the last bar.

Wolf rarely states a musical phrase in exactly the same way twice. The opening piano prelude of this song (Ex. 47-b) is therefore exceptional. Three times a three-note motive sounds above a throbbing bass, and on the fourth statement its interval narrows (see * in Ex. 47-b). As the singer begins, notice that only her first three pitches (see Ex. 47-d) are the same as those of the refrain. Schubert, too, changes the singer's melody (Ex. 47-c) from that of the opening prelude, but the changes seem far less significant because the harmony is the same, whereas Wolf alters his supporting harmonies considerably. Within Wolf's opening piano prelude, besides the three-note motive already cited, in bars 7-8 he presents another motive (A flat–E flat–D) that reappears later as the basis of the piano interlude between *Eingeweide* and the recurrence of *Nur . . . leide.* The two melodic motives and the persistent outline of octaves in the treble of the accompaniment, combined with the pulsating rhythm in the bass, provide the kind of musical cohesiveness for which Wolf is justly famous.

SCHUBERT: *Nur wer die Sehnsucht*

Nur wer die Sehn - sucht kennt, weiss, was ich lei - de,

c.

WOLF: *Nur wer die Sehnsucht*

Nur wer die Sehn - sucht kennt, weiss, was ich lei - de!

d.

The melody suggests a kind of perpetual *Sehnsucht*, unfulfilled long-ing. A flutter of optimism, and a moment later all hopes are dashed. Wolf achieves these emotions in his music by means of ultra-precise performance instructions. With them, he outdoes Schumann. Notice, for example, *immer belebter* and *immer zurückhaltender* (bars 18 and 21). Text underlay is extraordinary, particularly where we notice the voice remaining so inde-pendent of the piano. Examine *allein . . . Freude* (Ex. 47-e). *Allein* is set in a cross relation to the accompaniment; it also lies considerably lower than the upper treble at the piano. Most of the *Tonmalerei* appears in the vocal line: the leap at *abgetrennt*, the embellishment at *aller*, and the cynical plunge at *Freude*.

In still another attempt at concentration of material, Wolf restates the opening piano prelude to support a new melody at *Ach der mich liebt*. Again see how *weite* is underlined with the interval of a falling sixth. A rest occupies the first beat of each bar, and his maintaining this rhythmic feature until the very last bar of the piece serves as further means of unification.

Finally, Wolf's harmony reveals his striking originality. Tonal am-biguity persists throughout this lied. Despite the two flats in the signature, neither G minor nor B-flat major can be pinpointed as the definitive key. The composer avoids a full tonic chord until he lands on D. Most of the song sounds somewhere in modal limbo between transposed Phrygian on G or D.

Kennst du das Land

This ravishingly beautiful song on first hearing sounds like something by Liszt. Whereas *Mignon* shows Wolf in a very expansive mood and seems for all the world like one of his most complicated settings, it is in truth one of the most clearly defined strophic settings we have encountered. The formal scheme fascinates us because it is so exceptional for him. The pattern of the first stanza follows:

Section	Length	Meter	Key
Refrain (piano alone)	4 bars	$\frac{3}{4}$	G-flat major
Kennst du das Land (a)	8 bars 8 bars	$\frac{3}{4}$	G-flat major modulating to E-flat major
Kennst du es wohl (b)	11 bars	$\frac{9}{8}$	F minor
Dahin! (c)	3 bars 3 bars	$\frac{9}{8}$ $\frac{3}{4}$	B-flat minor modulating to G-flat major
Refrain (piano alone)	4 bars (includes preceding bar in overlap with part c)	$\frac{3}{4}$	

Each of the three stanzas follows a similar pattern. In other words, the interior *a b c* design is repeated with but slight changes. The refrain frames each stanza and brings the song to a close. Always after *Dahin!* Wolf modifies the quasi-recitative concluding pitches of this portion of the song. At the very end, he repeats the text *lass uns ziehn* in a codetta following the final stanza.

The most conspicuous alteration occurs in the music of the last stanza. The accompaniment becomes more orchestral and Wolf changes modes, moving from G-flat major to F-sharp minor, as Mignon puts her questions more insistently. A short transition links this material to the recurrent F minor section (*b*). Harmonically, the modulation from F-sharp minor to F minor is relatively uncommon. The song concludes with the restatement of the opening refrain, Mignon's repeated *lass uns ziehn,* and a four-bar piano postlude.

In contrast to Schubert's setting (p. 42), where the piano merely doubles the vocal line, here the voice and piano are completely independent of one another. Then too, the thicker texture in the Wolf song is markedly different from that employed by Schubert (cf. Exx. 48-a and 48-b). The vocal

Ex. 48

a.

b.

part in Wolf's setting lies midway between the two staves of the accompaniment. In our Ex. 48-b, notice that the small notes actually belong to Wolf's own orchestral transcription of this song, but many accompanists prefer to play them as a countertheme to the singer's melody. Unlike the regular rhythm and meter in the Schubert example, syncopated rhythmic patterns predominate. Each, however, is different within its own section. Compare the rhythmic designs of sections *a, b,* and *c.*

In addition to melodic independence, observe the multiple layers of rhythmic activity—three different profiles within the accompaniment alone (see * in Ex. 48-b) and another one for the singer! The impassioned *Kennst du es wohl* must be compared with Schubert's tame setting of these words. (See Exx. 48-c and 48-d.) *Leidenschaftlich* is Wolf's own direction

and perhaps the reason for his decision to repeat the text, a liberty he seldom takes.

The impatience of *Dahin!* (Ex. 48-e) is reflected in the accompaniment, which ceases abruptly as the voice alone concludes the stanza. It is here that Wolf modifies his closing material. Additional changes can be heard in the opening pitches of each stanza, and it is profitable to compare them to observe his technique. Variety in unity is the watchword here.

So lasst mich scheinen

Formally, the two settings of the poem by Schubert and Wolf resemble one another. Each composer has divided the four stanzas in a way that relates alternating stanzas: in other words, 1 and 3 correspond, as do 2 and 4. One might argue that such a pattern is merely strophic. The music, however, is not that distinctly shaped. In any event, after formal similarities, the resemblance ends. The two songs sound as if they were based on entirely different poems. (See commentary on p. 47.) Schubert's is a simple, hymnlike tune in symmetrical four-bar phrases which correspond to the mood and texture of the A-flat Major Impromptu, Op. 142. Rarely does the voice show any independence. Not only is it duplicated in the treble of the accompaniment, but occasionally both hands underline the singer's melody with doubled octaves.

Compare, for example, *dann öffnet sich der frische Blick* in both songs. Schubert apparently felt the need to exaggerate the meaning here and uses a very special modulation as well as textural change. Wolf makes the point more convincing through careful manipulation of music and text. He does not allow himself to get carried away by the music. Schubert's Mignon is resigned to her fate and entreats her friends to leave her as she is now. On the other hand, Wolf's impression of the girl reveals a more anguished soul—perhaps too tortured, according to some critics—who knows what is in store for her, but who also has an idea of what life is all about and resents the fact that she will soon be deprived of it.

Wolf's setting is so vastly different that it is hard to know where to begin comparisons. First, the entire piece has an exotic, otherworldly quality about it. A syncopated rhythmic figure courses through the entire lied as a kind of subliminal current. Here again, rhythm must be recognized as a significant factor in unification of the separate stanzas. Wolf actually changes his melody for each strophe, but interrelates them so that stanza 3 becomes a^1 and stanza 4 becomes b^1. In the third stanza, for example, the accompaniment remains fundamentally the same as it appeared earlier. At times, even the basic direction of the melody, too, parallels that of stanza 1. Intermittently, however, the composer surprises us with unexpected leaps in opposite directions. This startling absence of melodic inevitability becomes one of Wolf's particular trademarks.

Ewig is the climax of the song. It appears at the highest pitch of the piece. The voice then plunges down an octave and almost immediately afterward bounces up another octave, coming to rest for its final note on the dominant. Again the composer has avoided the tonic and the song is inconclusive. Dominant (V^9) harmony fills this entire bar (34), and Wolf resolves the chord in the accompaniment. Here an open-fifth tonic pedal sustains the gradual ritardando to the close.

Harmonic subtleties render this song exceptional for its time and show how Wolf occupied a position midway between Wagner and Schönberg. Like Wagner, he seemed unrestricted by tradition, but sought instead to expand the limits of tonality.

Heiss mich nicht reden

The curious harmonic ambiguity of the opening confuses the listener and reflects Mignon's attempt to conceal her secret. The juxtaposition of unrelated chords and the extensive use of appoggiaturas underline her discontent. Cross accents between the vocal line and the accompaniment add to the impression of listlessness. The figuration in the accompaniment is unpianistic; it simply provides the sonorous background colors out of which the voice rises. The vocal melody is in arioso style, with some recourse to sections in monotone. At the second stanza, beginning with *Zur rechten,* above a rising modal scale figure in octaves, the singer's part becomes more agitated. The long descent from *missgönnt* to *verborgnen* directs us to the source of Mignon's secret.

Innig is the style indication Wolf affixes to the music of the third stanza. Sensitive to the need for change in the return to *a,* he thickens the texture and modifies the harmonies. Wolf shows good control of the accelerated rate of pitch changes in this lied. Notice also the subtle means of unification: the last vocal phrase incorporates the same pitches employed in the rising scale figure at *Zur rechten,* but here sung in reverse. The voice ends on the leading tone, unresolved: Mignon has kept her secret.

A comparison of the opening of the two vocal parts by Schubert and Wolf reveals Schubert's weakness here. He has already offered a four-bar piano introduction, using his favorite funeral-march rhythmic figure. He repeats these bars (with slight modifications) in support of the voice. But he duplicates not only the pitch but also the rhythm of the singer. Wolf is far more sophisticated. The unnatural accents in his two-bar introduction immediately suggest uneasiness. The rhythmic profile of the opening bars adds to the sentiments. The leap on *Pflicht* is made deliberately. Schubert simply descends scalewise to the word. Wolf makes each of Mignon's statements a plea, and for this reason uses the monotone. Compare, also, in the last stanza *allein ein Schwur.* Notice Wolf's use of the leap at this cadence. Schubert misses the point. However, he does highlight the closing lines of the text, *nur ein Gott vermag sie aufzuschliessen,* through the change to recitative. Even here, however, he fails to achieve the desired result, because he has repeated the textual material several times, thereby making the words lose their effectiveness. Instead they drown in the musical elaboration of the line. Rhythmic and melodic motives serve to unify his piece. Despite these devices, however, this *Lied der Mignon* fails to show the best of Schubert.

Harfenspieler Lieder from *Wilhelm Meister*

Wolf's *Wilhelm Meister* songs rank among the finest he wrote. With one exception (*Der Sänger,* which he himself wanted to remove from the group), they are probably the best musical interpretations of these poems by Goethe. Wolf's music adds another dimension heretofore missing. Because these poems have inspired so many composers, a comparison at least with other settings by Schubert and Schumann is inevitable.

Wolf wrote a total of ten *Wilhelm Meister* songs. However, the seven usually referred to are the four Mignon songs and the three Harper songs. Schubert's *Mignon Lieder* are discussed above in the chapter on Schubert. Schumann treated these poems rather late in his career, long after he had already lost his initial approach to lieder composition and shortly before he became ill. His intellectual background as well as his acquaintance with literature surpassed Schubert's, and, perhaps for this reason, the range and depth of understanding that he brought to these songs make them—in particular *Heiss mich nicht reden*—superior to Schubert's. Unfortunately, they are not sung today nor are they available on recordings.

Because Wolf's settings are more often compared with Schubert's, it seemed worth while to search for some parallels in their settings of the same poems.

Schubert's three *Harfenspieler Lieder* stem from September, 1816, when he was nineteen years old. They are not typical of the work he was doing at this time, nor do they resemble any of the other songs we have discussed. A very elementary setting of *Wer sich der Einsamkeit ergibt* dates from 1815, but otherwise all variants of these songs—and all exist in at least two versions—were composed in 1816.

All of Schubert's Harper songs are in A minor, and all are set for tenor voice, perhaps because Schubert, like many other composers, regarded the tenor range as appropriate for an older man. None of these songs is strophic. Two of the songs, *Wer nie sein Brot mit Tränen ass* and *Wer sich der Einsamkeit ergibt,* contain similar accompaniments: harplike, vertical arpeggiated chords at strategic points. In both, the most extensive sections are set to a triplet figure reminiscent of the first movement of Beethoven's "Moonlight" Sonata. Another technique common to both songs is the persistent doubling of the vocal line, principally in those sections that do not feature the triplet figure. In these two songs, the melodic style is midway between lyrical and declamatory, more of an arioso.

Schubert sectionalizes *Wer sich der Einsamkeit ergibt* with four different textures; three of these appear before the start of the second stanza, *Es schleicht.* It is this second stanza that features the triplet figure exclusively. No piano interlude, indeed no real separation, occurs between the first and second stanzas. Instead, the weightier cadence, seemingly the end of a stanza, appears after *Pein* (bar 12), the middle of the first stanza. Here texture and harmony change. The composer extended the triplets through a repetition of the last three lines of text in the second stanza.

The predominant dynamic is piano to pianissimo; one *ff* emphasizes *Da lässt sie mich allein* at bars 35 ff. Schubert is inconsistent in his reflection of *einsam:* at bar 18 he has a tritone; at bars 28 and 30 he moves fluidly into a descending scale.

Wer nie sein Brot mit Tränen ass is more dramatic, more differentiated in texture and dynamics than the first song. The vocal style, however, is similar. One feature is unique to this song: the composer states each stanza twice. For example, the repeat of the first stanza is set in A major, with cadences in F major. Melody, harmony, and occasionally texture change for the repeat of the text. In the restatement of the second stanza, we notice even more alterations than those that had accompanied the repeat of the first stanza.

An die Türen offers a plodding, homorhythmic bass line similar to the basses of Purcell's laments of the seventeenth century. Also like these earlier arias, the basic direction of the melody is downward. In many settings of this poem (and Schubert's is no exception), the composer sought to imitate the sound of the footsteps of the wandering harper.

Harfenspieler I
Wer sich der Einsamkeit ergibt

Wer sich der Einsamkeit ergibt,
Ach! der ist bald allein;
Ein jeder lebt, ein jeder liebt,
Und lässt ihn seiner Pein.

Ja! lasst mich meiner Qual!
Und kann ich nur einmal
Recht einsam sein,
Dann bin ich nicht allein

Es schleicht ein Liebender lauschend sacht,
Ob seine Freundin allein?
So überschleicht bei Tag und Nacht
Mich Einsamen die Pein,

Mich Einsamen die Qual.
Ach werd' ich erst einmal
Einsam im Grabe sein,
Da lässt sie mich allein!

Until his identity becomes known, the harper is only a mysterious old man with a gray beard who seems partly out of his mind. He joins Wilhelm and Mignon and, a strange trio, they wander together. This song speaks of a terrible torment which haunts the poor harper wherever he goes, however solitary he may be in other respects. Only in the grave will he escape and be truly alone. This song does not hint that guilt is the source of his suffering.

Notes on the text:

3-4   I.e., everyone else is concerned with his own life and love, leaving him, the harper, to his suffering and pain.

8   He is never alone because his torment always accompanies him.
9   *sacht:* "softly" (a word of North German origin, the poetic equivalent of its cognate *sanft*).
10 *ob . . . allein:* to see whether his beloved is alone. Just as a jealous or zealous lover silently stalks his lady love to find out whether she is alone, so too is the harper stalked by his torment. The alternation of *a: ei,* not only in the final rhymes but also within verses, may be an intentional sound effect on Goethe's part.

To compare Schubert's settings of this text to Wolf's is grossly unfair, because Wolf's is not only one of his best Goethe songs, it is also one of the most extraordinary of his entire output. Wolf wrote all the Harper songs during four days in 1888 (October 27-30). *Wer sich der Einsamkeit ergibt* sets the stage for Berg's *Sieben frühe Lieder.* Harmony is the controlling element here, even more than rhythm. The entire lied reflects the kind of musico-literary concentration that enables the composer to enhance the poetry to the extent that the whole is greater than the sum of its parts.

The setting is extremely low, but the range is more than two and a half octaves, from low B to F above middle C. That F, the highest note in the song, underlies the second mention of *Pein* (bar 26). Voice and piano are completely independent of one another, moving in different, even unexpected directions, so that the few cadences, when they finally arrive, offer the only relief from sustained areas of unresolved tension. Using a declamatory melodic style, Wolf favors the monotone, but changes to jagged leaps when the text requires it. Observe the treble line of the accompaniment and notice that the opening motive, with its sharp rhythmic profile, recurs in different guises throughout the song. When the uppermost pitches of the treble descend seven steps in the first two bars of the introduction, the mood is set immediately. Chord spacing is unusual and most effective. Notice, for example, the layout on *allein,* in bar 8.

Wolf's control of new harmonic processes enables him to provide a sense of discontinuity. The three levels of activity (vocal line plus treble and bass of the accompaniment) seem disconcertingly out of focus. Even in the first bar, the chord on the third beat sounds wrong. When the accompaniment is repeated in augmentation as it supports the singer's entry in bar 6, that same chord sounds consonant, as if the conflicting parties were now at peace with one another. One of the most tender cadences appears at *nicht allein* (bar 17), where voice and piano join in sensual reunion. *Es schleicht* sounds as if it comes from another world; when well sung, this passage is extraordinarily beautiful. Wolf increases the tension beginning at *bei Tag und Nacht* through the use of chromatic sequences from bar 24 to bar 26, with the climax at *Pein,* bar 26. He obstinately refuses to resolve his dominant chord after *Qual* and detours before returning to G minor.

In the recurrence of the rhythmic motive of the opening bar, notice how Wolf starts on different beats, thus changing the accents. Compare bar 1 and bars 8 ff.

Very often Wolf will resolve to the tonic only at the piano, leaving his singer in tonal limbo. Exceptionally here, the singer's last note is the tonic, but the pianist, playing through the introductory material for the last time, ends on an unresolved dominant chord. Despite the prevalence of chromaticisms and tension-building devices, this song is undeniably in G minor. Yet Wolf's way of making the key sound refreshingly different demonstrates his remarkable talents.

Harfenspieler III
Wer nie sein Brot mit Tränen ass

Wer nie sein Brot mit Tränen ass,
Wer nie die kummervollen Nächte
Auf seinem Bette weinend sass,
Der kennt euch nicht, ihr himmlischen Mächte.

Ihr führt ins Leben uns hinein,
Ihr lasst den Armen schuldig werden,
Dann überlasst ihr ihn der Pein;
Denn alle Schuld rächt sich auf Erden.

In this song we learn that the old harper's suffering and torment are the result of a terrible sense of guilt. Only later is it revealed that he is the father of Mignon by his own sister, and the enormity of that feeling of guilt seems unmitigated by the fact that neither he nor she knew their relationship when they married. This is almost a Grecian sense of guilt— tragic because the offenders are ignorant of their offense. Ignorance is not equated with innocence under that harsh code, even though the harper recognizes the cruelty of the code and the mistreatment of humanity by the "heavenly powers."

Notes on the text:

1   *mit Tränen:* he who has never "eaten his bread with tears," i.e.,
wept at his meals because of his guilt.

3   or has been unable to sleep for the same reason.

4   A fortunate person does not know the heavenly powers and the
cruelty of their treatment of unfortunate wretches like the harper.

5-7   These lines virtually accuse the heavenly powers, fate, God, of
wrongdoing, of "stacking the cards." In line 5, *uns* means mankind in general, or suffering mankind. Line 6, *den Armen:* the
harper himself as a representative of his kind. "Poor" indicates
a partial realization that the guilt is imposed from without.

8   One need not wait for some punishment after death, because all
guilt is atoned for here on earth, where the heavenly powers can
make existence a hell.

Rhythmically, melodically, and harmonically, *Wer nie sein Brot mit
Tränen ass* resembles *Wer sich der Einsamkeit ergibt.* Formally, however,
its scheme corresponds more to *An die Türen.* The piano opens with a
rhythmic-melodic motive whose basic direction is downward, the melody
proceeding chromatically from the dominant to the tonic. As it reaches
the tonic (bar 5), the voice begins with the rhythmic motive sung on a
monotone. The motive, slightly altered at its close, returns in the piano
interlude that follows.

The singer starts the second stanza with full chordal support from
the pianist. Alternating bars for singer and pianist build to an emotional
and musical climax at *Pein* and recede once again at *Erden.* Instead of
lyricism, Wolf again shows preference for the arioso style. Indeed, the
isolated separate lines of the second strophe are projected as variants of
the basic rhythmic-melodic motive of the introduction. For this second
stanza, the piano proceeds in two-bar phrases in contrast to the single bar
for the voice. The singer begins each statement at a different pitch level;
the pianist's solo interjections assume greater importance as the music
surges to its climax. Notice that the formerly empty octaves have now
become thickly reinforced chords.

In his treatment of harmony, Wolf again defies tradition. Observe the
dubious progression from *Nächte* to *auf seinem,* the open end at *Mächte,*

and the striking sequence of unrelated key centers that heighten the tension underlining the second stanza. The voice concludes most unusually with a direct fall from the dominant to the tonic, but the piano does not resolve the unendurable anxiety of *alle Schuld rächt sich* and does not find release until the final bar.

This song represents an extreme emotional outburst for Wolf, many of whose friends felt that here he had been somewhat less than refined.

Harfenspieler II
An die Türen will ich schleichen

An die Türen will ich schleichen,
Still und sittsam will ich stehn,
Fromme Hand wird Nahrung reichen,
Und ich werde weiter gehn.

Jeder wird sich glücklich scheinen,
Wenn mein Bild vor ihm erscheint,
Eine Träne wird er weinen,
Und ich weiss nicht, was er weint.

Like all the songs of the old harper, this may be assumed to refer to himself; he is not merely singing a song about a beggar.

Notes on the text:

1 *schleichen:* "slink, sneak, go furtively," a word that can be applied to thieves, but not exclusively. He will steal up to people's doors partly with a sense of the great guilt besetting him, partly because of the embarrassment of being reduced to begging.

3 *fromme Hand: fromm* ("pious") = "good, kind, charitable." Since good works lead, in some theologies, to salvation, showing charity to a beggar can be a pious act. *Hand:* the figure of synecdoche (represents the person of which it is a part).

5 *sich glücklich scheinen:* in contrast to the wretchedness of the old beggar.

6 *mein Bild* = the sight of the harper—his form, not his image, although he is a sort of apparition. The man almost seems to view his form as separate from himself.

8   *Und ich weiss nicht, was er weint:* "And I won't know why [*was*] he weeps" (present for future, a common phenomenon in German). Each one may weep for some special reason in his own past (a relationship to a friend, a relative—a father, perhaps) or merely because of the unspeakably sad appearance of the old harper, as he begs the *Brot* which he will then eat with *Tränen.*

Both Schubert and Wolf, in their approach to *Wer sich der Einsamkeit ergibt* and *Wer nie sein Brot mit Tränen ass,* responded to the similarities of the two poems. The musical settings of these two poems show certain parallels. *An die Türen,* on the other hand, is different.

Wolf wrote his *An die Türen* in rondo form: *a b a¹ c a².* The *a,* which appears as prelude, interlude, and postlude, consists of a pattern of descending thirds characterized by a rest or tie on the first beat of each bar. This rhythmic feature (unaccented first beat) perhaps reflects the tired steps of the harper as he wanders from door to door. Wolf continues to manipulate rhythm to advantage as he sets equal quarters in the voice against the persistent off-beat sound of the accompaniment. The few instances of rhythmic flexibility in the vocal line occur at cadences and over significant words (e.g., *scheinen* and *weinen*). The modulation to F major before *Jeder wird sich glücklich* and the conclusion in C major mirror the new sentiment of the text. Observe that when the *Stimmung* changes, besides moving to the major mode, Wolf also regularizes the rhythm. Here (bars 17 ff.) the bass produces a vigorous half note on the first beat of each bar.

The narrow ambitus, the chromaticisms, and the circling introductory motive are characteristics of all three of Wolf's Harper songs. In this one, the unresolved dominant seventh chord that sustains the singer's last word, *weint,* provides the customary open-ended sound we find in Wolf's unhappy songs. Unlike Schubert, he has not altered or repeated a single word of the poet's text.

PAUL VON HEYSE (1830-1914)

A prolific writer of short stories, one of which, *L'Arrabbiata,* was long a favorite in American elementary German classes (though having nothing to do with Germany), Heyse was less successful with the drama and novel. A man of philological training, he was interested in French, Spanish, and

Italian, with a special predilection for Italy, which provided the setting for many of his original writings. Heyse was the first German poet to receive the Nobel prize (1910), ironically enough at a time when his esteem at home had fallen. His *Italienisches Liederbuch* (1860) includes translations of poems by Alfieri, Leopardi, and Manzoni, and evinces a high degree of skill, as does his earlier book of translations from Spanish, *Spanisches Liederbuch* (1852), in which he had the assistance of Emanuel Geibel.

In dem Schatten meiner Locken (from *Spanisches Liederbuch*)

In dem Schatten meiner Locken
Schlief mir mein Geliebter ein.
Weck' ich ihn nun auf?--Ach nein!

Sorglich strählt' ich meine krausen
Locken täglich in der Frühe,
Doch umsonst ist meine Mühe,
Weil die Winde sie zerzausen.
Lockenschatten, Windessausen
Schläferten den Liebsten ein.
Weck' ich ihn nun auf?--Ach nein!

Hören muss ich, wie ihn gräme,
Dass er schmachtet schon so lange,
Dass ihm Leben geb' und nehme
Diese meine braune Wange,
Und er nennt mich seine Schlange,
Und doch schlief er bei mir ein.
Weck' ich ihn nun auf?--Ach nein!

This song has no elusive poetic subtleties, and its meaning is clear from the text itself. Despite the pain suffered by the man because of the treachery of his sweetheart (who admits that he calls her a snake), he falls asleep "in the shadow of her tresses" and seems inescapably caught.

In his separation of the sacred and secular songs of the *Spanisches Liederbuch*, Wolf was simply following the original classifications of the poets. The composer generally treated the sacred poems to a more somber and austere setting, nevertheless bestowing upon them a variety of rhythmic and harmonic features not too different from those used for the secular poems. The secular poems, however, provided Wolf with an extraordinary opportunity to create an unlimited number of different textures and sonorities. The subject matter is exceedingly diversified.

In dem Schatten meiner Locken, the second of the *Weltliche Lieder,* begins with a piquant motive in the piano *(Leicht, zart, nicht schnell),* the voice picking up on the last two eighth notes of the bar (see Ex. 49). Wolf demonstrates his excellent control of rhythm, alternating light, rapid notes with a single chord of a whole measure's duration. (See * Ex. 49.) Observe how he builds tension by extending the section containing the shorter note values. What began as a three-bar statement (see opening of Ex. 49) is soon lengthened to sixteen bars.

Ex. 49

WOLF: *In dem Schatten*

In dem   Schatten meiner Locken schlief mir mein Geliebter ein.

Weck' ich ihn nun auf?

Wolf's songs are often described as miniature music dramas. Within the limits of a single lied, the composer was able to compress so much concentrated material, employing a wide variety of different figurations and textures. Look, for example, at the question asked in bar 6 (** in Ex. 49). It is pure recitative! Wolf deftly paints the girl's movements—very cautious, lest she wake her lover. The composer later inserted this song into his opera *Der Corregidor*. As a young man, Brahms set this poem also, but with entirely different results. He viewed it as a simple folk song, using a rather innocuous accompaniment, most exceptional for him.

Schweig' einmal still
(from *Italienisches Liederbuch*)

Schweig'einmal still, du garst'ger Schwätzer dort!
Zum Ekel ist mir dein verwünschtes Singen.
Und triebst du es bis morgen früh so fort,
Doch würde dir kein schmuckes Lied gelingen.
Schweig'einmal still und lege dich aufs Ohr!
Das Ständchen eines Esels zög'ich vor.

"The Donkey Serenade" might serve as a suitable title for this poem, a humorous, almost comical variation on the *Vergebliches Ständchen* theme. Here the serenaded lady, acting as critic, roughly orders the wretched singer to be silent, for she is sick of his croaking. She urges him to go home and get a good night's sleep, because if he were to sing all night he would never succeed in producing a decent song. She would prefer the serenade of a donkey.

Among the forty-six songs of the *Italienisches Liederbuch,* we find no noticeably Italian elements in the music. The sentiments of the poets, however, are invariably intensified by Wolf's musical settings, which leave no doubt as to their Germanic origin. Seven of the songs were written in 1890; fifteen more appeared at the end of 1891, after a year of scarcely any creative work. These two groups were published as Volume I in 1892. In 1896, in little more than a month's time, Wolf completed the twenty-four songs of Volume II.

Schweig' einmal still, one of the last songs in the group (No. 43), is a piece that evokes immediate laughter. Wolf admirably captures the high-pitched voice of the distraught maiden as she rebukes the lover who serenades her. Persistently repeated staccato chords in a homorhythmic pattern contrast with the more diversified rhythm of the vocal part. The composer writes a jagged melody, clearly derived from speech inflection, and proceeds to treat the same basic notes to several permutations. (Compare *einmal still* and *Schwätzer dort* in Ex. 50.) Melody and accompaniment are relatively independent of one another, at times sounding dissonantly together (e.g., bars 11 and 13), at other times fighting each other with cross accents. See * in Ex. 50 where the music imitates the sound of the donkey's braying.

Ex. 50

WOLF: *Schweig einmal still*

Schweig'_____ein - mal still, du garst'ger Schwätzer dort! Zum

E - kel ist mir dein verwünsch - tes Singen.

The pianist begins with the material found in the accompaniment in the second bar of our Ex. 50. The vocalist enters at bar 6 with a completely independent melody, which appears again at bar 15, sung to the same text. The pianist plays a variant of this theme to conclude the song. This lied is nearly *durchkomponiert*, but the recurrence of the opening theme makes for a quasi-rondo form. Notice how the irregular phrase structure also contributes to the general feeling of dissatisfaction. Observe the effective use of the Neapolitan sixth chord in bar 19 as Wolf ends with élan. This lied is a fine example of the composer's highly concentrated musical style. Indeed, most of the songs of the *Italienisches Liederbuch* are short, terse statements in music, unlike the more extensive lieder in the *Spanisches Liederbuch*.

SUMMARY

With the perspective of history, we can see clearly that while Wolf's songs represent the zenith of lieder composition, they also incorporate within themselves the beginning of the end of that particular art form. Both Mahler and Wolf orchestrated their songs, a technique which led to the eventual composition of orchestral songs. (Orchestral transcriptions of works written originally for voice and piano appear as early as Berlioz's setting of Théophile Gautier's *Nuits d'été* [1843-56]; but songs conceived initially for voice and orchestra are a development of the late nineteenth century.) The intimacy formerly captured in this concentrated genre was thus lost. The concert singer, supported by an orchestra of fifty to one hundred players, performed in a large hall before a sophisticated audience. The picture of two artists, a singer and a pianist, playing before friends— or at most giving recitals for small groups—became a thing of the past. The traditional lied was gone. Several features of Wolf's lieder, however, found their way into the music of the next century.

The startling extension of the realm of tonality that occurred shortly after 1900 was hinted at by Wagner and endorsed by Wolf. Schönberg and his followers charted completely unknown paths in both their lieder and instrumental compositions. Whereas theorists recognize that Wolf's songs set the stage for Schönberg's *Das Buch der hängenden Gärten* (1908) and Berg's *Sieben frühe Lieder* (1905-08), it is difficult for the lay listener to hear the relationship between the style of singing in Schönberg's *Pierrot Lunaire* (1912) and Wolf's *Wer sich der Einsamkeit ergibt* (p. 290).

The era of lieder composition was a relatively short one. The music produced was extremely beautiful. We can hope only that the time will come again when beauty of sound rather than mathematical or electrical accuracy will be the criterion for the composition of fine music.

Bibliography

Most of the material specifically covering the subject will be found only in German scholarly journals or *Festschriften*. (See Walter Gerboth's *An Index to Musical Festschriften,* New York: 1969, under "Poetry and music" for numerous relevant articles.) Histories of the lied have been written by Abert, Bücken, Kretzschmar, and Moser, but no extensive work deals with both the poetry and the music of the ninteenth-century lied in the way that Friedländer studied its eighteenth-century predecessor. Detailed essays treat lieder of individual composers, but these monographs are not readily available in this country. Then too, the Goethe literature is so vast that it is difficult to make a selection. We have decided therefore to suggest supplementary material in four categories: lieder texts, music scores, literature concerned exclusively with poetry and music and their relationship to one another, and literature dealing with German lyric poetry.

LIEDER TEXTS

Fischer-Dieskau, Dietrich. *Texte deutscher Lieder* (Munich: 1968). A collection of more than 1300 texts arranged alphabetically by title and preceded by an essay on the history of the lied. Includes three indexes: composer, poet, and title and first line.

Lerche, Julius. *Das Wort zum Lied. 2000 der beliebsten Konzertlieder im Texte* (Berlin: n.d.). A collection organized alphabetically by composer, but indexed by title and first line.

Miller, Philip L. *The Ring of Words* (New York: 1963). A collection of about 300 art songs from seven countries, arranged alphabetically by poet within each country. Includes English translations.

Prawer, S. S. *The Penguin Book of Lieder* (Baltimore: 1964). A collection of about 250 lieder texts arranged by composer—from Haydn to Hindemith—and including English translations and notes on the poets.

Stein, Franz A. *Verzeichnis deutscher Lieder seit Haydn* (Bern: 1967). A catalogue of lieder arranged alphabetically by composer. No texts, just titles, opus numbers, dates, and keys are given.

SCORES

Loewe's ballads and all of the lieder of Mozart, Beethoven, Schubert, Schumann, Mendelssohn, Brahms, and Wolf are available in Peters Edition. Mahler's songs are the property of International Music Co.

Lea Pocket Scores reprint in miniature the lieder of Mozart, Beethoven, Schubert, Schumann, and Brahms.

MUSICAL LITERATURE

Blume, Friedrich. *Goethe und die Musik* (Kassel: 1948).

Capell, R. *Schubert's Songs,* 2nd rev. ed. (New York: 1957).

Draheim, Hans. *Goethes Balladen in Loewes Komposition* (Langensalza: 1905).

Friedländer, Max. *Brahms Lieder,* trans. C. Leonard Leese (London: 1929).

——. *Das deutsche Lied im 18. Jahrhundert* (Beriin: 1902; repr. 1968).

——. *Gedichte von Goethe in Kompositionen seiner Zeitgenossen* (Schriften der Goethe Gesellschaft, v. 11, Weimar: 1896).

Kinsey, Barbara. "Mörike Poems set by Brahms, Schumann, and Wolf" in *Music Review* XXIX (1968) 257 ff.

Kneisel, Jessie H. *Mörike and Music* (New York: 1949).

Longyear, R. M. *Schiller and Music* (Chapel Hill: 1966).

Sams, Eric. *The Songs of Robert Schumann* (London: 1969).

——. *The Songs of Hugo Wolf* (London: 1961).

Schnapp, F. "Robert Schumann and Heinrich Heine" in *The Musical Quarterly* XI (1925) 615 ff.

Sietz, Reinhold. *Carl Loewe: ein Gedenkbuch zum 150. Geburtstag* (Cologne: 1948).

Stein, Jack M. "Poem and Music in Hugo Wolf's Mörike Songs" in *The Musical Quarterly* LIII (1967) 22 ff.

Sternfeld, Frederick W. *Goethe and Music* (New York: 1954).

Walker, Frank. "Hugo Wolf's Spanish and Italian Songs" in *Music & Letters* XXV (1944) 194 ff.

LITERARY BIBLIOGRAPHY

The following works treat such subjects as interpretation, versification, poetic analysis, form and content, etc., but independently of musical settings save for a rare reference.

Atkins, H. G. *A History of German Versification* (London: 1923).

Boehringer, Robert. *Das Leben von Gedichten,* 2nd ed. (Breslau: 1934).

Browning, Robert M. *German Poetry. A Critical Anthology* (New York: 1962).

Bruns, Friedrich. *Modern Thought in the German Lyric Poets from Goethe to Dehmel* (Madison: 1921).

Buchheim, C. A. *Balladen und Romanzen* (London and New York: 1895). An old work but with some useful material, including notes and introduction.

Closs, August. *The Genius of the German Lyric* (London: 1938).

——. and T. Pugh Williams. *The Heath Anthology of German Poetry* (Boston and London, n.d. [post-1957]).

Echtermeyer, Theodor. *Deutsche Gedichte von den Anfängen bis zur Gegenwart* revised by Benno von Wiese (Düsseldorf: 1966).

Ermatinger, Emil. *Die deutsche Lyrik in ihrer geschichtlichen Entwicklung von Herder bis zur Gegenwart.* 2nd printing, 3 vols. (Leipzig and Berlin: 1925).

Fiedler, H. G. *A Book of German Verse from Luther to Liliencron* (Oxford: 1916, with numerous reprintings). Valuable introduction. Brief explanatory notes.

——. *The Oxford Book of German Verse.* 2nd ed. (London: 1927, with subsequent reprintings).

Forster, Leonard, ed. *The Penguin Book of German Verse* (Harmondsworth, Middlesex: 1957). Good anthology with prose translation.

Hederer, Edgar. *Das deutsche Gedicht vom Mittelalter bis zum 20. Jahrhundert* (Frankfurt: 1958). Anthology with good introduction.

Hirschenauer, Rupert, and Albrecht Weber. *Wege zum Gedicht* (Munich and Zurich: 1956). Includes a detailed bibliography on interpretation of the German lyric.

Holthusen, Hans Egon, and Friedhelm Kemp. *Ergriffenes Dasein. Deutsche Lyrik 1900-1950.* (Ebenhausen/Munich: 1953).

Kayser, Wolfgang. *Kleine deutsche Verslehre.* 2nd rev. printing (Bern: 1949) = *Sammlung Dalp,* vol. 21.

Klein, J. *Geschichte der deutschen Lyrik von Luther bis zum Ausgang des zweiten Weltkrieges* (Wiesbaden: 1957).

Litzmann, Berthold. *Goethes Lyrik* (Berlin: 1903 and subsequently). Aesthetic criticism of Goethe's lyric poetry.

Pfeiffer, Johannes. *Wege zur Dichtung. Eine Einführung in die Kunst des Lesens* (Hamburg: 1953).

Prawer, S. S. *German Lyric Poetry* (London: 1952).

Schneider, Wilhelm. *Liebe zum deutschen Gedicht. Ein Begleiter für alle Freunde der Lyrik.* 2nd rev. ed. (Freiburg: 1954).

Witkop, Philipp. *Die deutschen Lyriker von Luther bis Nietzsche.* 2 vols. 3rd rev. ed. (Leipzig: 1921-25).

Index

Abendlied (Claudius), 69
Abgesang, 5
Aeolian harp, 268-269
Aelst, Paul van der (fl. c. 1600), 32
Ahnung und Gegenwart (Eichendorff), 143, 150-151, 155
Alfieri, Vittorio (1749-1803), 295
Am Rhein (Heine/Liszt), 208
Amalie. *See* Heine, Amalie.
An der Saale hellem Strande (Kugler), 245
An die ferne Geliebte (Jeitteles/Beethoven), 18, 139
An mein Klavier (Schubart/Schubert), 79
Anacreontic poets, 41, 277
Andersen, Hans Christian (1805-1875), 100
Arabeske, Op. 18 (Schumann), 99, 121
Arabic poetry, 4, 76, 113
Aria, 16-17, 289
Arioso, 42, 55, 62, 118, 286, 288, 292
Ariosto, Ludovico (1474-1533), 179
Arndt, Ernst Moritz (1769-1860), 79
Arnim, Achim von (1781-1831), 143, 248, 252
Asmus (pseudonym). *See* Claudius.
Aufenthalt (Rellstab/Schubert), 80
Aufschwung. *See Fantasiestücke*, Op. 12 (Schumann).
Aus dem Leben eines Taugenichts (Eichendorff), 143, 151, 156

Bach, Johann Sebastian (1685-1750), 6, 180
Ballad, 29-31, 34-38, 100, 153, 167, 172-176, 182-207, 209-212, 214-217

Balladen und Romanzen (Brahms), 192
Bar form, 5-7 (incl. Ex. 1), 31, 78, 81, 178, 242
Beethoven, Ludwig van (1770-1827), 12, 13, **18-19**, 21, 43, 45-46, 53, 58, 70, 79, 139, 207, 288
Béranger, Pierre Jean de (1780-1857), 127
Berg, Alban (1885-1935), 161, 208, 290, 299
Berlioz, Hector (1803-1869), 30, 212, 251, 299
Bhartṛhari (fl. 7th century), 113
Blumen, 7-8
Bopp, Franz (1791-1867), 113, 177
Brahms, Johannes (1833-1897), 9, 13, 45, 82, 87, 125, 161, 164, 192, 207, 218, **225-250**, 252, 255, 269, 278, 297
Brentano, Bettina (1785-1859), 179
Brentano, Clemens (1778-1842), 143, 248, 252
Brion, Friederike (1752-1813), 32
Buch der Lieder (Heine), 88-98
Burns, Robert (1759-1796), 100, 164
Byron, George Gordon, Lord (1788-1824), 82, 100, 164, 167, 219

Carnaval, Op. 9 (Schumann), 99, 124, 126, 166
Challier's *Liederlexikon*, 272
Chamisso, Adelbert (1781-1838), 18, 100, 118, **127-142**, 246,
Chanson du roi de Thulé (Gounod), 31
Chinese poetry and literature, 76

Chopin. See Carnaval, Op. 9 (Schumann).
Church, influence of, on German literature, 3
Church music, 4, 6-8
Claudius, Matthias (1740-1815), 68-71
Common-tone modulation, 61, 166
Craigher, Jakob Nikolaus de Jachelutta (1797-1855), 74-76

Danish folk song, 35-36
Das Buch der hängenden Gärten (Schönberg), 299
Daumer, Georg Friedrich (1800-1875), 225, 233-235, 243
"Death and the Maiden" Quartet (Schubert), 70-71
Debussy, Claude (1862-1918), 208, 224
Declamation, declamatory style, 55, 73, 118, 120-122, 139, 141-142, 160, 162, 174-176, 183, 208, 213, 235, 269, 288, 290
Der Corregidor (Wolf), 297
Der Dichter spricht. See Kinderscenen, Op. 15 (Schumann).
Der du von dem Himmel bist (Goethe/Liszt), 208
"Der du von dem Himmel bist." *See Wanderers Nachtlied I* (Goethe/Schubert).
Der Freischütz (Weber), 93
Der frohe Wandersmann (Eichendorff/Schumann), 158
Der Genesene an die Hoffnung (Mörike/Wolf), 259
Der Jüngling an der Quelle (Salis/Schubert), 84
Der Jüngling und der Tod (Spaun/Schubert), 71
"Der Mond ist aufgegangen." *See Abendlied* (Claudius).
Der Müller und der Bach (Müller/Schubert), 84
Der Sänger (Goethe/Wolf), 287
Des Baches Wiegenlied (Müller/Schubert), 84
Des Knaben Wunderhorn (Arnim & Brentano), 143, 248, 251-255

Deutsche Volkslieder (Zuccalmaglio), 249
Dichter und ihre Geselle (Eichendorff), 152
Dichtung und Wahrheit (Goethe), 58
Die Fischerin (Goethe), 35
Die Heimkehr (Heine), 243
Die Leiden des jungen Werthers (Goethe), 14, 18
Die Meistersinger (Wagner), 260
Die schlanke Wasserlilie (Heine), 170-171
Die Taubenpost (Seidl/Schubert), 89
Die weinende Braut (Eichendorff), 153
Die Winterreise (Müller/Schubert), 20, 89
Die Zauberflöte Mozart, 16
Divan (Hafiz), 63-65
Du bist wie eine Blume (Heine), 114
Du neue Welt (Lenau), 219
Durchkomponiert form, 10-11, 17, 33, 38, 125, 172, 175, 270, 278, 298. *See also* Through-composed form

Edward (Herder/Brahms), 192
Edward (Herder/Schubert), 192
Edward, Ballade, Op. 10, No. 1 (Brahms), 192
Egmont (Beethoven), 58
Egmont (Goethe), 14, 56
Eichendorff, Joseph von (1788-1857), 81, 83, 100, 117, **142-164**, 176, 219, 229, 246, 260, **273-277**
Ein Mädchen oder Weibchen (Mozart), 16
Ein Vogelfänger bin ich ja (Mozart), 16
Eine altschottische Ballade (Herder/Schubert), 192
Einstein, Alfred, 79
Ellerkone, 35-36
Er ist's (Mörike/Franz), 265-266
Er ist's (Mörike/Schumann), 265-266
"Eroica" Symphony, No. 3 (Beethoven), funeral march, rhythmic motive of, 46, 70
Erwin und Elmire (Goethe), 15-16
Es war ein König in Thule (Goethe/Liszt), 207
Es zogen drei Burschen wohl über den Rhein (Uhland), 209
Ethiopic poetry and literature, 76

Etudes symphoniques, Op. 13 (Schumann), 99, 126

Evers, Carl (1819-1875), 43

Expression of the text. *See* Text reflection.

Faber, Bertha. *See* Porubsky.

Fantasiestücke, Op. 12 (Schumann), 99, 166

Faust (Goethe), 13-14, 22-32, 52, 63

Faust (Gounod), 23, 31

Faust (Marlowe), 23

Florestan. See Carnaval, Op. 9 (Schumann).

Folk poems and poetry, 4, 32, 96, 112, 125, 182-183, 185, 199-202, 240, 251, 261, 271. *See also Volkslied,* etc.

Folk song (folk melody, folk tune, etc.), 7, 10, 31-33, 35-36, 69, 82, 101, 108-109, 112, 114, 126, 141, 143, 150, 158, 167, 176, 182-183, 196, 204, 207-210, 225, 236, 239, 245-255, 261, 297

Folk style, 68-84, 92, 100, 164, 183, 193, 196, 200, 240, 252

Franz, Robert (1815-1892), 87, 207, 265-266

Frauenliebe und -leben (Chamisso/Kugler), 245

Frauenliebe und -leben (Chamisso/Loewe), 138, 245

Freiheit, die ich meine (Schenkendorf), 229

Freiligrath, Ferdinand (1810-1876), 184, 203-207

French poetry and poets, 4, 127-128

Freudvoll und Leidvoll (Goethe/Liszt), 207

Friedländer, John, 110-111, 113

Frommann, Carl Friedrich Ernst (1765-1837), 179

Frühling und Liebe (Eichendorff), 151

Gautier, Théophile (1811-1872), 299

Gedichte (Lenau), 218

Gedichte aus Liebesfrühling, Op. 37 (Rückert/Schumann), 166

Gefrorne Tränen (Müller/Schubert), 84

Geibel, Emanuel (1815-1884), 260, 295

German lied: definition of nineteenth-century or romantic lied, 9-12; early

growth of, 3, 8-9; eighteenth-century lied, 5, 8-9, 11-12, 16-18

Gesangsweise (Sachs), 7-8

Gluck, Christoph Willibald von (1714-1787), 45

Goethe, August (1789-1830), 195

Goethe, Johann Wolfgang von (1749-1832), 7, **11-66,** 68, 73, 79, 83, 87, 100, 110, 113, 129, 164, **178-180,** 184-185, **192-203,** 207-209, 219, 225, 234, 260-261, 271, 274, **277-294**

Goncharov, Ivan Alexandrovich (1812-1891), 219

Gottfried von Strassburg (13th century), 108

Göttinger Hain (Bund), 227

Gounod, Charles (1818-1893), 23, 31

Greek poetry and literature, 113, 189, 277

Grenzen der Menschheit (Goethe/Schubert), 53, 73

Grieg, Edvard Hagerup (1843-1907), 87

Grimm, Jacob (1785-1863) and Wilhelm (1786-1859), 199

Grossvatertanz, 126

Groth, Klaus (1819-1899), 225, 232, 235-239

Gypsy elements, 208, 219-222, 273-275

Hafiz (Mohammed Shams ud-Din, 1300-1388), 63-65, 234

Hammer, Josef von (1774-1856), 63

Hark, Hark, the Lark (Shakespeare/Schubert), 53

Haslinger, Tobias (1787-1842), 21, 89

Hauptmann, Moritz (1792-1868), 52

Hebbel, Friedrich (1813-1863), 222, 232, 235

Heidenröslein (Goethe/Werner), 33

Heine, Amalie, 86, 88, 92-93, 96, 101, 110-113, 117, 170, 177-178

Heine, Heinrich (1797-1856), 21, 79, 83, **86-98,** 100-129, 134, 139, 144, 164-165, **170-178,** 181, 190, 207-208, **212-213,** 225, **242-244,** 256

Heine, Salomon, 86, 92, 111-112

Heine, Therese, 86

Heiss mich nicht reden (Goethe/Schubert), 287

Herder, Johann Gottfried (1744-1803), 32, 35, 63, 69, 173, **184-192**, 252, 277

Herrmann, Robert (1869-1912), 87

Herzlieb, Wilhelmina (1789-1865), 179

Heyse, Paul von (1830-1914), 260, 295-298

Highlighting of text. *See* Text reflection.

Hiller, Ferdinand (1811-1885), 43

Himmel, Friedrich (1765-1814), 87

Hoffmann, E. T. A. (1776-1822), 177

Hoffmann von Fallersleben, H. A. (1798-1874), 100

Höfische Dorfpoesie, 4

Hölty, L. C. H. (1748-1776), 225, 227-229

Horace (65 B.C.—8 B.C.), 113, 269

Hugo, Victor (1802-1885), 207

Hungarian minor scale, 222

Hungarian Rhapsodies (Liszt), 221

Hymn, 4, 7, 152, 230

Ich hatt' einen Kameraden (Uhland), 209

Ich träum' als Kind mich zurücke (Chamisso), 128

Il Trovatore (Verdi), 245

Illustriertes deutsches Kinderbuch (Scherer), 248

Indian poetry and literature, 23, 113, 116, 150, 170, 177-178

Irony. *See* Stimmungsbrechung.

Istel, Edgar (1880-1948), 52

Italian vocal style, 16, 120, 124

Ja, du bist elend (Heine), 110

Jeitteles, Aloys (1764-1858), 18

John, Ernst Karl Christian (1788-1856), 198

Kafka, Franz (1883-1924), 239

Kalidasa (5th century?), 23, 63

Kampf der Sänger (Hoffmann), 177

Kerner, Justinus (1786-1862), 100, 218

Keudell, Robert von (1824-1903), 43

Kinderland figure (Schubert), 34, 44, 54

Kinderscenen, Op. 15 (Schumann), 99, 118

Kindertotenlieder (Rückert/Mahler), 251

Klein, Bernhard (1793-1832), 43

Klopstock, Friedrich (1724-1803), 68

Kreutzer, Konradin (1780-1849), 43, 245

Kugler, Franz (1808-1858), 245-247

Kuh, Emil (1828-1876), 222-224

Kunstvolkspoesie, 271. *See also* Folk poetry, Folk song, Folk style, and *Volkslied.*

Ländler, 203, 251

Lang, Josephine (1815-1880), 43

Lassen, Eduard (1830-1904), 87

Leander, Richard (1830-1889), 252, 255-258

Leisewitz, Johann Anton (1752-1806), 91

Lemcke, Carl (1831-1913), 225

Lenau, Nikolaus (1802-1850), 208, 218-222, 233, 273

Leopardi, Giacomo (1798-1837), 219, 295

Lermontov, Mikhail Yurievich (1814-1841), 219

Les deux Grenadiers (Heine/Wagner), 174

Les Huguenots (Meyerbeer), 61

Lessing, Gotthold Ephraim (1729-1781), 68

Liebesfrühling (Rückert), 165-166

Liebestraum No. 3 (Liszt), 207

Lied. *See* German lied.

Lieder eines fahrenden Gesellen (Mahler), 251

Liederkreis, Op. 24 (Heine/Schumann), 100, 117, 157

Liszt, Franz (1811-1886), 30, 87, 183, **207-224**, 275, 282

Lochner, Stephan (c. 1400-1451), 109-110

Loewe, Karl (1796-1869), 38, 43, 52, 87, 138, **183-207**, 259

Lotosblume (Heine), 171

Low German, 232, 235-237

Luther, Martin (1483-1546), 7

Magelone Lieder (Tieck/Brahms), 225, 242

Mahler, Gustav (1860-1911), 166, 203, 251-258, 299

Manzoni, Alessandro (1785-1873), 219, 295

"March of the Davidsbündler against the Philistines." *See Carnaval,* Op. 9 (Schumann).

Marlowe, Christopher (1564-1593), 23
Marseillaise, 174-176
Marx, Karl (1818-1883), 203
Mastersinger, Mastersong, 6-8
Mauke, Wilhelm (1867-1930), 52
Mayrhofer, Johann (1787-1836), 73, 89
Medieval German poetry, 3-5, 69, 108-109, 248
Meeres Stille (Goethe/Schubert), 84
Mein (Müller/Schubert), 84
Melismata, melismatic text setting, 53, 183
Melodic declamation. *See* Declamation.
Melodic recurrence (between songs in a cycle), 18, 139, 142
Mendelssohn, Felix (1809-1847), 13, 87, 126, 143, **176-181**
Meyerbeer, Giacomo (1791-1864), 61, 87
Mignon Lieder (Goethe/Schumann), 287
Mignons Lied (Goethe/Liszt), 207
Milder-Hauptmann, Anna (1785-1838), 65
Miller, Philip, 262
Minnesinger, Minnesong, 3-7
Mirroring of the text. *See* Text reflection.
Modality, modes, 122, 162, 217, 226, 258, 264, 281
Modified strophic form, 10-11, 48, 68, 95, 118, 121, 123-126, 139, 142, 162-163, 181, 226, 238-239, 250
Mohammed Shams ud-Din. *See* Hafiz.
Monophonic music, 5-9
Monotone, 73, 89, 98, 120-121, 125, 141, 157, 174-176, 183, 193, 286-287, 290, 292
"Mood-breaking." *See Stimmungsbrechung.*
Moor, Emanuel (1863-1931), 43
Moore, Thomas (1779-1852), 100, 165
Morgens steh' ich auf und frage (Heine/Liszt), 207
Mörike, Eduard (1804-1875), 100, 218-119, **259-273**
Mosen, Julius (1803-1867), 100, 164, **167-170**
Moszkowski, Moritz (1854-1925), 87
Motto theme, 76, 97
Mozart, Wolfgang Amadeus (1756-1791), 11-12, 16-18, **32-33**, 45
Müller, Max (1823-1900), 113
Müller, Sophie (1803-1830), 75

Müller, Wilhelm (1794-1827), 20, **82-84,** 101, 113, 144

Neidhart von Reuenthal (c.1180-c.1240), 4-5
Neumatic text setting, 82, 171, 202, 254
Newman, Ernest, 260
Niembsch. *See* Lenau.
Nikolaus (pseudonym). *See* Craigher.
Nodnagel, E. O. (1870-1909), 43
Novalis (Friedrich Leopold, Freiherr von Hardenburg, 1772-1801), 115
Nuits d'été (Gautier/Berlioz), 299

Ode, classical and Horatian, 269
Opera, 8, 16, 124, 208
Operatic scena, 16, 38, 53, 65
Oral tradition in literature, 3-4, 10, 32, 183
Orchestration, 212, 251, 254, 257, 283, 299
Oriental literature, 23, 62-65, 76-77, 113, 116, 150, 165, 168, 170-171, 177-178, 234

Papillons, Op. 2 (Schumann), 99, 126
Parlando, 160, 212, 221
Parrish, Carl, 7
Patter song, 120, 160
Paumgartner, Sylvester (c. 1763-1841), 68
Persian poetry and language, 63-65, 76, 234
Peter Schlemihls wundersame Geschichte (Chamisso), 128-129
Petrarch, Francesco (1304-1374), 179, 207, 223
Pierrot Lunaire (Schönberg), 299
Plattdeutsch. See Low German.
"Plucked guitar" accompaniment, 82, 125, 246
Poetische Betrachtungen (Craigher), 74
Polyphonic music, definition of, 7-8
Porubsky, Fräulein Bertha, 248
Purcell, Henry (1659-1695), 289
Pushkin, Alexander (1799-1837), 219

Rahel. *See* Varnhagen von Ense.
Ravel, Maurice (1875-1937), 208, 212, 224
Recitative (recitative-like, recitativo style,

etc.), 17, 31, 38, 42, 46, 54-55, 94, 118, 125, 139, 142, 163, 174, 193-194, 208, 269, 282, 287, 297

Redwitz, Oskar von (1823-1891), 217-218

Reflection of the text. See Text reflection.

Refrain, 5, 27, 29, 174-176, 280, 282-285

Reichardt, Johann Friedrich (1752-1814), 38, 43, 52

Reisenauer, Alfred (1863-1907), 43

Reiter, Josef (1862-1939), 52

Rellstab, Ludwig (1799-1860), 79-82, 89

Rhapsody, 182, 208-224

"Rhenish" Symphony (Schumann), 122, 162

Riemer, Friedrich Wilhelm (1774-1845), 195

Rilke, Rainer Maria (1875-1926), 239

Ring (Wagner), 122, 245

Romances (Tieck), 225

Rondo form, 294, 298

Rossini, Gioacchino (1792-1868), 120

Rückert, Friedrich (1788-1866), 76-78, 100, 164-167, 251

Sachs, Hans (1494-1576), 6-8

Šakuntala (Kalidasa), 23, 63

Sams, Eric, 161-162

Sängerleben (Eichendorff), 150, 154-155

Sanskrit, 23, 76, 113, 170

Schenkendorf, Max von (1783-1817), 229-232

Scherer, Georg (1828-1909), 248

Schiller, Friedrich von (1759-1805), 66-67, 71-73, 100, 214-217

Schlegel, August Wilhelm (1767-1845), 113, 177

Schlegel, Friedrich (1772-1829), 143

Schober, Franz von (1796-1882), 78-79, 89

Schönberg, Arnold (1874-1951), 286, 299

Schubart, Christian Friedrich Daniel (1739-1791), 66-68, 79

Schubert, Andreas (1823-1893), 71

Schubert, Ferdinand (1794-1859), 89

Schubert, Franz (1797-1828), 9, 11, 13, 20-100, 118, 123, 160, 162, 164, 176, 183-184, 192-194, 207, 225, 257, 259-260, 273, 279-280, 283-285, 287-289

Schubertiads, 89

Schumann, Clara Wieck (1819-1896), 99, 164

Schumann, Robert (1810-1856), 5, 9, 11, 13, 18, 21, 43, 61, 87, 99-176, 181, 207, 209, 218, 225-226, 245-246, 252, 259-260, 264-266, 271-273, 275, 281, 287

Schwind, Moritz von (1804-1871), 89

Scottish Ballad, 30, 184-192

Searle, Humphrey, 208

Seidl, Johann Gabriel (1804-1875), 89

Sieben frühe Lieder (Berg), 290, 299

Simrock, Fritz (1838-1870), 248

Singspiel, 5, 8, 15-16

Skizzenbuch (Kugler), 246

Song cycle, 18, 20-21, 79-98, 99-172, 181, 225, 251

Sonnet, 176, 178-180, 207, 223

Spaun, Josef von (1788-1865), 71, 89

"Spiritual Poems" (Eichendorff), 152

Sprechgesang, 55, 259

Staël, Madame de (1766-1817), 128

Stimmen der Völker (Herder), 184

Stimmung, 126, 166, 279, 294

Stimmungsbrechung, 86, 94-95, 118, 128, 144, 173, 213

Stöhr, Richard (1874-1967), 52

Stollen, 5

Storm, Theodor (1817-1888), 232-233, 235

Strauss, Richard (1864-1949), 161, 212, 251

Strophic form, 10-11, 16, 27, 31, 79, 84, 119, 139, 141, 162, 190, 196, 226, 245, 282, 285, 288

Strophic variation form, 10-11, 141

Sturm und Drang, 13-14, 18-19, 48-52, 56, 60, 262

Suleika I (Goethe/Schubert), 65

Syllabic text setting, 5, 7, 17, 19, 33, 82, 84, 120, 158, 160, 180, 183, 191-192, 202-203, 205, 221, 224, 254

Tchaikovsky, Piotr Ilyitch (1840-1893), 43

Ternary form, 10-11, 89-92, 120, 141-142, 159-161, 164, 166-167, 169-170, 247, 254-255, 258, 262, 271, 279

Text reflection, 11, 17, 19, 29, 37, 43, 66, 89, 91, 119, 123, 125, 139-140, 163, 166,

171, 180, 183, 193-194, 197, 213, 218, 247, 264, 287-288. *See also Tonmalerei.*

Text repetition in the lied, 5, 17, 19, 27, 66, 81, 84, 90, 91, 107, 134, 137, 140, 154, 160, 164, 166-167, 180, 193-194, 210, 217-218, 224, 237, 255, 261-262, 266, 279-280, 282-285, 287-288, 294

Thalberg, Sigismond (1812-1871), 87

Thomas, Dylan (1914-1953), 57

Thomson, James (1700-1748), 41

Through-composed form, 10-11, 27, 62, 97, 118, 125-126, 139, 158, 162, 180, 188, 191, 196, 206, 208, 218, 232. *See also Durchkomponiert* form.

Tieck, Ludwig (1773-1853), 79, 225

Tonmalerei, 1, 21, 53, 73, 95, 98, 123, 164, 217, 225, 235, 251, 258, 278, 281. *See also* Text reflection.

Totenopfer (Eichendorff), 149

Traditional poem, 247-249

Tristan und Isolde (Wagner), 260

Trost im Liede (Schober/Schubert), 79

Troubadour, 4

"Trout" Quintet (Schubert), 68

Trouvère, 4

Über allen Gipfeln ist Ruh (Goethe/ Liszt), 207

Uhland, Johann Ludwig (1787-1862), 209-212, 225, 244-245

Varnhagen von Ense, Karl August (1785-1858) and Rahel (1771-1833), 127

Verdi, Giuseppe (1813-1901), 245

Viennese waltz, 248

Volkmann. *See* Leander.

Volkslied, 7, 16, 32, 69, 86, 101, 128, 144, 149, 154, 209, 249

Volkspoesie. See Folk poetry.

Volkstümliches Lied, 8

Wagner, Richard (1813-1883), 6, 38, 55, 122, 174, 208, 245, 259-260, 270, 286, 299

Walther von der Vogelweide (1165-1230), 4, 32, 109

Wanderers Nachtlied I (Goethe/Schubert), 62

Wanderlieder (Eichendorff), 152-153, 155

"Was bedeutet die Bewegung." *See Suleika I* (Goethe/Schubert).

Water figures (Schubert), 20, 21, 68, 70, 84-85, 95, 162

Weber, Carl Maria von (1786-1826), 79, 93

Weill, Kurt (1900-1950), 206

Wenn ich ein Vöglein wär' (Eichendorff), 151

Wenzig, Josef (1807-1876), 225, 239-242

Wer nie sein Brot mit Tränen ass (Goethe/Liszt), 208

Werfel, Franz (1890-1945), 239

Werner, Eric, 180

Werner, Heinrich (1800-1833), 33

Werner, Zacharias (1707-1788), 179

Wieck, Friedrich (1785-1873), 99

Wilhelm Tell (Schiller), 67, 71, 216

Willemer, Marianne von (c. 1784-1860), 64-65

Wir wandelten (Daumer/Brahms), 243

Wolf, Hugo (1860-1903), 9, 13, 42-44, 52, 87, 164, 208, 252, **259-299**

Zelter, C. F. (1758-1832), 30-31, 43, 176

Zigeuner (Goethe), 274

Zu Mantua in Banden (Mosen), 167

Zuccalmaglio, A. W. F. von (1803-1869), 225, 248-250

Zumsteeg, Johann Rudolph (1760-1802), 38, 183

Zuschauer, Freimund (pseudonymn). *See* Rellstab.

Song Index

Songs are indexed here by title and first line. The following abbreviations are used:

DL   *Dichterliebe*
FL   *Frauenliebe und -leben*
LK   *Liederkreis, Op. 39*
M   *Myrten*
SG   *Schwanengesang*
SM   *Die schöne Müllerin*

"Ach, um deine feuchten Schwingen." *See Suleika II* (Willemer/Schubert).

"Ach, wer nimmt von meiner Seele." *See Todessehnen* (Schenkendorf/Brahms).

Allnächtlich im Traume (Heine/Mendelssohn) 105, 181, (incl. Ex. 26)

Allnächtlich im Traume (Heine/Schumann) DL 14, 105, 115, 126, 181 (incl. Ex. 26)

"Am fernen Horizonte." *See Die Stadt* (Heine/Schubert) SG 11.

"Am Kreuzweg, da lausche ich." *See Die Zigeunerin* (Eichendorff/Wolf).

Am leuchtenden Sommermorgen (Heine/Schumann) DL 12, 105, 114, 125

Am Meer (Heine/Schubert) SG 12, 84, 94-95

An die Musik (Schober/Schubert), 78-79

An die Türen (Goethe/Schubert), 288-289, 294

An die Türen (Goethe/Wolf), 292-294

An eine Äolsharfe (Mörike/Wolf), 267-270

An meinem Herzen, an meiner Brust (Chamisso/Schumann) FL 7, 133, 137-138, 142

An Schwager Kronos (Goethe/Schubert), 53, 55-58, 60

Anakreons Grab (Goethe/Wolf), 262, 277-278 (incl. Ex. 46)

Andenken. See Intermezzo (Eichendorff/Schumann).

"Angelehnt an die Efeuwand." *See An eine Äolsharfe* (Mörike/Wolf).

Auf dem Wasser zu singen (Stollberg/Schubert), 84-85 (incl. Ex. 12)

Auf einer Burg (Eichendorff/Schumann) LK 7, 122, 147, 153, 162-163

Auf Flügeln des Gesanges (Heine/Mendelssohn), 176-178

Aus alten Märchen winkt es (Heine/Schumann) DL 15, 106, 115-116, 126

"Aus der Heimat hinter den Blitzen rot." *See In der Fremde* (Eichendorff/Schumann) LK 1.

Aus meinen Tränen spriessen (Heine/Schumann) DL 2, 101-102, 108, 120

"Bedecke deinen Himmel, Zeus." *See Prometheus* (Goethe/Schubert).

Buch der Lieder (Heine), 88-98

"Dämmrung will die Flügel spreiten." *See Zwielicht* (Eichendorff/Schumann) LK 10.

Das Fischermädchen (Heine/Schubert) SG 10, 91-92

Das ist ein Flöten und Geigen (Heine/Schumann) DL 9, 61, 104, 112, 124

"Das Meer erglänzte weit hinaus." *See Am Meer* (Heine/Schubert) SG 12.

Das Veilchen (Goethe/Mozart), 12, 15-18 (incl. Ex. 2), 32-33

Das verlassene Mägdlein (Mörike/Wolf), 270-273 (incl. Ex. 44)

Das verlassne Mägdelein (Mörike/Schumann), 271-273 (incl. Ex. 44)

Das Wandern (Müller/Schubert) SM 1, 20, 83-85 (incl. Ex. 12)

"Dein Bildnis wunderselig." *See Intermezzo* (Eichendorff/Schumann) LK 2.

"Dein Schwert, wie ist's von Blut so Rot?" *See Edward* (Herder/Loewe).

Der Alpenjäger (Schiller/Liszt), 208, 214-217 (incl. Ex. 33)

Der Atlas (Heine/Schubert) SG 8, 88-91 (incl. Ex. 13), 93, 111

Der Doppelgänger (Heine/Schubert) SG 13, 95-98 (incl. Ex. 15)

Der getreue Eckart (Goethe/Loewe), 184, 198-203 (incl. Ex. 30)

Der König in Thule (Goethe/Schubert), 29-31

"Der Mond steht über dem Berge." *See Ständchen* (Kugler/Brahms).

Der Musensohn (Goethe/Schubert), 58-61 (incl. Ex. 8)

Der Nussbaum (Mosen/Schumann) M 2, 167-170

Der Schmied (Uhland/Brahms), 244-245

Der Tod, das ist die kühle Nacht (Heine/Brahms), 242-244

Der Tod und das Mädchen (Claudius/Schubert), 69-71 (incl. Ex. 10)

Des Knaben Wunderhorn (Mahler), 251-255

Dichterliebe (Heine/Schumann), 5, **100-127** (incl. Exx. 16-22), 157, 161-164, 170, **181** (incl. Ex. 26)

Die alten, bösen Lieder (Heine/Schumann) 106-107, 116-117, 127

Die beiden Grenadiere (Heine/Schumann), 172-176 (incl. Ex. 25), 190

Die drei Zigeuner (Lenau/Liszt), 208, 219-222 (incl. Ex. 34), 275

Die Forelle (Schubart/Schubert), 11, 53, **66-68** (incl. Ex. 9), 79, 84

Die junge Nonne (Craigher/Schubert), 74-76 (incl. Ex. 11)

Die Liebende schreibt (Goethe/Mendelssohn), 176, 178-180

Die Lorelei. See Waldesgespräch (Eichendorff/Schumann) LK 3

Die Lotosblume (Heine/Schumann) M 7, 170-172

Die Mainacht (Hölty/Brahms), 227-229 (incl. Ex. 35), 241

Die Rose, die Lilie, die Taube (Heine/Schumann) DL 3, 102, 108-109, 120 (incl. Ex. 17)

Die schöne Müllerin (Müller/Schubert), 20, 83-85 (incl. Ex. 12), 101, 154

Die Stadt (Heine/Schubert) SG 11, 92-95 (incl. Ex. 14)

Die Stille (Eichendorff/Schumann) LK 4, 145-146, 151, 160

Die Vätergruft (Uhland/Liszt), 209-212 (incl. Ex. 32)

Die wandelnde Glocke (Goethe/Loewe), 184, 194-197 (incl. Ex. 29), 202

Die Zigeunerin (Eichendorff/Wolf), 264, 274-277 (incl. Ex. 45)

"Drei Zigeuner fand ich einmal." *See Die drei Zigeuner* (Lenau/Liszt).

Du bist die Ruh (Rückert/Schubert), 77-78

"Du holde Kunst, in wieviel grauen Stunden." *See An die Musik* (Schober/Schubert).

"Du meine Seele, du mein Herz." *See Widmung* (Rückert/Schumann) M 1.

Du Ring an meinem Finger (Chamisso/ Schumann) FL 4, 130-131, 135-136, 141

"Du schönes Fischermädchen." *See Das Fischermädchen* (Heine/Schubert) SG 10.

"Dunkel, wie dunkel im Wald und in Feld!" *See Von ewiger Liebe* (Wenzig/ Brahms).

"Durch Feld und Wald zu schweifen." *See Der Musensohn* (Goethe/Schubert).

Edward (Herder/Loewe), 173, 183-192 (incl. Ex. 27), 207

"Ein Blick von deinen Augen in die meinen." *See Die Liebende schreibt* (Goethe/Mendelssohn).

"Eingeschlafen auf der Lauer." *See Auf einer Burg* (Eichendorff/Schumann) LK 7.

Ein Jüngling liebt ein Mädchen (Heine/ Schumann) DL 11, 104, 113-114, 125

"Ein Veilchen auf der Wiese stand." *See Das Veilchen* (Goethe/Mozart).

Er, der Herrlichste von allen (Chamisso/ Schumann) FL 2, 129-130 (incl. Ex. 23), 134, 140-141

Erinnerung (Leander/Mahler), 252, 256-258 (incl. Ex. 41)

Er ist's (Mörike/Wolf), 164, 264-267 (incl. Ex. 43)

Erlkönig (Goethe/Loewe), 184, 192-195 (incl. Ex. 28)

Erlkönig (Goethe/Schubert), 34-38 (incl. Ex. 6), 57, 150, 184, 192-194

"Es ging wohl über die Haide." *See Die Vätergruft* (Uhland/Liszt).

"Es grünet ein Nussbaum vor dem Haus." *See Der Nussbaum* (Mosen/Schumann) M 2.

"Es ist schon spät, es ist schon kalt." *See Waldesgespräch* (Eichendorff/Schumann) LK 3.

Es muss ein Wunderbares sein (Redwitz/ Liszt), 208, 217-218

"Es rauschen die Wipfel und schauern."

See Schöne Fremde (Eichendorff/Schumann) LK 6.

"Es war, als hätt' der Himmel." *See Mondnacht* (Eichendorff/Schumann) LK 5.

"Es war ein Kind, das wollte nie." *See Die wandelnde Glocke* (Goethe/Loewe).

"Es war ein König in Thule." *See Der König in Thule* (Goethe/Schubert).

"Es wecket meine Liebe die Lieder immer wieder!" *See Erinnerung* (Leander/ Mahler).

"Es weiss und rät es doch keiner." *See Die Stille* (Eichendorff/Schumann) LK 4.

"Es zog eine Hochzeit den Berk entlang." *See Im Walde* (Eichendorff/Schumann) LK 11.

Frauenliebe und -leben (Chamisso/Schumann), 18, 117-118, 129-142 (incl. Ex. 23), 164, 245

"Früh, wann die Hähne krähn." *See Das verlassene Mägdlein* (Mörike/Schumann & Wolf).

"Frühling lässt sein blaues Band." *See Er ist's* (Mörike/Wolf).

Frühlingsnacht (Eichendorff/Schumann) LK 12, 149, 156-157, 164

Ganymed (Goethe/Schubert), 48-54 (incl. Ex. 7), 58, 60

Gedichte von Eduard Mörike (Mörike/ Wolf), 259-273 (incl. Exx. 42-44)

Gretchen am Spinnrade (Goethe/Schubert), 22-23, 26-30 (incl. Ex. 4), 57, 129, 273

Gruppe aus dem Tartarus (Schiller/Schubert), 71-73

"Guten Abend, gut' Nacht." *See Wiegenlied* (Traditional/Brahms).

Gute Nacht, mein Kind. See Wiegenlied (Traditional/Brahms).

"Guten Abend, mein Schatz, guten Abend, mein Kind!" *See Vergebliches Ständchen* (Traditional/Brahms).

Harfenspieler Lieder (Goethe/Schubert), 287-294

Harfenspieler Lieder (Goethe/Wolf), 260, 287-294

Harfenspieler I. See *Wer sich der Einsamkeit ergibt* (Goethe/Schubert & Wolf).

Harfenspieler II. See *An die Türen* (Goethe/Schubert & Wolf).

Harfenspieler III. See *Wer nie sein Brot mit Tränen ass* (Goethe/Schubert & Wolf).

Heidenröslein (Goethe/Schubert), 31-34 (incl. Ex. 5), 54, 271

Heiss mich nicht reden (Goethe/Schubert), 45-46, 48, 279, 287

Heiss mich nicht reden (Goethe-Wolf), 45, 279, 286-287

Helft mir, ihr Schwestern (Chamisso/Schumann) FL 5, 131-132, 136-137, 141

"Horch—wie Murmeln des empörten Meeres." See *Gruppe aus dem Tartarus* (Schiller/Schubert).

Hör' ich das Liedchen klingen (Heine/Schumann) DL 10, 104, 112-113, 124-125

Ich ging mit Lust durch einen grünen Wald (*Des Knaben Wunderhorn*/Mahler), 252-255 (incl. Ex. 40)

Ich grolle nicht (Heine/Schumann) DL 7, 103, 110-111, 123 (incl. Ex. 20), 134, 166, 212

Ich hab' im Traum geweinet (Heine/Schumann) DL 13, 105, 114, 125-126 (incl. Ex. 22)

"Ich hör die Bächlein rauschen." See *In der Fremde* (Eichendorff/Schumann) LK 8.

"Ich hör meinen Schatz." See *Der Schmied* (Uhland/Brahms).

Ich kann's nicht fassen, nicht glauben (Chamisso/Schumann) FL 3, 130, 135, 141

"Ich kann wohl manchmal singen." See *Wehmut* (Eichendorff/Schumann) LK 9.

"Ich stand in dunklen Träumen." See *Ihr Bild* (Heine/Schubert) SG 9.

"Icht unglückseliger Atlas." See *Der Atlas* (Heine/Schubert) SG 8.

Ich will meine Seele tauchen (Heine/Schumann) DL 5, 102, 109, 121

Ihr Bild (Heine/Schubert) SG 9, 90-91

Ihr Glocken von Marling (Kuh/Liszt), 223-224

Im Rhein, im heiligen Strome (Heine/Schumann) DL 6, 102-103, 109-110, 122 (incl. Ex. 19), 162

Im Walde (Eichendorff/Schumann) LK 11, 148-149, 156, 163-164

Im wunderschönen Monat Mai (Heine/Schumann) DL 1, 5, 101, 107, 118-119 (incl. Ex. 16)

In dem Schatten meiner Locken (Heyse & Geibel/Wolf), 295-297 (incl. Ex. 49)

In der Fremde (Eichendorff/Schumann) LK 1, 144, 149, 158

In der Fremde (Eichendorff/Schumann) LK 8, 147, 153-154, 162-163

"In einem Bächlein helle." See *Die Forelle* (Schubart/Schubert).

Intermezzo (Eichendorff/Schumann) LK 2, 145, 150, 159 (incl. Ex. 24)

Italienisches Liederbuch (Heyse/Wolf), 260, 295, 297-298 (incl. Ex. 50)

Kennst du das Land (Goethe/Schubert), 39-44, 279, 283-284 (incl. Ex. 48)

Kennst du das Land (Goethe/Wolf), 40-43, 279-285 (incl. Ex. 48)

"Lass, o Welt, o lass mich sein!" See *Verborgenheit* (Mörike/Wolf).

"Leise flehen meine Lieder." See *Ständchen* (Rellstab/Schubert) SG 4.

Lied der Mignon (Op. 62, No. 4). See *Nur wer die Sehnsucht kennt* (Goethe/Schubert).

Lied der Mignon, No. 1 (Op. 62, No. 2). See *Heiss mich nicht reden* (Goethe/Schubert).

Lied der Mignon, No. 2 (Op. 62, No. 3). See *So lasst mich scheinen* (Goethe/Schubert).

Liederkreis, Op. 39 (Eichendorff/Schumann), 117, 122, 144-164 (incl. Ex. 24), 275

Lieder und Gesänge aus der Jugendzeit (Des Knaben Wunderhorn, Leander/ Mahler), 252-258 (incl. Exx. 40-41)

Lyrisches Intermezzo (Heine), 101-127, 170, 177, 181, 212

"Meine Ruh ist hin." *See Gretchen am Spinnrade* (Goethe/Schubert).

Mignon. See Kennst du das Land (Goethe/ Wolf).

Mignon I. See Heiss mich nicht reden (Goethe/Wolf).

Mignon II. See Nur wer die Sehnsucht kennt (Goethe/Wolf).

Mignon III. See So lasst mich scheinen (Goethe/Wolf).

Mignon Lieder (Goethe/Schubert), 39-48, 279-287 (incl. Exx. 47-48)

Mignon Lieder (Goethe/Wolf), 279-287 (incl. Exx. 47-48)

Mignons Gesang. See Kennst du das Land (Goethe/Schubert).

Mondnacht (Eichendorff/Schumann) LK 5, 146, 152, 158, 161

Myrten, Op. 25 (Rückert, Mosen, Heine/ Schumann), 117, 164-172

"Nach Frankreich zogen zwei Grenadier'." *See Die beiden Grenadiere* (Heine/ Schumann).

Nicht mehr zu dir zu gehen (Daumer/ Brahms), 234-235

Niederrheinisches Volkslied. See Vergebliches Ständchen (Traditional/Brahms).

Nun has du mir den ersten Schmerz getan (Chamisso/Schumann) FL 8, 133, 138-139, 142

Nur wer die Sehnsucht kennt (Goethe/ Schubert), 43-46, 279-280 (incl. Ex. 47)

Nur wer die Sehnsucht kennt (Goethe/ Wolf), 43-44, 279-281 (incl. Ex. 47)

"O wären wir weiter, o wär' ich zu Haus!" *See Der getreue Eckart* (Goethe/Loewe).

O wüsst' ich doch den Weg zurück (Groth/ Brahms), 236-239 (incl. Ex. 37)

Prinz Eugen, der edle Ritter (Freiligrath/ Loewe), 184, 203-207 (incl. Ex. 31)

Prometheus (Goethe/Schubert), 48-55, 58, 73

"Sah ein Knab' ein Röslein stehn." *See Heidenröslein* (Goethe/Schubert).

Schöne Fremde (Eichendorff/Schumann) LK 6, 146, 152, 161-162

Schwanengesang (Rellstab, Heine/Schubert), 21, 79-82, 88-98 (incl. Exx. 14-15)

Schweig' einmal still (Heyse/Wolf), 297-298 (incl. Ex. 50)

Seit ich ihn gesehen (Chamisso/Schumann) FL 1, 129, 133-134, 139

"Serenade." *See Ständchen* (Rellstab/Schubert) SG 4.

So lasst mich scheinen (Goethe/Schubert), 46-48, 279, 285

So lasst mich scheinen (Goethe/Wolf), 46-47, 279, 285-286

Spanisches Liederbuch (Heyse & Geibel/ Wolf), 260, 295-298 (incl. Ex. 49)

"Spute dich, Kronos!" *See An Schwager Kronos* (Goethe/Schubert).

Ständchen (Kugler/Brahms), 245-247

Ständchen (Rellstab/Schubert) SG 4, 79-82, 89

"Still ist die Nacht, es ruhen die Gassen." *See Der Doppelgänger* (Heine/Schubert) SG 13.

Suleika II (Willemer/Schubert), 64-66

Süsser Freund, du blickest mich verwundert an (Chamisso/Schumann) FL 6, 132, 137, 142

Todessehnen (Schenkendorf/Brahms), 230-232

"Trocknet nicht, trocknet nicht." *See Wonne der Wehmut* (Goethe/Beethoven).

"Über allen Gipfeln." *See Wanderers Nachtlied II* (Goethe/Schubert).

Über die Heide (Storm/Brahms), 232-233
"Überm Garten durch die Lüfte." *See Frühlingsnacht* (Eichendorff/Schumann) LK 12.
Und wüssten's die Blumen, die kleinen (Heine/Schumann) DL 8, 103, 111, 123-124

Verborgenheit (Mörike/Wolf), 261-264 (incl. Ex. 42)
Vergebliches Ständchen (Traditional/Brahms), 248-250 (incl. Ex. 39), 297
Vergiftet sind meine Lieder (Heine/Liszt), 207, 212-213
Von ewiger Liebe (Wenzig/Brahms), 239-242 (incl. Ex. 38)
"Vorüber! ach, vorüber." *See Der Tod und das Mädchen* (Claudius/Schubert).

Waldesgespräch (Eichendorff/Schumann) LK 3, 145, 150-151, 153, 160, 243
Waldvögelein. See Ich ging mit Lust (Des Knaben Wunderhorn/Mahler).
Wanderers Nachtlied II (Goethe/Schubert), 61-62
Wanderschaft. See Das Wandern (Müller/Schubert) SM 1.
"Wann der silberne Mond durch die Gesträuche blinkt." *See Die Mainacht* (Hölty/Brahms).
Wehmut (Eichendorff/Schumann) LK 9, 148, 154-155, 163
Wenn ich in deine Augen seh' (Heine/Schumann) DL 4, 102, 109, 120-121 (incl. Ex. 18)
Wer nie sein Brot mit Tränen ass (Goethe/Schubert), 288, 291, 294

Wer nie sein Brot mit Tränen ass (Goethe/Wolf), 291-294
"Wer reitet so spät durch Nacht und Wind?" *See Erlkönig* (Goethe/Schubert).
Wer sich der Einsamkeit ergibt (Goethe/Schubert), 288-289, 294
Wer sich der Einsamkeit ergibt (Goethe/Wolf), 289-292, 294, 299
West-östlicher Divan (Goethe), 62-66, 234
"Why dois your brand sae drap wi bluid." *See Edward* (Herder/Loewe).
Widmung (Rückert/Schumann) M 1, 164-167
"Wie braust durch die Wipfel der heulende Sturm!" *See Die junge Nonne* (Craigher/Schubert).
"Wie im Morgenglanze." *See Ganymed* (Goethe/Schubert).
Wiegenlied (Traditional/Brahms), 247-248
Wilhelm Meisters Lehrjahre (Goethe), 14, 39-48, 260, 279-294
Willkommen Mayenschein (Neidhart von Reuenthal), 5 (incl. Ex. 1)
"Willst du nicht das Lämmlein hüten?" *See Der Alpenjäger* (Schiller/Liszt).
"Wo die Rose hier blüht." *See Anakreons Grab* (Goethe/Wolf).
Wohin? (Müller/Schubert) SM 2, 84-85 (incl. Ex. 12)
Wonne der Wehmut (Goethe/Beethoven), 18-19 (incl. Ex. 3)

"Zelte, Posten, Werdarufer!" *See Prinz Eugen, der edle Ritter* (Freiligrath/Loewe).
Zwielicht (Eichendorff/Schumann) LK 10, 148, 155-156, 164